NEGOTIATORS
OF
CHANGE

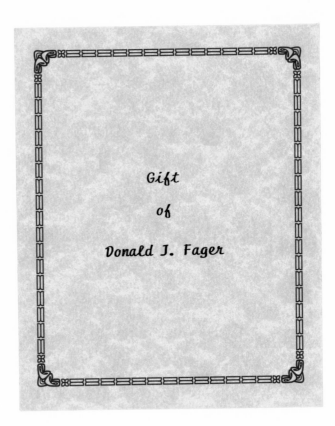

NANCY SHOEMAKER

NEGOTIATORS
OF
CHANGE

HISTORICAL
PERSPECTIVES
ON
NATIVE
AMERICAN
WOMEN

ROUTLEDGE   NEW YORK   LONDON

Published in 1995 by

Routledge
29 West 35th Street
New York, NY 10001

Published in Great Britain by

Routledge
11 New Fetter Lane
London EC4P 4EE

#30735855

Copyright © 1995 by Routledge, Inc.

Printed in the United States of America on acid free paper

Library of Congress Cataloging-in-Publication Data

    Shoemaker, Nancy.
    Negotiators of change : historical perpsectives on Native American Women / Nancy Shoemaker, editor.
        p.   cm.
    Includes index.
    ISBN 0-415-90992-9. (acid-free paper). — ISBN 0-415-90993-7 (acid-free paper).
    1. Indian women—North America—History—Sources. 2. Indian women—North America—Economic conditions. 3. Indian women—North America—Public opinion. 4. Indian women—North America. 5. Sex role—North America—History. I. Shoemaker, Nancy, 1958–.
E98.W8N44 1994   94-15774
305.48'897—dc20   CIP

British Library Cataloguing-in-Publication Data also available

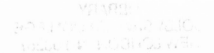

CONTENTS

INTRODUCTION   1
Nancy Shoemaker

1   THE ANGLO-ALGONQUIAN GENDER FRONTIER   26
    Kathleen M. Brown

2   KATERI TEKAKWITHA'S TORTUOUS   49
    PATH TO SAINTHOOD
    Nancy Shoemaker

3   AUTONOMY AND THE ECONOMIC ROLES OF   72
    INDIAN WOMEN OF THE FOX-WISCONSIN
    RIVERWAY REGION, 1763–1832
    Lucy Eldersveld Murphy

4   WOMEN, MEN AND AMERICAN INDIAN POLICY: 90
    THE CHEROKEE RESPONSE TO "CIVILIZATION"
    Theda Perdue

5   CHOCTAW WOMEN AND CULTURAL PERSISTENCE   115
    IN MISSISSIPPI
    Clara Sue Kidwell

6 THE LAND INCARNATE: NAVAJO WOMEN   135
     AND THE DIALOGUE OF COLONIALISM, 1821–1870
     CAROL DOUGLAS SPARKS

7 "DEAR FRIEND AND EX-HUSBAND":   157
     MARRIAGE, DIVORCE, AND WOMEN'S PROPERTY
     RIGHTS ON THE SOUTHERN UTE RESERVATION, 1887–1930
     KATHERINE M.B. OSBURN

8 HORSES AND CATTLE, BUGGIES AND HACKS: 176
     PURCHASES BY YAKIMA INDIAN WOMEN, 1909–1912
     CLIFFORD E. TRAFZER

9 PATCHWORK AND POLITICS: THE EVOLVING ROLES OF   193
     FLORIDA SEMINOLE WOMEN IN THE TWENTIETH CENTURY
     HARRY A. KERSEY, JR. AND HELEN M. BANNAN

10 MOTHERS AND COMMUNITY BUILDERS: SALT RIVER   213
     PIMA AND MARICOPA WOMEN IN COMMUNITY ACTION
     PÄIVI H. HOIKKALA

CONTRIBUTORS   235

NANCY SHOEMAKER

INTRODUCTION

In the process of soliciting articles for this volume in native women's history, I had an interesting conversation with one potential contributor. After I described the project to him—a collection of original research articles, each on some aspect of Indian women's history, covering the experience of women from different tribal groups, and spanning the period from the seventeenth century to the twentieth—he asked, "But why do we need a book in Indian women's history? There already is one."[1] His assumption that one book, or a more accurate tally of seven or eight books, would be enough to say everything there was to say surprised me but reveals much about the state of scholarly research in this area. It is at such an early stage of development that we have yet to realize its full potential. I imagine that twenty or so years ago, when women's history in general began intruding on more traditional ways of researching and writing about the past, many scholars responded in just the same way, unable to understand that women's lives have been just as rich and varied as men's.

The articles collected here will help recover American Indian women's history from an invisible past and illuminate, by example, new avenues for further research. This volume is not the last word in Indian women's history. Neither is it the first word. But the breadth of approaches and insights offered here will be a valuable stepping stone to more in-depth historical investigations into Indian women's experiences.

The ten original research essays that follow show the many ways in which native women influenced and were influenced by the changing world around them. These women were grandmothers, mothers, daughters, sisters, and wives. They planted corn, ground corn into meal, tanned hides, gathered food, traded, produced fancy quill or beadwork, and wove rugs. They were clan mothers, mothers of the nation, beloved women, medicine women, brave-hearted women, and women warriors. They were also cast in the roles of squaw and princess. Several Indian women, Pocahontas and Sacajawea, appear prominently in the standard narratives of American history. We also know that Indian women travelled the Trail of Tears, died at the Wounded Knee Massacre, and occupied Alcatraz. Although we know this much about the experience of Native American women and the roles they have played, we do not know much more than this. Native women were important in their communities for more profound reasons than the above list implies. Native women maintained the cultural traditions of their people. They also, on other occasions, advocated change.[2] They were, in short, crucial participants in the ongoing struggle for the survival of Indian cultures and communities.

Besides autobiographies, biographies, and some outdated ethnographies, there are few books that deal explicitly with Indian women's history. However, there are a growing number of research articles available in journals and books, covering a broad array of time periods, cultural groups, and issues.[3] Thus far, three questions have dominated scholarly research in Indian women's history. First, in native societies, did women have status and power equivalent to that of men? Since the answer to that question has often been "yes," the second question asks why? What was the source of women's authority? And third, how did European settlement of the Americas affect the gender balance within native societies? The essays in this volume deal primarily with the third question, but—obviously—answering the third question depends on how one has answered the other two.

Although scholars disagree on the position of women in native societies before European contact, most do agree that Indian women had more authority and were more respected than their counterparts in Europe. However, the lack of written records for precolumbian America hinders historical research in this area. From Columbus's initial descriptions of "India" up through the twentieth century, most of the available written records have been produced by Euro-American men—explorers, traders, missionaries, and government policymakers. Robert Berkhofer has shown how European observers saw Indians (by implication, Indian men) as either "brutal savages" or "noble savages."[4] Euro-Americans used a similarly dichotomous imagery to describe Indian women. Historical accounts of Indian women usually depict them as "squaw drudges," beasts of burden bowed down with overwork and spousal oppression, or as "Indian princesses," voluptuous and promiscuous objects of white and Indian men's sexual desire.[5] Sifting through these stereotyped images to appreciate Indian women's viewpoints and motivations is our greatest challenge.[6]

Under the rubric of ethnohistory, historians and anthropologists have developed creative and culturally sensitive approaches to mining the documentary record left by Euro-Americans. Along with using the written record, ethnohistorians have turned to archaeology, oral traditions, and anthropological fieldwork from the late nineteenth and twentieth centuries.[7] Still, the resource materials available for Indian history are almost entirely the product of a post-conquest world. We will probably never know as much about the history of Indian women, whether before or after European contact, as we would like to. Moreover, the cultural and gender biases of our sources and the paucity of Indian voices from the past naturally allow considerable room for debate.

Early ethnographic studies, followed by feminist theories of anthropology in the 1970s, established the parameters of the debate on gender in Indian cultures and posed many of the questions that still concern us today. Of the ethnographic studies, Ruth Landes's *The Ojibwa Woman* offered a multilayered, and ultimately controversial, approach to understanding Indian gender roles and socialization processes. After doing fieldwork among the Ojibwas in the 1930s, Landes concluded that Ojibwa boys underwent a rigorous training to learn the adult male role, and through this process men became achievement-oriented. Women, however, were left to "spontaneous and confused behavior." While men's achievements were honored publicly, "women form a closed world where each woman is distinctive, where women's work is valued explicitly, and where women's values are pursued. It is completely dissociated from the world of men where women's work is conventionally ignored and where no individual woman is distinctive." Although Landes laid the groundwork for a "separate spheres" theory of gender, she also demonstrated that these spheres were flexible. Some women did men's work, by choice or by necessity. They were, however, not trained in these tasks and could not expect to be honored for their achievements in the same way that men were.[8]

Landes's ethnographic observations fit Michelle Rosaldo's later theory of how separate spheres for men and women formed a basis for nearly universal male dominance. According to Rosaldo, in many cultures women's childbearing and childrearing responsibilities confined them to a

4 | domestic, private sphere, while men dominated in the public sphere of political decisionmaking and community recognition of their achievements. More egalitarian gender relations might prevail under certain conditions. If the public and private spheres were not very differentiated (if the domestic sphere, the family, was the locus of decisionmaking), men and women might share authority. Ranked societies might allow elite women to assume positions of power. In some societies, women might be able to gain authority by taking on male roles and would probably be identified by others as a woman who acted like a man. Or, women could exercise informal power (gossiping, manipulating kin relations, becoming "the woman behind the man"). And, finally, women might be able to exercise authority by accentuating their differences from men to enlarge the powers and responsibilities of the domestic sphere.[9]

The anthropologist Eleanor Leacock was the foremost critic of Landes and Rosaldo. Interpreting Montagnais history through the lens of Marxist (or really, "Engelsist") theory, Leacock argued that the separate spheres for men and women, which Landes observed among the Ojibwa and which Rosaldo theorized about, were historical developments fed by the rise of capitalism. In "non-class-societies" or "egalitarian societies," Leacock contended, there were no separate spheres. Instead, "there was a rough and ready division of labor, based on expediency, with the men doing most of the large game hunting, and the women preparing the food, making the clothes and tents, and tending the small children. When necessary, the women helped with the hunting, and if a woman was busy elsewhere, a man would readily look after the children."[10] In political matters, the principle of individual autonomy outweighed gender distinctions.

Leacock's critique was most compelling in its insistence that scholars be aware of their own cultural biases and pay attention to historical processes. She accused Landes of being ethnocentric.[11] However, Leacock could easily be accused of the same shortcoming. Marx and Engels saw historical processes in Western terms. In his history of the development of the family, Engels borrowed from Lewis Henry Morgan's research on the Iroquois and shared in Morgan's speculations about how matrilineal kinship was an intermediary stage between "primitive promiscuity" and the patrilineality of more developed societies.[12] Engels was not a cultural relativist, as most of us who currently study Indian history and anthropology are, and his encapsulation of all human history into stages of development obscures the diversity and complexity of change within Indian societies. Leacock approached Indian history from a Marxist perspective, and was therefore wedded to the idea of separate spheres being a product of capitalism. However, her refutal of gender distinctions in "non-class-societies" contradicts the evidence, which overwhelmingly points to gender, age, and kin as the three essential organizing principles determining one's identity and role within Indian societies.

Theories, in their absoluteness, rarely satisfy anyone for very long. But in this case, Rosaldo's and Leacock's theoretical perspectives both offer insights; they just need to be synthesized. Their theories face each other at opposite ends of a paradox, and our inability to look at the paradox in two-dimensional terms, instead of one-dimensional, reflects our own ethnocentrism. Gender differences were crucially important in Indian cultures for organizing behavior and activities but gender was also flexible and variable.

All Indian societies defined certain economic, political, and ceremonial activities as male or female.[13] Even though there was much variety across cultures as to whether men or women planted corn, fished, wove cloth, or made clay pots, it is still possible to make some generalizations. All Indian societies had a gendered division of labor and authority. Men were primarily responsible for hunting, warfare, and interacting with outsiders. Women managed the household. They usually owned the home (the tipi, hogan, longhouse, wickiup); engaged in such non-hunting forms of food production as agriculture or gathering; distributed food to family members and guests; and bore and raised children. Men received public honor for achievement in hunting and warfare. Women received public honor for achievements in fancy beadwork or other arts, exceptional farming or gathering productivity, and coming of age at menarche. Men often had more visible public roles, but that does not mean they were necessarily more powerful. Much of the recent literature on Indian women views gender as a fundamental, yet non-hierarchical, social category. Women and men had complementary roles of equal importance, power, and prestige.

Despite clear cultural guidelines differentiating between male and female tasks and behavior, individual men and women were free to choose and improvise. From the Indian perspective, gender was a socially constructed category and not biologically determined. Many Indian societies had an institutionalized acceptance of gender variation, sometimes referred to as a third gender, or more commonly, berdache.[14] The literature on berdache has been most closely associated with the history of sexuality; however, the essential signifier of one's gender identity was the kind of work one did. Scholars use the word "berdache" to refer to Indian men who chose to do women's work, and who accordingly adopted the symbols, especially the style of dress, of the female gender. Although most of the literature on berdache is about men assuming women's roles, women also could assume men's roles. Historical accounts usually refer to male chiefs, warriors, and councils, but also occasionally mention women chiefs, women warriors, and sometimes even women's councils.[15] Some Indian women held positions which fell into what Rosaldo would have called the public sphere.

Unfortunately, not all of the research on women chiefs and women warriors distinguishes between an institutionalized form of power and the occasional, exceptional woman who opted to take on the male role, who was of high rank (in northwest coast Indian cultures, for instance), or who for some other reason wielded political powers that usually fell to men. For example, clan mothers among the Iroquois had the right to appoint and depose chiefs, but to the best of my knowledge no woman ever held the position of chief. Thus, some women—clan mothers—had an institutionalized form of political authority, but there do not seem to have been any individual women among the Iroquois who rose to prominence by assuming the male role. In contrast, in her autobiography the Crow woman Pretty-Shield, rather defiantly, told the battle stories of a woman and a "half-woman" who "fought with Three-stars on the Rosebud." Among the Crow, women and berdaches could go to war if they chose, but not many did. Women generally did not go to war, since their culture defined that as a male activity. Indeed, Pretty-Shield told this particular story because women and berdaches in battle were a notable exception and because it was a story women told but men did not. As Pretty-Shield said, "All the men saw these things, and yet they have never told you about them."[16] I doubt any scholar would use the prominence of Queen Elizabeth I and Joan of Arc to suggest that women in medieval Europe were equally or more powerful than men, and yet this kind of conclusion is common in Indian history.

To truly understand Indian women's history, we need to look simultaneously at Indian cultural ideas about gender difference and how these ideas related to the experience of individual women. Moreover, we need to accept the inevitability, or at least potentiality, of ambivalence *within* a culture. As Oscar Lewis demonstrated in his essay on "manly-hearted women" among the Piegan, women who were economically, sexually, and socially aggressive, like men, were simultaneously admired and feared. These women were allowed complete independence and could behave in ways deemed inappropriate for women in general, and yet mothers anxiously raised daughters with the hope that they would not become manly-hearted women.

Although many scholars now assert that Indian women and men had complementary roles and powers, there is still much debate about why. What was the source of women's independence and authority? There are three equally persuasive explanations. As Eleanor Leacock argued, within most Indian cultures there was a basic principle of individual autonomy which structured social and political relationships, including relations between men and women. Second, women's work was vital to native economies. And third, women's responsibilities in bearing and raising children brought women certain kinds of authority within the community at large.

One of the most common observations made by Europeans when they first encountered native people was the freedom allowed women and children. In Europe, patriarchy ordered social relations under a hierarchical system: women and children were the obedient dependents of a patriarch who, ideally, used his power benevolently to protect them but who also had the uncontested privilege of forcible coercion. In native North America, coercion was rare. In political matters, Indian groups valued consensus above all, and if consensus failed separation could resolve most disputes. Within families the same principle applied. Parents rarely turned to physical punishment to control their children, and relied instead on logical argument and instructive stories. If all else failed, parents shamed and teased children into socially acceptable behavior.[17] In contrast to Euro-American women living under patriarchy, Indian women were not categorized as dependents who fell somewhere between men and children in the social hierarchy. Women, men, and children were all recognized as autonomous beings; however, the extended family or clan bound individuals together within a system of mutual obligation and respect. Therefore, lineage was more important than marriage in determining significant relationships and corresponding responsibilities, and consent, not contractual obligation, held marriages together. The independence of women and children, which struck European observers as odd, even anarchic, arose primarily from an inherent respect for individual autonomy and from different kinship systems.

Scholars have usually argued that it was either women's productive or reproductive role that explained their authority. For example, the more than one-hundred-year-old debate on the power of Iroquois women has drawn on both economics and matrilineality to explain Iroquois women's political powers. Perhaps more than any other tribe, the Iroquois delegated definite political decisionmaking powers to women. Several scholars and popular writers have claimed, as did George Murdock, compiler of the voluminous ethnographic bibliography of peoples around the globe, that the Iroquois "of all the peoples of the earth" came the closest to being a "matriarchate."[18] Although few scholars today would credit Iroquois women with that much power (they did not rule over men), Iroquois women did control certain decisions. Clan mothers appointed chiefs, could tell warriors when to go to war, and decided the fate of war captives.[19]

Judith Brown's widely cited article, "Economic Organization and the Position of Women Among the Iroquois," argued that Iroquois women had these rights because of their vital economic contribution of corn, beans, and squash to the Iroquois diet.[20] By comparing the Iroquois to the Bemba, a matrilineal society in Africa, Brown tried to hold matrilineality constant. Since Bemba women did not have a political role equivalent to that of Iroquois clan mothers, Brown concluded that Iroquois women's ability to control economic resources bestowed them with these decision-making powers. However, Brown provided other evidence about the Bemba that weakens her argument. According to Brown, the Bemba had a ranked society headed by one supreme ruler. In contrast, the Iroquois used the metaphor of the matrilocal longhouse to structure the council and the larger, multitribal alliance, the Confederacy. Chiefs represented their clans in council and in the Confederacy. And warriors went to war avowedly to avenge the deaths of clan members and to take captives who were then adopted into the clan. Since the matrilineal clan was the decisive political unit, it was most likely Iroquois women's status as heads of clans that determined their political powers. However, this does not exclude women's economic contributions from being an equally important avenue through which women earned respect and influence.[21]

Many Indian cultures conceptually tied women's economic activities to childbearing, and so perhaps the debate over whether economics or motherhood was the determining factor in women's status overstates the difference between the two. From the Indian cultural perspective, women's economic productivity and their reproductivity were expressions of fertility. In many native origin stories, women initiate the creation of life. They give birth to a child (or children), and their body becomes the earth from which plants and animals spring. Women gave life, in contrast to men, whose primary tasks of hunting and warfare involved taking life. In native stories and rituals, women's reproductivity was often metaphorically identified with food, nurturing, and life itself.[22]

As a by-product of the women's movement, many of us view work and childbearing as separate and competing activities. Indeed, the idea of motherhood as a source of power is anathema to many feminists, who see motherhood as the source of women's subjugation. However, if highly valued, motherhood could bring women status and power. The rise of Republican Motherhood, an ideology embraced by women in early national America, is an example of women expanding their influence by emphasizing the importance of their childrearing role.[23] By emphasizing their role as mothers of male citizens within a republican government, women in early national America gained a political voice. Indian women made similar claims to political authority. As one Cherokee woman, Katteuha, said to Benjamin Franklin in a 1787 letter advocating peace between their two nations,

> I am in hopes if you Rightly consider it that woman is the mother of All—and that woman Does not pull Children out of Trees or Stumps nor out of old Logs, but out of their Bodies, so that they ought to mind what a woman says, and look upon her as a mother—and I have Taken the privelage to Speak to you as my own Children, & the same as if you had sucked my Breast—and I am in hopes you have a beloved woman amongst you who will help to put her Children Right if they do wrong, as I shall do the same . . .[24]

Appealing to her role as mother was probably just one of many sources of authority Katteuha could claim. Depending on the situation, Indian women might have referred to themselves as mothers, heads of clans, or producers of certain foods as a means to give weight to their point of view.

The principle of autonomy (as it functioned within an extended family kin system), economic power, and the high status accorded motherhood, especially in matrilineal systems, all emerge as factors in scholars' assessments of the impact of European colonization on native women. Most of the historical literature about the changes in Indian communities during the past several hundred years has argued that there was a steady decline in the status and power of women. However, some scholars have noted a brief rise before the decline. And then there is other literature, much of it about Indian women in the twentieth century, which contends that Indian men had to make more radical changes in their accustomed roles than women did.

Research into how assimilationist policies affected women has usually found that there was a decline in women's status and power. Missionaries, government policymakers, and reformers often saw gender and the family as the focal point of the assimilation process. Assimilationist policies that were explicitly about education, land ownership, and religion also called for aligning Indian gender roles to fit Euro-American expectations and intended to restructure the extended family into a patriarchal, nuclear unit.[25] Most of the literature on Indian women and assimilation argues, or in some cases only implies, that these programs worked. Indian women and men, in the view of this scholarship, accepted the new gender ideology. At the very least, policymakers succeeded in introducing confusion into native beliefs about gender by attacking traditional attitudes without offering a viable replacement. Other scholars have emphasized women's resistance to change. However, even this scholarship asserts that women eventually gave in and accepted their place within the Euro-American gender ideology.[26]

Many of the scholars arguing that the position of Indian women declined after European contact use a materialist or Marxist perspective. Thus, they emphasize the introduction of new trading patterns and capitalist ideas as the underlying cause of an emerging male dominance. Eleanor Leacock, for instance, traced a decline in the power and status of Montagnais women to the economic disruptions of the fur trade, which left the Montagnais vulnerable to the new gender ideology prescribed by Jesuit missionaries.[27] Another anthropologist, Alan Klein, posited a similar decline in the status of Plains Indian women after European contact. He asserted that by the nineteenth century, the introduction of the horse had enhanced men's ability to hunt and trade but disempowered women. No longer the provisioners of essential foods, women in the nineteenth century now devoted most of their labor to processing hides, which men then controlled in trade.[28]

One does not need to use a Marxist perspective to see that capitalism did alter women's and men's economic roles in significant ways, especially in the twentieth century when wage work became the primary source of income for most Indians in the United States. Historically, the gendered division of labor has favored men in defining the kinds of work one does and in the amount of wages paid. Most Indian men and women entered the workforce as unskilled laborers, but for Indian women this meant domestic service, consistently the lowest paid and lowest status form of employment. As Laila Shukry Hamamsy showed in her study of Navajo women in the 1950s, the wage work opportunities available to men transformed women's traditional domestic role into one of economic dependency. Whereas previously Navajo women had themselves owned many sheep (the basis of wealth in the Navajo economy), as more of the family's income derived from wages, women had less control over their own and their families' source of livelihood.[29] Other research attests to more variability in Navajo responses to wage work as Navajos living in different places developed different kinds of mixed economies, all of which depended to some extent on wage work.[30]

Since Euro-American men traded with and employed native laborers from their own gendered perspective about appropriate economic behavior, they insisted on dealing with Indian men and therefore succeeded to some extent in limiting women's economic opportunities.[31] However, there is some evidence that Indian women may have benefitted from Euro-American contact, especially in the initial stages. In the early days of the fur trade, for instance, native women were crucial players in the development of the North Atlantic fur trade. Women processed hides, manufactured and sold pemmican (buffalo and berry jerky), and through alliances with French and British traders became the bilingual, bicultural intermediaries between Indians and Europeans. As the fur trade expanded, European gender and racial ideologies pushed native women to the bottom of fur trade society. European traders wanted wives who were white, decorative, and fragile, not the hard-working native women whose skills were so closely tied to the productive aspects of the fur trade economy.[32]

In contrast to the usual argument that European contact eventually led to a decline in Indian women's position, some research has suggested that colonial economic policies had the opposite effect on women's access to economic and political power. Jo-Anne Fiske's study of changes facing the Carrier Indians in Canada found that state policies and wage work constrained men's economic activities but ignored women's fishing and other subsistence activities. Over the years, women's control over certain important resources brought women more political power, visibility, and respect.[33] In *Oglala Women*, Marla Powers discerned a related pattern in women's lives at Pine Ridge Reservation.[34] Powers contended that Oglala women survived the economic stresses of the transition to reservation life more easily than men because their roles required less adjustment. Men could no longer hunt buffalo. Women, however, had been caretakers of the home and children in the nineteenth century, and those responsibilities have continued to be of high value in the twentieth century.[35] Locating the origins of women's traditional authority elsewhere, Laura F. Klein argued that contemporary Tlingit women's political influence in community affairs stemmed from the longstanding Tlingit respect for individual autonomy.[36]

Despite these few maverick interpretations of Indian women's authority and its survival into the present, most of the research in Indian women's history has pointed to a decline in women's status, either abruptly or gradually after European contact. But it is then difficult to explain the prominence of Indian women in the political and social life of their communities throughout the twentieth century. The best-known contemporary example of an Indian woman leader is Wilma Mankiller, formerly Principal Chief of the Cherokee Nation (one of the largest Indian tribes in the United States), but there have been many other equally note-worthy Indian women. Indian women have served as tribal officers, staffed tribal and federal Indian programs, worked with government pol-icymakers to improve U.S.-Indian relations, and been respected as educators and innovators in their reservation and urban communities.[37]

While it is true that the odds were stacked against Indian women as they began to participate in the American economy, many women avoided or rejected the dismal domestic service route to become professionals. Indian women in higher education, like other American women, usually trained in areas stereotypically defined as women's work: education, health care, and social welfare. Although some women may have felt frustrated by the gendered limitations on their educational and professional choices, for most this meant they became the experts in those areas of increasing importance to Indian communities. Indians living on reservations and many of those living in cities have been plagued by excessively high poverty rates accompanied by an obviously related host of other problems, such as high rates of unemployment, alcoholism, fetal alcohol syndrome, infant mortality, and children dropping out of school at early ages. Indian women's visibility and activism in contemporary politics and social pro-grams can be viewed as a continuation of their traditional role as important decisionmakers within the family.

Partly because Indian women were among the most active and respected leaders in their communities, the Indian response to the "wom-en's movement" of the 1970s was one of ambivalence. For instance, in a recently published autobiography, American Indian Movement (AIM) activist Mary Crow Dog referred to feminism as irrelevant to Indian women. And yet, much like the Crow woman Pretty-Shield, Crow Dog insisted on telling a woman's story of such events as the 1973 takeover of Wounded Knee, AIM's most militant action and one in which AIM's male leaders dominated in the public eye, in the media spotlight, and now in historical accounts of the Red Power movement.[38] Many Indian women share with Mary Crow Dog a skepticism about feminism and consider the issues raised by the "women's movement" not only alien to the Indian experience but also potentially harmful to the Indian community as a whole. However, some Indian women writers and scholars have worked to define a distinctively Indian feminism. This Indian feminism would acknowledge the achievements and leadership of Indian women while taking into account the uniqueness of the Indian situation, the continuing importance of the extended family, and the need to improve conditions for all Indians (not just for Indian women).[39]

◆　◆　◆

Research in Native American women's history has reached a critical juncture. The previous literature provides us with a solid base of knowledge and ideas from which to expand the breadth and depth of our approaches. The articles in this collection will help achieve new directions in Indian women's history.

Even though these articles together span several centuries and cover the experience of ten different Indian groups, common themes unite them. Most notably, these essays show that we cannot answer questions about the effects of European colonization on Indian women's power and status without separating power into its many parts. Power is not tangible, measurable, immediately observable and knowable, but instead the many different manifestations of power need to be situated and contextualized to be understood. Power could mean authority in some community activities but not in others, authority in the family, autonomy, having a voice in public activity, having an independent income, having the opportunity to earn respect. Indian women could have simultaneously lost and gained power. Although the issue of Indian women's power may be too multi-faceted to answer simply, these articles do show that Indian women continually worked to enhance their position within native societies.

Organized chronologically, the collection begins with two essays about the early years of Indian-European relations on the eastern seaboard of North America. Kathleen Brown's essay examines the "gender frontier" structuring Indian-white relations in Jamestown, Virginia, the first permanent Anglo settlement in North America. My essay on Mohawk saint Kateri Tekakwitha explores missionized Indian women's reasons for choosing Christianity in seventeenth-century New France.

Four articles cover the period from the mid-eighteenth century to the mid-nineteenth century. Lucy Eldersveld Murphy describes how Winnebago, Mesquakie, and Sauk women adapted their traditional, gender-defined economic activities to meet the needs of the new market economy brought to the Fox-Wisconsin Riverway area by European traders, settlers, and miners. Theda Perdue looks at how Cherokee women and men accepted U.S. policies aimed at assimilating Indians but in ways that complemented traditional gender roles. Clara Sue Kidwell argues that Mississippi Choctaw women continued in their role as heads of matrilineal clans despite intermarriage with whites, pressure to remove to Indian Territory, and land loss. Finally, Carol Douglas Sparks documents Anglos' changing images of Navajo women as they fought for possession of the Southwest.

Four articles covering the period from the turn of the century to the 1960s complete the collection. Katherine Osburn examines the impact of the 1887 Dawes (Allotment) Act on the Southern Ute Reservation in Colorado and Ute women's efforts to thwart the patriarchal intent of the land distribution process. Based on a quantitative analysis of purchasing records from the Yakima Reservation in Washington State for the early twentieth century, Clifford Trafzer shows that Yakima women were active traders in the reservation economy. Harry Kersey, Jr., and Helen Bannan trace Florida Seminole women's history from the late nineteenth century to the present and demonstrate how women's traditional political influence has now revived, partly because many Seminole women have sought higher education and developed useful skills for tribal governance. Observing a similar situation among Pima and Maricopa women in Arizona, Päivi Hoikkala's article emphasizes the critical role played by the Office of Economic Opportunity programs in the 1960s and 1970s in bringing more women into leadership positions.

Many of these articles discuss women's relationships to the changing economy, a familiar issue in the historical and anthropological literature on native women. Whereas most previous researchers have claimed that the male-dominated market economy introduced by Euro-Americans favored men and excluded women, these authors have found that native women adapted traditional roles to participate in market-oriented economic activity.

Murphy's study of several native groups in the midwest is particularly interesting for its discussion of women lead miners. Native women in other regions of North America had to adapt to a market economy centered on the fur trade or deerskin trade, which meant that men, because they were the hunters, became the primary producers of goods for the market. However, the Fox-Wisconsin Riverway region had rich lead resources as well as furs. Sauk, Mesquakie, and Winnebago women adapted their traditional agricultural, gathering, and domestic manufacturing tasks to produce surpluses for trade with Euro-Americans. They also began mining lead, a kind of labor which could be considered women's work since it was a form of gathering and could be integrated in the seasonal round of maple sugaring and corn planting. Consequently, these women also stood at the front lines, on the frontier of Anglo-American expansion. As white farmers and miners swarmed into the region in the 1820s and 1830s, abuses against native women and men mounted, culminating in an Indian defeat in the 1832 Black Hawk War. Women seem to have eagerly and successfully participated in the emerging regional economy until competition with white men, who did the same kind of work, squeezed native women out of mining and deprived native women and men of their land and resources.

Theda Perdue examines the economic changes in Cherokee society during the same time period. Unlike the midwestern tribes in Murphy's article, the Cherokees had to cope simultaneously with the development of a market economy and an assimilationist United States Indian policy. Cherokee women responded to assimilationist interventions by incorporating some aspects of women's work as defined by Euro-Americans. They learned to spin and weave. However, Cherokee women recast the design of the assimilationist project by adding the buying, raising, and selling of livestock to their agricultural role. Within Cherokee society in the 1820s and 1830s, women continued to engage in their traditional work roles but also learned new skills that enabled them to earn income in a market economy. As Perdue shows, both Cherokee men and women took on new economic roles in the early eighteenth century, but did not accept the gendered division of labor U.S. policymakers outlined for them. Men resisted farming, probably because it was considered women's work, but extended their traditional role as traders to engage in entrepreneurial business activity, and many hired laborers or bought slaves to farm for them. Cherokee women do not seem to have pursued wealth on a vast scale, as some Cherokee men did, but certainly retained independence as producers within the economy. As Perdue has discussed elsewhere, race ultimately united Cherokee women and men under a common economic disadvantage. White miners and landseekers flocked to the Cherokee Nation in the 1820s and 1830s, pressuring the U.S. government into forcibly removing the Cherokees to west of the Mississippi River in the winter of 1838–39.[40]

In his analysis of Yakima purchasing records, Clifford Trafzer assesses women's participation in an early-twentieth-century reservation economy. The horse had become an important feature of Yakima culture in the nineteenth century, and economic adaptations to reservation life carried on this tradition as many Yakimas turned to ranching. Trafzer shows that women were at least as active as men in making what seem to be capital investments in the emerging ranching and farming industry—horses, livestock, wagons, and farm equipment. Trafzer suggests that women's traditional role as provisioners of important foods adapted to a new form of economic activity as the confines of the reservation forced the Yakimas to look for alternative ways of making a living.

Later in the twentieth century, Indian communities had to make even more dramatic adjustments to their traditional economies. Kersey and Bannan's research on the Seminole points to the 1920s and 1930s as a crucial period in their economic and political history. Increasingly hemmed in by white settlements, Seminole income came to depend on their participation in the Florida tourist industry, the sale of craft items to tourists, and agricultural wage work. These opportunities, though limited and low-paying, were available to both men and women, and in some cases, Seminole women were more active at seeking wage work than men. Indeed, women may have had more access to income than men, since tourists especially prized Seminole patchwork, a style of sewing different fabrics together that was invented by Seminole women. Kersey and Bannan connect women's economic and educational parity with men to their rising visibility in the traditionally male sphere of politics beginning in the 1930s.

Although these four articles are about the experiences of different Indian peoples in different times and places, they hint at changes that may have affected all native economies. Euro-Americans created a demand for natural resources and manufactured items that Indians could satisfy by extending or transforming some economic activities, though perhaps at the expense of other activities. Indians also participated in the Euro-American market economy as they traded, raised, and invested in livestock. In the twentieth century, wage work became necessary, and education came to be seen as a means to better jobs and higher wages. As Indian groups became more involved in the global economy introduced by Euro-Americans, their short-term adaptations to economic change could be termed successful but also carried the potential for economic dependency and marginalization. The Seminoles could in the twentieth century earn income through tourism and agricultural wage work, but they could not earn much income. These articles show that native people had to continually struggle to find new ways of making a living, and that this struggle had a gender dimension. Both women and men reinvented the traditional gendered division of labor to find new economic roles for themselves in the nineteenth and twentieth centuries.

Other articles in this collection further explore the issue of separate spheres, focusing on women's domestic role, especially the role of mother. The articles by Kidwell, Osburn, and Hoikkala reveal how "motherhood" as a cultural construct could be preserved or reconstructed to meet changing social conditions.

Clara Sue Kidwell compares the experience of two groups of Choctaws during the removal period of the 1820s and 1830s: the main body of Choctaws who removed to Indian Territory, now Oklahoma, and the small number of families who chose to remain behind in Mississippi. The majority of Choctaws, politically organized as the Choctaw Nation, adhered to new laws that did away with the Choctaws' traditional, matrilineal social organization. The Choctaw Nation adopted patrilineage, new landholding and residence patterns, and the use of an Anglo kinship system to explain relationships. But the families left behind in Mississippi, perhaps because they fell outside of the Choctaw Nation's state-building efforts, retained matrilineage and matrilocal residence patterns for much longer. The Choctaws who removed seem to have willingly countered U.S. assimilationist policies by conforming somewhat to Anglo-American family ideals, but the Mississippi Choctaws, left to their own devices, found there was no need to reform a household structure that granted respect and authority to the matrilineal head.

Katherine Osburn's article on Ute women and the Dawes Act presents a contrasting situation, one in which U.S. assimilationist policies directly threatened women's traditional economic and social roles. The Dawes Act, which allotted communal land to individuals, intended to make property-owning, yeoman farmers out of Indians. When implemented on the Southern Ute Reservation in the late-nineteenth century, allotment favored men as heads of households, and married women's rights to allotments were subsumed within their husbands' ownership. Osburn's essay focuses on the problems experienced by divorced women claiming land legally owned by their ex-husbands. Osburn argues that women probably considered their claims to land valid because of their traditional economic role as gatherers. However, in their appeals to U.S. Indian agents, women explained their rights in terms of motherhood (they were the mothers of their ex-husbands' children), a social role of high value in Ute culture. Neither of these roles—women as important economic producers and women as mothers—resonated with Indian agents. Agents persisted in believing that the land belonged to the women's husbands. Agents were sympathetic, however, to divorced women's claims, but primarily because they saw these women as wives, who in the Euro-American, patriarchal tradition were economic dependents of their husbands.

Based largely on oral history research on the Salt River Pima-Maricopa Indian Community in Arizona, Päivi Hoikkala's essay looks at how, in the 1960s and 1970s, grant money from the Office of Economic Opportunity (OEO) transformed women's political role in the reservation community. Women dominated in the development and maintenance of social welfare programs funded by the OEO. Their involvement can in part be traced to the traditional complementarity of women's and men's work. Both the women and men whom Hoikkala interviewed explained women's prominence in social welfare programs and their emergence as leaders in tribal governance as an extension of their role as caretakers, nurturers, mothers. However, as Hoikkala shows, women had already ventured into wage work, on and off the reservation, before the OEO-funded programs opened up new employment opportunities, and many of the women who sought employment with the new programs did so out of economic necessity. Indeed, the skills, educational opportunities, and self-confidence that women acquired at their new jobs might prove to have the longterm effect of eliminating the gendered division of labor and the previous pattern of a male public sphere versus a female domestic sphere. As one of her interviewees said, "today women 'work as heavy equipment operators, in tribal law enforcement and other occupations that would have been unimaginable twenty years ago.'" Women have also moved into positions in tribal government that manage economic development and tribal resources, leadership positions that do not fall within a traditionally defined women's sphere and its contemporary counterpart, social welfare work. Still, it is women's caretaking role that justifies their employment outside the home and their authority as community leaders.

Kidwell, Osburn, and Hoikkala discuss the meaning of motherhood and separate spheres from three different angles. Motherhood sometimes had significance in structuring social relationships, and may have been especially important in matrilineal and matrilocal societies. Even in bilateral societies, such as the Southern Utes, motherhood was a social role demanding respect, and a role which women might have emphasized as a means to gain economic independence and an equality with men. Unfortunately for the Ute women discussed in Osburn's article, Indian agents put women who saw themselves as "mothers" into the category of "wives," a social role which Euro-Americans considered inferior to that of "husbands." And finally, as Hoikkala shows, the belief that women have special caretaking abilities can be a powerful political force within reservation communities. In contrast to the women's movement of the 1960s and 1970s, Pima-Maricopa women became more active and visible in the community by emphasizing women's domestic qualities.

All seven of the articles discussed so far suggest that Indian women have not found the idea of separate spheres for men and women confining. In contrast to the Marxist model of separate spheres, however, Indian women continued to be economic producers and sought to maximize their economic opportunities while shouldering much of the responsibility for the well-being of their families. Women's economic independence and the cultural ideal of women's difference from men worked together to provide a base of strength and identity from which women could seek more political influence.

Three other articles in the collection deal with the cultural conflict in gender ideologies between Indians and Euro-Americans. Although all the previously mentioned articles dealt with this theme, the articles by Brown, Sparks, and Shoemaker address more specifically the issue of gender as a cultural system shaping the contact experience. Brown and Sparks discuss the consequences of imagining the Other through gender-tinted glasses, while my article on Tekakwitha examines the native appropriation of Christian symbols.

Brown coins the term "gender frontier" to explain how Algonguians and Anglo settlers in Colonial Virginia saw each other in gendered ways. Powhatan, who headed a powerful alliance of native peoples, sought to incorporate the new arrivals under his "mantle." As men without women, Anglo settlers, from the Algonquian perspective, appeared to be warriors in need of women. Powhatan's people gave the Englishmen the services of women: women provided corn, sexual intimacy, and adoption into Indian families, a native ceremony in which women played a prominent role. Resisting Powhatan's claims to leadership in this Algonquian-Anglo alliance, the English settlers tried to subjugate the Algonquians by "feminizing" them. Provisioning Englishmen with corn placed the Algonquians, as a people, in a female role in relation to English warriors. This "gender frontier" mediated the tense diplomatic and economic relationships between Algonguians and Anglo settlers in the tidewater region.

Carol Douglas Sparks describes how real Navajo women in the documentary record are overshadowed by figurative Navajo women created to fit the plotline of Anglo conquest. A romanticized trope of beautiful, young Navajo women awaiting rescue prevails in Anglo accounts of the southwestern landscape before Anglos acquired the territory from Mexico. As Anglos tried to subdue and contain the Navajo people, Navajo women were seen as threatening harridans reigning over a hostile land. When once the Navajos were later confined to a reservation at Bosque Redondo, New Mexico, the dominant image employed in Anglo descriptions was that of the "squaw drudge," the faithful, hard-working wife of a lazy Indian man. In tracing this transition in Anglo images of Navajo women, Sparks's article shows how deliberate and malleable misinterpretations of Indian gender systems assisted in the Euro-American conquest of native people.

My article on Kateri Tekakwitha argues the same thing but from the Indian perspective. Tekakwitha and other women at the Christian Indian community of Kahnawake near Montreal seem to have interpreted Christianity as a set of rituals and stories that empowered women. The Jesuits made patriarchy explicit in the new social customs they tried to impose at Kahnawake, but they also brought imagery, stories, and rituals that portrayed women (e.g., the Virgin Mary, women saints, and nuns) as powerful and respected members of European communities. Indian women saw what they wanted to see in Christianity, and probably selectively appropriated Christian symbols and rituals without necessarily accepting Jesuit patriarchy.

Cultural constructions of gender had as much influence on the contact experience as economic, political, and social interactions. Cultural ideas about gender difference provided a lens through which people looked at the Other and interpreted, or misinterpreted, the meaning of the Other's actions and words.

The four-hundred-year period covered by this volume reveals surprising continuity in native women's experiences. Where scholars have previously seen a history of decline and increasing marginality, these articles show that native women actively, creatively, and often successfully resisted marginality. In responding to the changing world around them, Indian women did not conform to the Euro-American gender ideal. Sometimes native women were forced to adapt to Euro-American gender expectations, but more often they sought alternatives and created a new understanding of their roles by merging traditional beliefs with cultural innovation.

NOTES

1. He was referring to Patricia Albers and Beatrice Medicine, eds., *The Hidden Half: Studies of Plains Indian Women* (Lanham: University Press of America, 1983).

2. Kathryn E. Holland Braund makes this point in her article on Creek women, "Guardians of Tradition and Handmaidens to Change: Women's Roles in Creek Economic and Social Life During the Eighteenth Century," *American Indian Quarterly* 14 (1990): 239–258.

3. There are two excellent annotated bibliographies listing materials on Indian women: Gretchen M. Bataille and Kathleen M. Sands, *American Indian Women: A Guide To Research* (NY: Garland Publishing, 1991); Rayna Green, *Native American Women* (Bloomington: Indiana University Press, 1983). There are several review essays, each with a different focus, which are also useful: Patricia C. Albers, "From Illusion to Illumination: Anthropological Studies of American Indian Women," in *Gender and Anthropology: Critical Reviews for Research and Teaching*, ed. Sandra Morgan (Washington, D.C.: American Anthropological Assocation, 1989), 132–170; Deborah Welch, "American Indian Women: Reaching Beyond the Myth," in *New Directions in American Indian History*, ed. Colin G. Calloway (Norman: University of Oklahoma, 1988), 31–48; Kathleen M. Brown, "Brave New Worlds: Women's and Gender History," *William and Mary Quarterly* 50 (1993): 311–328. Also see Gretchen M. Bataille and Kathleen Mullen Sands, *American Indian Women: Telling Their Lives* (Lincoln: University of Nebraska Press, 1984), which gives a thorough assessment of Indian women's autobiographies, an important resource for Indian women's history.

4. Robert F. Berkhofer, Jr., *The White Man's Indian: Images of the American Indian from Columbus to the Present* (NY: Alfred A. Knopf, 1978).

5. Rayna Green, "The Pocahontas Perplex: The Image of Indian Women in American Culture," in *Unequal Sisters: A Multicultural Reader in U.S. Women's History*, eds. Ellen Carol DuBois and Vicki L. Ruiz (NY: Routledge, 1990), 15–21; David Smits, "The 'Squaw Drudge': A Prime Index of Savagism," *Ethnohistory* 29 (1982): 281–306; Katherine M. Weist, "Beasts of Burden and Menial Slaves: Nineteenth Century Observations of Northern Plains Indian Women," in *The Hidden Half*, 29–52.

6. Clara Sue Kidwell, "Indian Women as Cultural Mediators," *Ethnohistory* 39 (Spring 1992): 97–107.

7. See, for example, Janet D. Spector, "Male/Female Task Differentiation Among the Hidatsa: Toward the Development of an Archeological Approach to the Study of Gender," in *The Hidden Half*, 77–99; Martha L. Sempowski, "Differential Mortuary Treatment of Seneca Women: Some Social Inferences," *Archaeology of Eastern North America* 14 (1986): 35–44; Paula Gunn Allen, *The Sacred Hoop: Recovering the Feminine in American Indian Traditions* (Boston: Beacon Press, 1986).

8. Ruth Landes, *The Ojibwa Woman* (NY: Norton, 1971), v, 18. Another classic ethnographic study of Indian women is Louise S. Spindler, *Menomini Women and Culture Change*, American Anthropological Association, Memoir 91 (February 1962).

9. Michelle Zimbalist Rosaldo, "Woman, Culture, and Society: A Theoretical Overview," in *Woman, Culture, and Society*, eds. Michelle Zimbalist Rosaldo and Louise Lamphere (Stanford: Stanford University Press, 1974), 16–42.

10. Eleanor Burke Leacock, "Women in an Egalitarian Society: The Montagnais-Naskapi of Canada," in *Myths of Male Dominance: Collected Articles on Women Cross-Culturally* (NY: Monthly Review Press, 1981), 37. Also see her essay "Women's Status in Egalitarian Society: Implications for Social Evolution," in *Myths of Male Dominance*, 133–182.

11. Leacock, 147.

12. Frederick Engels, *The Origin of the Family, Private Property and the State, in the Light of the Researches of Lewis H. Morgan* (NY: International Publishers, 1942); Lewis Henry Morgan, *Ancient Society, or Researches in the Lines of Human Progress from Savagery Through Barbarism to Civilization* (Tucson: University of Arizona Press, 1985); Leacock, "Introduction to Lewis Henry Morgan, Ancient Society, Parts I, II, III, IV," in *Myths of Male Dominance*, 85–132.

13. See for example, Spector, "Male/Female Task Differentiation Among the Hidatsa"; Raymond J. DeMallie, "Male and Female in Traditional Lakota Culture," in *The Hidden Half*, 237–265; Priscilla Buffalohead, "Farmers, Warriors, and Traders: A Fresh Look at Ojibway Women," *Minnesota History* 48 (1983): 236–244; Loraine Littlefield, "Women Traders in the Maritime Fur Trade," in *Native People, Native Lands: Canadian Indians, Inuit and Métis*, ed. Bruce Alden Cox (Ottawa: Carleton University Press, 1987), 173–185; Nancy J. Parezo, "Navajo Sandpaintings: The Importance of Sex Roles in Craft Production," *American Indian Quarterly* 6 (1982), 125–148.

14. An especially good account of a particular berdache, described within the context of Zuni gender roles, is Will Roscoe's *The Zuni Man-Woman* (Albuquerque: University of New Mexico Press, 1991); also see Walter L. Williams, *The Spirit and the Flesh: Sexual Diversity in American Indian Culture* (Boston: Beacon Press, 1986).

15. For more on women assuming a male role, see Evelyn Blackwood, "Sexuality and Gender in Certain Native American Tribes: The Case of Cross-gender Females," *Signs* 10 (1984): 27–42; Oscar Lewis, "Manly-Hearted Women Among the North Piegan," *American Anthropologist* 43 (1941): 173–187; Bea Medicine, "'Warrior Women'—Sex Role Alternatives for Plains Indian Women," in *The Hidden Half*, 267–280. For more on politically or ceremonially prominent women in general, see Gretchen Bataille, ed., *Native American Women: A Biographical Dictionary* (NY: Garland, 1993); Priscilla Buffalohead, "Farmers, Warriors and Traders"; Robert Grumet, "Sunksquaws, Shamans, and Tradeswomen: Middle Atlantic Coastal Algonkian Women During the 17th and 18th Centuries," in *Women and Colonization: Anthropological Perspectives*, eds. Mona Etienne and Eleanor Leacock (NY: Praeger, 1980), 43–62; Valerie Sherer Mathes, "Native American Women in Medicine and the Military," *Journal of the West* 21 (1982): 41–48; Martha W. McCartney, "Cockacoeske, Queen of Pamunkey: Diplomat and Suzeraine," in *Powhatan's Mantle: Indians in the Colonial Southeast*, eds. Peter H. Wood, Gregory A. Waselkov, and M. Thomas Hatley (Lincoln: University of Nebraska Press, 1989), 173–195; Theda Perdue, "Nancy Ward," in *Portraits of American Women: From Settlement to the Present*, eds. C.J. Barker-Benfield and Catherine Clinton (NY: St. Martin's Press, 1991), 83–100; Helen Hornbeck Tanner, "Coocoochee: Mohawk Medicine Woman," *American Indian Culture and Research Journal* 3 (1979), 23–42.

16. Frank B. Linderman, *Pretty-Shield: Medicine Woman of the Crows* (Lincoln: University of Nebraska Press, 1972), 228, 229.

17. Margaret Connell Szasz, "Native American Children," in *American Childhood: A Research Guide and Historical Handbook*, eds. Joseph M. Hawes and N. Ray Hiner (Westport, Connecticut: Greenwood Press, 1985), 311–342.

18. George Peter Murdock, *Our Primitive Contemporaries* (NY: Macmillan, 1934), 302.

19. Cara B. Richards argued that Iroquois women's power to determine the fate of war captives and freedom to choose marriage partners were post-contact developments, but her evidence does not entirely support this. For instance, the Jesuit accounts she uses mention different people (warriors, chiefs, councils, clan mothers, sisters) making decisions about captives. Richards spliced together a series of brief references to captives and claimed they showed change over time, when they could also be interpreted as being different stages of a process. Moreover, she does not offer any explanation as to why these changes might have occurred. See her article "Matriarchy or Mistake: The Role of Iroquois Women through Time," in *Cultural Stability and Cultural Change*, Proceedings of the 1957 Annual Spring Meeting of the American Ethnological Society, ed. Verne F. Ray (Seattle: University of Washington Press, 1957), 36–45.

20. Judith K. Brown, "Economic Organization and the Position of Women Among the Iroquois," *Ethnohistory* 17 (1970): 151–167.

21. Elisabeth Tooker, "Women in Iroquois Society," in *Extending the Rafters: Interdisciplinary Approaches to Iroquoisan Studies*, eds. Michael K. Foster, Jack Campisi, Marianne Mithun (Albany: State University of New York Press, 1984), 109–123. Cherokee women also had a voice in the fate of war captives and early land sales. As Theda Perdue shows, these powers originated in both the Cherokees' matrilineal social organization and in women's proprietary, agricultural relationship with the land. See Theda Perdue, "The Traditional Status of Cherokee Women," *Furman Studies* 26 (1980): 19–25; Theda Perdue, "Cherokee Women and the Trail of Tears," *Journal of Women's History* 1 (1989): 14–30.

22. Mary E. Black, "Maidens and Mothers: An Analysis of Hopi Corn Metaphors," *Ethnology* 23 (1984): 279–288; Sam D. Gill, *Mother Earth: An American Story* (Chicago: University of Chicago Press, 1987); M. Jane Young, "Women, Reproduction, and Religion in Western Puebloan Society," *Journal of American Folklore* 100 (1987): 436–445.

23. Linda K. Kerber, *Women of the Republic: Intellect and Ideology in Revolutionary America* (NY: W.W. Norton, 1986); also see Paula Baker, "The Domestication of Politics: Women and American Political Society, 1780–1920," *American Historical Review* 89 (1984): 620–647.

24. Samuel Hazard, ed., *Pennsylvania Archives*, 1787, Volume 11 (Philadelphia: J. Severns, 1852–56), 181.

25. For more on the gender aspects of assimilationist policies, see Helen M. Bannan, "'True Womanhood' on the Reservation: Field Matrons in United States Indian Service," Working Paper #18 (Tucson: Southwest Institute for Research on Women, 1984), 1–25; Lisa E. Emmerich, "'Right in the Midst of My Own People': Native American Women and the Field Matron Program," *American Indian Quarterly* 15 (1991): 201–216; Theda Perdue, "Southern Indians and the Cult of True Womanhood," in *The Web of Southern Social Relations: Women, Family, and Education*, eds. Walter J. Fraser, Jr., R. Frank Saunders, Jr., John L. Wakelyn (Athens: University of Georgia Press, 1985), 35–51; Carolyn Garrett Pool,

"Reservation Policy and the Economic Position of Wichita Women," *Great Plains Quarterly* 8 (1988): 158–171; Margaret Connell Szasz, "'Poor Richard' Meets the Native American: Schooling for Young Indian Women in Eighteenth-Century Connecticut," *Pacific Historical Review* 49 (1980): 215–235; Robert A. Trennert, "Educating Indian Girls at Nonreservation Boarding Schools, 1878–1920," in *Unequal Sisters*, 224–249; Robert A. Trennert, "Victorian Morality and the Supervision of Indian Women Working in Phoenix, 1906–1930," *Journal of Social History* 22 (1988): 112–128; Mary E. Young, "Women, Civilization, and the Indian Question," in *Clio Was a Woman: Studies in the History of American Women* (Washington, D.C.: Howard University Press, 1980), 98–110. For an account of an indigenous school that promoted values similar to those advocated by assimilationist programs, see Devon A. Mihesuah, *Cultivating the Rosebuds: The Education of Women at the Cherokee Female Seminary, 1851–1909* (Urbana: University of Illinois Press, 1993).

26. Karen Anderson, *Chain Her By One Foot: The Subjugation of Women in Seventeenth-Century New France* (NY: Routledge, 1991); Carol Devens, *Countering Colonization: Native American Women and Great Lakes Missions, 1630–1900* (Berkeley: University of California Press, 1992); Diane Rothenberg, "The Mothers of the Nation: Seneca Resistance to Quaker Intervention," in *Women and Colonization*, 66–72. For a critique of these kinds of declension arguments, see Nancy Shoemaker, "The Rise or Fall of Iroquois Women," *Journal of Women's History* 2 (1991): 39–57.

27. Eleanor Leacock, "Montagnais Women and the Jesuit Program for Colonization," *Myths of Male Dominance*, 43–62.

28. Alan M. Klein, "The Plains Truth: The Impact of Colonialism on Indian Women," *Dialectical Anthropology* 7 (1983): 299–313; Alan M. Klein, "The Political-Economy of Gender: A 19th Century Plains Indian Case Study," *The Hidden Half*, 143–173.

29. Laila Shukry Hamamsy, "The Role of Women in a Changing Navaho Society," *American Anthropologist* 59 (1957): 101–111.

30. Christine Conte, "Ladies, Livestock, Land and Lucre: Women's Networks and Social Status on the Western Navajo Reservation," *American Indian Quarterly* 6 (1982): 105–124; Louise Lamphere, "Historical and Regional Variability in Navajo Women's Roles," *Journal of Anthropological Research* 45 (1989): 431–456.

31. See for instance, Ellice B. Gonzalez, "An Ethnohistorical Analysis of Micmac Male and Female Economic Roles," *Ethnohistory* 29 (1982): 117–129.

32. Sylvia Van Kirk, *Many Tender Ties: Women in Fur-Trade Society, 1670–1870* (Norman: University of Oklahoma Press, 1980); Jennifer S.H. Brown, *Strangers in Blood: Fur Trade Company Families in Indian Country* (Vancouver: University of British Columbia Press, 1980); also see Richard Perry, "The Fur Trade and the Status of Women in the Western Subarctic," *Ethnohistory* 26 (1979): 363–375; Perry argued that the fur trade had varying effects on the status of women depending on tribes' differing pre-fur-trade cultural attitudes towards women, geography and its relation to women's work, and the availability of pack animals; for women and the fur trade in the Pacific Northwest, see Mary C. Wright, "Economic Development and Native American Women in the Early Nineteenth Century," *American Quarterly* 33 (1981): 525–536.

33. Jo-Anne Fiske, "Fishing is Women's Business: Changing Economic Roles of Carrier Women and Men," in *Native People, Native Lands*, 186–198.

34. Marla N. Powers, *Oglala Women: Myth, Ritual and Reality* (Chicago: University of Chicago Press, 1986).

35. Clara Sue Kidwell also makes this point in "The Power of Women in Three American Indian Societies," *Journal of Ethnic Studies* 6 (1979): 113–121.

36. Laura F. Klein, "'She's One of Us, You Know' The Political Life of Tlingit Women: Traditional, Historical, and Contemporary Perspectives," *The Western Canadian Journal of Anthropology* 6 (1976): 164–183.

37. Bataille, *Native American Women: A Biographical Dictionary*; Ruth McDonald Boyer and Narcissus Duffy Gayton, *Apache Mothers and Daughters: Four Generations of a Family* (Norman: University of Oklahoma Press, 1992); Gae Whitney Canfield, *Sarah Winnemucca of the Northern Paiutes* (Norman: University of Oklahoma Press, 1983); Laurence Hauptman, "Alice Jemison: Seneca Political Activist," *Indian Historian* 12 (1979): 15–40; Robert N. Lynch, "Women in Northern Paiute Politics," *Signs* 11 (1986): 352–366; John Terreo, "Minerva Allen: Educator, Linguist, Poet," *Montana: The Magazine of Western History* 41 (1991): 58–68. Alison Bernstein argued that the Indian New Deal of the 1930s gave Indian women more access to political participation; however, she also mentions that a number of already influential Indian women activists and spokespeople, such as Ruth Muskrat Bronson and Gertrude Bonnin, were excluded from the BIA's planning and implementation of New Deal policies. See her article "A Mixed Record: The Political Enfranchisement of American Indian Women During the Indian New Deal," *Journal of the West* 23 (1984): 13–20.

38. Mary Crow Dog and Richard Erdoes, *Lakota Woman* (NY: HarperCollins, 1990).

39. Rayna Green, "Diary of a Native American Feminist," *Ms. Magazine* (July–August 1982): 170–172, 211–213; Kathryn Shanley, "Thoughts on Indian Feminism," in *Modern American Women: A Documentary History*, ed. Susan Ware (Dorsey Press, 1989), 349–354.

40. Perdue, "Cherokee Women and the Trail of Tears."

1

KATHLEEN M. BROWN

THE ANGLO-ALGONQUIAN GENDER FRONTIER

In 1607, when English colonists made their first permanent settlement at Jamestown, Virginia, many of the Algonquian-speaking peoples living in the Chesapeake Bay area belonged to an alliance of different tribal groups headed by the powerful Indian leader Powhatan. By the end of the seventeenth century, intermittent warfare between Virginia Algonquians and English settlers had resulted in the destruction of Powhatan's confederacy, substantial loss in land and population, and the confinement of the few remaining Algonquians to reservations. Kathleen Brown's article focuses on early Algonquian-English relations.

Recent scholarship has improved our understanding of the relationship between English settlers and Indians during the early seventeenth century. We know, for instance, that English expectations about American Indians were conditioned by Spanish conquest literature, their own contact with the Gaelic Irish, elite perceptions of the lower classes, and obligations to bring Christianity to those they believed to be in darkness.[1]

Largely unacknowledged by historians, gender roles and identities also played an important role in shaping English and Indian interactions. Accompanied by few English women, English male adventurers to Roanoake and Jamestown island confronted Indian men and women in their native land. In this cultural encounter, the gender ways, or what some feminist theorists might call the "performances," of Virginia Algonquians challenged English gentlemen's assumptions about the naturalness of their own gender identities. This interaction brought exchanges, new cultural forms, created sites of commonality, painful deceptions, bitter misunderstandings, and bloody conflicts.[2]

Identities as English or Indian were only partially formed at the beginning of this meeting of cultures; it required the daily presence of an "other" to crystallize self-conscious articulations of group identity. In contrast, maleness and femaleness within each culture provided explicit and deep-rooted foundations for individual identity and the organization of social relations. In both Indian and English societies, differences between men and women were critical to social order. Ethnic identities formed along this "gender frontier," the site of creative and destructive processes resulting from the confrontations of culturally-specific manhoods and womanhoods. In the emerging Anglo-Indian struggle, gender symbols and social relations signified claims to power. Never an absolute barrier, however, the gender frontier also produced sources for new identities and social practices.[3]

In this essay, I explore in two ways the gender frontier that evolved between English settlers and the indigenous peoples of Virginia's tidewater. First, I assess how differences in gender roles shaped the perceptions and interactions of both groups. Second, I analyze the "gendering" of the emerging Anglo-Indian power struggle. While the English depicted themselves as warriors dominating a feminized native population, Indian women and men initially refused to acknowledge claims to military supremacy, treating the foreigners as they would subject peoples, cowards, or servants. When English warrior discourse became unavoidable, however, Indian women and men attempted to exploit what they saw as the warrior's obvious dependence upon others for the agricultural and reproductive services that ensured group survival.

The indigenous peoples who engaged in this struggle were residents of Virginia's coastal plain, a region of fields, forests, and winding rivers that extended from the shores of the Chesapeake Bay to the mountains and waterfalls near present-day Richmond. Many were affiliated with Powhatan, the *werowance* who had consolidated several distinct groups under his influence at the time of contact with the English.[4] Most were

Algonquian-speakers whose distant cultural roots in the Northeast distinguished them from peoples further south and west where native economies depended more on agriculture and less on hunting and fishing.[5] Although culturally diverse, tidewater inhabitants shared certain features of social organization, commonalities that may have become more pronounced with Powhatan's ambitious chiefdom-building and the arrival of the English.

◆   ◆   ◆

Of the various relationships constituting social order in England, those between men and women were among the most contested at the time the English set sail for Virginia in 1607. Accompanied by few women before 1620, male settlers left behind a pamphlet debate about the nature of the sexes and a rising concern about the activities of disorderly women. The gender hierarchy the English viewed as "natural" and "God-given" was in fact fraying at the edges. Male pamphleteers argued vigorously for male dominance over women as crucial to maintaining orderly households and communities. The relationship between men and women provided authors with an accessible metaphor with which to communicate the power inequities of abstract political relationships such as that of the monarch to the people, or that of the gentry to the lower orders.[6] By the late sixteenth century, as English attempts to subdue Ireland became increasingly violent and as hopes for a profitable West African trade dimmed, gender figured increasingly in English colonial discourses.[7]

English gender differences manifested themselves in primary responsibilities and arenas of activity, relationships to property, ideals for conduct, and social identities. Using plow agriculture, rural Englishmen cultivated grain while women oversaw household production, including gardening, dairying, brewing, and spinning. Women also constituted a flexible reserve labor force, performing agricultural work when demand for labor was high, as at harvest time. While Englishmen's property ownership formed the basis of their political existence and identity, most women did not own property until they were no longer subject to a father or husband.[8]

By the early seventeenth century, advice-book authors enjoined English women to concern themselves with the conservation of estates rather than with production. Women were also advised to maintain a modest demeanor. Publicly punishing shrewish and sexually aggressive women, communities enforced this standard of wifely submission as ideal and of wifely domination as intolerable.[9] The sexual activity of poor and unmarried women proved particularly threatening to community order; these "nasty wenches" provided pamphleteers with a foil for the "good wives" female readers were urged to emulate.[10]

How did one know an English good wife when one saw one? Her body and head would be modestly covered. The tools of her work, such as the skimming ladle used in dairying, the distaff of the spinning wheel, and the butter churn reflected her domestic production. When affixed to a man, as in community-initiated shaming rituals, these gender symbols communicated his fall from "natural" dominance and his wife's unnatural authority over him.[11]

Advice-book authors described men's "natural" domain as one of authority derived from his primary economic role. A man's economic assertiveness, mirrored in his authority over wife, child and servant, was emblematized by the plow's penetration of the earth, the master craftsman's ability to shape his raw materials, and the rider's ability to subdue his horse. Although hunting and fishing supplemented the incomes of many Englishmen, formal group hunts—occasions in which associations with manual labor and economic gain had been carefully erased—remained the preserve of the aristocracy and upper gentry.

The divide between men's and women's activities described by sixteenth- and seventeenth-century authors did not capture the flexibility of gender relations in most English communities. Beliefs in male authority over women and in the primacy of men's economic activities sustained a perception of social order even as women marketed butter, cheese and ale, and cuckolded unlucky husbands.

◆   ◆   ◆

Gender roles and identities were also important to the Algonquian speakers whom the English encountered along the three major tributaries of the Chesapeake Bay. Like indigenous peoples throughout the Americas, Virginia Algonquians invoked a divine division of labor to explain and justify differences between men's and women's roles on earth. A virile warrior god and a congenial female hostess provided divine examples for the work appropriate to human men and women.[12] Indian women's labor centered on cultivating and processing corn, which provided up to seventy-five percent of the calories consumed by residents of the coastal plain.[13] Women also grew squash, peas, and beans, fashioned bedding, baskets, and domestic tools, and turned animal skins into clothing and household items. They may even have built the houses of semi-permanent summer villages and itinerant winter camps. Bearing and raising children and mourning the dead rounded out the range of female duties. All were spiritually united by life-giving and its association with earth and agricultural production, sexuality and reproduction. Lineage wealth and political power passed through the female line, perhaps because of women's crucial role in producing and maintaining property. Among certain peoples, women may also have had the power to determine the fate of captives, the nugget of truth in the much-embellished tale of Pocahontas's intervention on behalf of Captain John Smith.[14]

Indian women were responsible not only for reproducing the traditional features of their culture, but for much of its adaptive capacity as well. As agriculturalists, women must have had great influence over decisions to move to new grounds, to leave old grounds fallow, and to initiate planting. As producers and consumers of vital household goods and implements, women may have been among the first to feel the impact of new technologies, commodities, and trade. And as accumulators of lineage property, Indian women may have been forced to change strategies as subsistence opportunities shifted.

Indian men assumed a range of responsibilities that complemented those of women. Men cleared new planting grounds by cutting trees and burning stumps. They fished and hunted for game, providing highly valued protein. After the last corn harvest, whole villages traveled with their hunters to provide support services throughout the winter. Men's pursuit of game shaped the rhythms of village life during these cold months, just as women's cultivation of crops determined feasts and the allocation of labor during the late spring and summer. By ritually separating themselves from women through sexual abstinence, hunters periodically became warriors, taking revenge for killings or initiating their own raids. This adult leave-taking rearticulated the *huskanaw*, the coming of age ritual in which young boys left their mothers' homes to become men.[15]

Men's hunting and fighting roles were associated with life-taking, with its ironic relationship to the life-sustaining acts of procreation, protection and provision. Earth and corn symbolized women, but the weapons of the hunt, the trophies taken from the hunted, and the predators of the animal world represented men. The ritual use of *pocones*, a red dye, also reflected this gender division. Women anointed their bodies with *pocones* before sexual encounters and ceremonies celebrating the harvest, while men wore it during hunting, warfare, or at the ritual celebrations of successes in these endeavors.[16]

The exigencies of the winter hunt, the value placed on meat, and intermittent warfare among native peoples may have been the foundation of
male dominance in politics and religious matters. Women were not without their bases of power in Algonquian society, however; their important
roles as agriculturalists, reproducers of Indian culture, and caretakers of
lineage property kept gender relations in rough balance. Indian women's
ability to choose spouses motivated men to be "paynefull" in their hunting and fishing. These same men warily avoided female spaces the English
labeled "gynaeceum," in which menstruating women may have gathered.
By no means equal to men, whose political and religious decisions directed village life, Indian women were perhaps more powerful in their
subordination than English women.[17]

Even before the English sailed up the river they renamed the James,
however, Indian women's power may have been waning, eroded by
Powhatan's chiefdom-building tactics. During the last quarter of the sixteenth century, perhaps as a consequence of early Spanish forays into the
region, he began to add to his inherited chiefdom, coercing and manipulating other coastal residents into economic and military alliances. Powhatan
also subverted the matrilineal transmission of political power by appointing
his kinsmen to be *werowances* of villages recently consolidated into his chiefdom. The central military force under his command created opportunities
for male recognition in which acts of bravery, rather than matrilineal property or political inheritance, determined privileges. Traditions of gift-giving
to cement alliances became exchanges of tribute for promises of protection
or non-aggression. Powhatan thus appropriated corn, the product of wom-
en's labor, from the villages he dominated. He also communicated power
and wealth through conspicuous displays of young wives. Through marriages to women drawn from villages throughout his chiefdom, Powhatan
emblematized his dominance over the margins of his domain and created
kinship ties to strengthen his influence over these villages. With the arrival
of the English, the value of male warfare and the symbolism of corn as tribute only intensified, further strengthening the patriarchal tendencies of
Powhatan's people.[18]

◆　◆　◆

Almost every writer described the land west and south of Chesapeake Bay
as an unspoiled "New World."[19] Small plots of cultivated land, burned
forest undergrowth, and seasonal residence patterns often escaped the

notice of English travelers habituated to landscapes shaped by plow agriculture and permanent settlement. Many writers believed the English had
"chanced in a lande, even as God made it," which indigenous peoples had
failed to exploit.[20]

Conquest seemed justifiable to many English because Native Americans had failed to tame the wilderness according to English standards.
Writers claimed they found "only an idle, improvident, scattered people . . . carelesse of anything but from hand to mouth."[21] Most authors
compounded impressions of sparse indigenous populations by listing only
numbers of fighting men, whom they derided as impotent for their failure
to exploit the virgin resources of the "bowells and womb of their Land."[22]
The seasonal migration of native groups and the corresponding shift in
diet indicated to the English a lack of mastery over the environment,
reminding them of animals. John Smith commented, "It is strange to see
how their bodies alter with their diet; even as the deare and wild beastes,
they seem fat and leane, strong and weak."[23]

The English derision of Indian dependence on the environment and
the comparison to animals, while redolent with allusions to England's own
poor and to the hierarchy of God's creation, also contained implicit gender meanings. Women's bodies, for example, showed great alteration
during pregnancy from fat to lean, strong to weak. English authors often
compared female sexual appetites and insubordination to those of wild
animals in need of taming. Implicit in all these commentaries was a critique of indigenous men for failing to fulfill the responsibility of economic
provision with which the English believed all men to be charged. Lacking
private property in the English sense, Indian men, like the Gaelic Irish
before them, appeared to the English to be feminine and not yet civilized
to manliness.[24]

For many English observers, natives' "failure" to develop an agricultural
economy or dense population was rooted in their gender division of labor.
Women's primary responsibility for agriculture merely confirmed the abdi-
cation by men of their proper role and explained the "inferiority" of native
economies in a land of plenty. Smith commented that "the land is not
populous, for the men be fewe; their far greater number is of women and
children," a pattern he attributed to inadequate cultivation.[25] Of the significance of women's work and Indian agriculture, he concluded, "When
all their fruits be gathered, little els they plant, and this is done by their
women and children; neither doth this long suffice them, for neere 3 parts
of the yeare, they only observe times and seasons, and live of what the
Country naturally affordeth from hand to mouth."[26] In Smith's convoluted

analysis, the "failure" of Indian agriculture, implicitly associated in other parts of his text with the "idleness" of men and the reliance upon female labor, had a gendered consequence; native populations became vulnerable and feminized, consisting of many more women and children than of "able men fitt for their warres."[27]

English commentators reacted with disapproval to seeing women perform work relegated to laboring men in England while Indian men pursued activities associated with the English aristocracy. Indian women, George Percy claimed, "doe all their drugerie. The men takes their pleasure in hunting and their warres, which they are in continually."[28] Observing that the women were heavily burdened and the men only lightly so, John Smith similarly noted "the men bestowe their times in fishing, hunting, wars and such manlike exercises, scorning to be seene in any woman like exercise," while the "women and children do the rest of the worke."[29] Smith's account revealed his discomfort with women's performance of work he considered the most valuable.

The English were hard pressed to explain other Indian behavior without contradicting their own beliefs in the natural and divinely-sanctioned characteristics of men and women. Such was the case with discussions of Indian women's pain during childbirth. In judgements reminiscent of their descriptions of Irish women, many English writers claimed that Indian women gave birth with little or no pain.[30] English readers may have found this observation difficult to reconcile with Christian views of labor pains as the source of maternal love and as punishment for the sins of Eve. Belief in indigenous women's closer proximity to nature—an interpretive stance that required an uncomfortable degree of criticism of civilization—allowed the English to finesse Indian women's seeming exemption from Eve's curse.[31] This is also why the association of Native American gender norms with animals proved so powerful for the English; it left intact the idea of English gender roles as "natural," in the sense of fulfilling God's destiny for civilized peoples, while providing a similarly "natural" explanation for English dominance over indigenous peoples.

The English were both fascinated and disturbed by other aspects of Native American society through which gender identities were communicated, including hairstyle, dress and make-up. The native male fashion of going clean-shaven, for example, clashed with English associations of beards with male maturity, perhaps diminishing Indian men's claims to manhood in the eyes of the English. Upon seeing an Indian with a full "blacke bush beard," Smith concluded that the individual must be the son of a European as "the Salvages seldome hav any at all." It probably did not enhance English respect for Indian manhood that female barbers sheared men's facial hair.[32]

Most English writers found it difficult to distinguish between the sexual behavior of Chesapeake dwellers and what they viewed as sexual potency conveyed through dress and ritual. English male explorers were particularly fascinated by indigenous women's attire, which seemed scanty and immodest compared to English women's multiple layers and wraps. John Smith described an entertainment arranged for him in which "30 young women came naked out of the woods (only covered behind and before with a few greene leaves), their bodies al painted."[33] Several other writers commented that Native Americans "goe altogether naked," or had "scarce to cover their nakednesse."[34] Smith claimed, however, that the women were "alwaies covered about their midles with a skin and very shamefast to be seene bare." Yet he noted, as did several other English travelers, the body adornments, including beads, paintings, and tattoos, that were visible on Indian women's legs, hands, breasts, and faces. Perhaps some of the "shamefastness" reported by Smith resulted from Englishmen's close scrutiny of Indian women's bodies.[35]

For most English writers, Indian manners and customs reinforced an impression of sexual passion. Hospitality that included sexual privileges, for instance sending "a woman fresh painted red with *Pocones* and oile" to be the "bedfellow" of a guest, may have confirmed in the minds of English men the reading of Indian folkways as sexually provocative. Smith's experience with the thirty women, clad in leaves, body paint, and buck's horns and emitting "hellish cries and shouts," undoubtedly strengthened the English association of Indian culture with unbridled passion:

> . . . they solemnly invited Smith to their lodging, but no sooner was hee within the house, but all these Nimphes more tormented him than ever, with crowding, and pressing, and hanging upon him, most tediously crying, *love you not mee.*[36]

These and other Indian gender ways left the English with a vivid impression of unconstrained sexuality that in their own culture could mean only promiscuity.

The stark contrast between Indian military techniques and formal European land stratagems reinforced English judgements that indigenous peoples were animalistic by nature.[37] George Percy's description of one skirmish invoked a comparison to the movement of animals : "At night, when we were going aboard, there came the Savages creeping upon all foure, from the Hills, like Beares, with their Bowes in their mouthes."[38] While writers regaled English readers with tales of Indian men in hasty retreat from English guns, thus reconfirming for the reader the female vulnerability of Indians and the superior weaponry of the English, they also recounted terrifying battle scenes such as the mock war staged for the entertainment of John Smith, which included "horrible shouts and screeches, as though so many infernall helhounds could not have made them more terrible."[39] Englishmen were perhaps most frightened, however, by reports of Caribbean Indians that echoed accounts of Irish cannibalism; George Percy claimed that Carib men scalped their victims, or worse still, that certain tribes "will eate their enemies when they kill them, or any stranger if they take them."[40] Stories like these may have led Smith to believe he was being "fattened" for a sacrifice during his captivity in December 1607.[41]

Although the dominant strand of English discourse about Indian men denounced them for being savage and failed providers, not all Englishmen shared these assessments of the meaning of cultural differences. Throughout the early years of settlement, male laborers deserted military compounds to escape puny rations, disease and harsh discipline, preferring to take their chances with local Indians whom they knew had food aplenty. Young boys like Henry Spelman, moreover, had nearly as much to fear from the English, who used him as a hostage, as he did from his Indian hosts. Spelman witnessed and participated in Indian culture from a very different perspective than most Virginia chroniclers. While George Percy and John Smith described Indian entertainments as horrible antics, Spelman coolly noted that Patawomeck dances bore a remarkable resemblance to the Darbyshire hornpipe.[42]

Even among men more elite and cosmopolitan than Spelman, a lurking and disquieting suspicion that Indian men were like the English disrupted discourses about natural savagery and inferiority. John Smith often explained Indian complexions and resistance to the elements as a result of conditioning and daily practice rather than of nature.[43] Smith also created areas of commonality with Algonquians through exchanges of gifts, shared entertainments, and feasts. Drawn into Indian cultural expressions despite himself, Smith gave gifts when he would have preferred to barter and concocted Indian explanations for English behavior.[44] Despite the flamboyant rhetoric about savage warriors lurking in the forests like animals, Smith soon had Englishmen learning to fight in the woods.[45] He clearly thought his manly English, many of whom could barely shoot a gun, had much to learn from their Indian opponents.

Most English did not dwell on these areas of similarity and exchange, however, but emphasized the "wild" and animalistic qualities of tidewater peoples. English claims to dominance and superiority rested upon constructions of Indian behavior as barbaric. Much as animals fell below humans in the hierarchy of the natural world, so the Indians of English chronicles inhabited a place that was technologically, socially, and morally below the level of the civilized English. Anglo-Indian gender differences similarly provided the English with cultural grist for the mill of conquest. Through depictions of feminized male "naturalls," Englishmen reworked Anglo-Indian relations to fit the "natural" dominance of men in gender relations. In the process, they contributed to an emerging male colonial identity that was deeply rooted in English gender discourses.

The gendering of Anglo-Indian relations in English writing was not without contest and contradiction, however, nor did it lead inevitably to easy conclusions of English dominance. Englishmen incorporated Indian ways into their diets and military tactics, and Indian women into their sexual lives. Some formed close bonds with Indian companions, while others lived to father their own "naturall" progeny. As John Rolfe's anguish over his marriage to Pocahontas attested, colonial domination was a complex process involving sexual intimacy, cultural incorporation and self-scrutiny.[46]

◆　　◆　　◆

The Englishmen who landed on the shores of Chesapeake Bay and the James River were not the first European men that Virginia Algonquians had seen. During the 1570s, Spanish Jesuits established a short-lived mission near the James River tributary that folded with the murder of the clerics. The Spaniards who revenged the Jesuit deaths left an unfavorable impression upon local Chickahominy, Paspegh, and Kecoughtan Indians. At least one English ship also pre-empted the 1607 arrival of the Jamestown settlers; its captain was long remembered for killing a Rappahanock river *werowance*.[47]

The maleness of English explorers' parties and early settlements undoubtedly raised Indian suspicions of bellicose motives. Interrogating Smith at their first meeting about the purpose of the English voyage, Powhatan was apparently satisfied with Smith's answer that the English presence was temporary. Smith claimed his men sought passage to "the backe Sea," the ever-elusive water route to India which they believed lay beyond the falls of the Chesapeake river system. Quick to exploit native assumptions that they were warriors, Smith also cited revenge against Powhatan's own mortal enemies, the Monacans, for their murder of an Englishman as a reason for their western explorations. The explanation may have initially seemed credible to Powhatan because the English expedition consisted only of men and boys. Frequent English military drills in the woods and the construction of a fort at Jamestown, however, may have aroused his suspicions that the English strangers planned a longer and more violent stay.[48]

Equipped with impressive blasting guns, the English may have found it easy to perpetuate the warrior image from afar; up close was a different matter, however. English men were pale, hairy, and awkward compared to Indian men. They also had the dirty habit of letting facial hair grow so that it obscured the bottom part of their faces where it collected food and other debris. Their clumsy stomping through the woods announced their presence to friends, enemies, and wildlife alike and they were forced, on at least one very public occasion, to ask for Indian assistance when their boats became mired in river ooze. Perhaps worst of all from the perspective of Indian people who valued a warrior's stoicism in the face of death, the Englishmen they captured and killed died screaming and whimpering. William Strachey recorded the mocking song sung by Indian men sometime in 1611, in which they ridiculed "what lamentation our people made when they kild him, namely saying how they [the Englishmen] would cry whe, whe."[49]

Indian assumptions about masculinity may have led Powhatan to overestimate the vulnerability of Smith's men. The gentlemen and artisans who were the first to arrive in Virginia proved to be dismal farmers, remaining wholly dependent upon native corn stores during their first three years and partially dependent thereafter. They tried, futilely, to persuade Indians to grow more corn to meet their needs, but their requests were greeted with scorn by Indian men who found no glory in the "woman-like exercise" of farming. Perhaps believing that the male settlement would always require another population to supply it, Powhatan tried to use the threat of starvation to level the playing field with the English. During trade negotiations with Smith in January 1609, Powhatan held out for guns and swords, claiming disingenuously that corn was more valuable to him than copper trinkets because he could eat it.[50]

When Powhatan and other Indian peoples reminded Smith of his dependence upon Indian food supplies, Smith reacted with anger. In his first account of Virginia, he recalled with bitterness the scorn of the Kecoughtan Indians for "a famished man": they "would in derision offer him a handfull of Corne, a peece of bread."[51] Such treatment signified both indigence and female vulnerability to the English, made worse by the fact that the crops they needed were grown by women. At Kecoughtan, Smith responded by "let[ting] fly his muskets" to provoke a Kecoughtan retreat and then killing several men at close range. The survivors fell back in confusion, allowing the image of their god Okeus to fall into English hands. After this display of force, he found the Kecoughtan "content" to let the English dictate the terms of trade: Kecoughtan corn in exchange for copper, beads, hatchets, and the return of Okeus.[52] The English thus used their superior weaponry to transform themselves from scorned men into respected warriors and to recast the relationship: humble agriculturists became duty-bound to produce for those who spared their lives.[53]

Powhatan's interactions with Englishmen may also have been guided by his assessment of the gender imbalance among them. His provision of women to entertain English male guests was a political gesture whose message seems to have been misunderstood as sexual license by the English.[54] Smith, for example, believed the generosity stemmed from Powhatan's having "as many women as he will," and thereby growing occasionally "weary of his women."[55] By voluntarily sharing his wealth in women and thus communicating his benign intent, Powhatan invoked what he may have believed to be a transcendent male political bond, defined by men's common relationship to women.[56] Powhatan may also have believed that by encouraging English warriors' sexual activity, he might diminish their military potency. It was the fear of this loss of power, after all, that motivated Indian warriors' ritual abstinence before combat. Ultimately, Powhatan may have hoped that intimacy between native women and English men would lead to an integration of the foreigners and a diffusion of the threat they presented. Lacking women with whom to reciprocate and unfettered by matrilineage ties, the English, Powhatan may have reasoned, might be rapidly brought into alliance. Powhatan's gesture, however, only reinforced the English rationale for subjugating the "uncivilized" and offered English men an opportunity to express the Anglo-Indian power relationship sexually with native women.[57]

Indian women were often more successful than Powhatan in manipulating Englishmen's desires for sexual intimacy. At the James River village of Appocant in late 1607, the unfortunate George Cawson met his death when village women "enticed [him] up from the barge into their howses."[58] Oppossunoquonuske, a clever *werowansqua* of another village, similarly led fourteen Englishmen to their demise. Inviting the unwary men to come "up into her Towne, to feast and make Merry," she convinced them to "leave their Armes in their boat, because they said how their women would be afrayd ells of their pieces."[59]

Although both of these accounts are cautionary tales that represent Indians literally as feminine seducers capable of entrapping Englishmen in the web of their own sexual desires, the incidents suggest Indian women's canny assessment of the men who would be colonial conquerors. Exploiting Englishmen's hopes for colonial pleasures, Indian women dangled before them the opportunity for sexual intimacy, turning a female tradition of sexual hospitality into a weapon of war. Acknowledging the capacity of English "pieces" to terrorize Indian women, Oppossunoquonuske tacitly recognized Englishmen's dependence on their guns to construct self-images of bold and masculine conquerors. Her genius lay in convincing them to rely on other masculine "pieces." When she succeeded in getting Englishmen to set aside one colonial masculine identity—the warrior—for another—the lover of native women—the men were easily killed.

Feigned sexual interest in Englishmen was not the only tactic available to Indian women. Some women clearly wanted nothing to do with the English strangers and avoided all contact with them. When John Smith traveled to Tappahannock in late 1607, for example, Indian women fled their homes in fear.[60] Other Indian women treated the English not as revered guests, to be gently wooed into Indian ways or seduced into fatal traps, but as lowly servants. Young Henry Spelman recorded such an incident during his stay at the house of a Patawomeck *werowance*. While the *werowance* was gone, his first wife requested that Spelman travel with her and carry her child on the long journey to her father's house. When Spelman refused, she struck him, provoking the boy to return the blows. A second wife then joined in the fray against Spelman, who continued to refuse to do their bidding. Upon the *werowance*'s return, Spelman related the afternoon's events and was horrified to see the offending wife brutally punished. In this Patawomeck household, women's and men's ideas about the proper treatment of English hostages differed dramatically.[61]

In addition to violence and manipulations of economic dependence and sexual desire, Algonquians tried to maneuver the English into positions of political subordination. Smith's account of his captivity, near-execution, and rescue by Pocahontas was undoubtedly part of an adoption ritual in which Powhatan defined his relationship to Smith as one of patriarchal dominance. Smith became Powhatan's prisoner after warriors easily slew his English companions and then "missed" with nearly all of the twenty or thirty arrows they aimed at Smith himself. Clearly, Powhatan wanted Smith brought to him alive. Smith reported that during his captivity he was offered "life, libertie, land and women," prizes Powhatan must have believed to be very attractive to Englishmen, in exchange for information about how best to capture Jamestown.[62] After ceremonies and consultations with priests, Powhatan brought Smith before an assembly where, according to Smith, Pocahontas risked her own life to prevent him from being clubbed to death by executioners. It seems that Smith understood neither the ritual adoption taking place nor the significance of Powhatan's promise to make him a *werowance* and to "for ever esteeme him as [he did] his son Nantaquoud."[63]

Powhatan subsequently repeated his offer to Smith, urging the adoptive relationship on him. Pronouncing him "a werowance of Powhatan, and that all his subjects should so esteeme us," Powhatan integrated Smith and his men into his chieftancy, declaring that "no man account us strangers nor Paspaheghans, but Powhatans, and that the Corne, weomen and Country, should be to us as to his owne people."[64]

Over the next weeks and months the two men wrangled over the construction of their short-lived alliance and the meaning of Powhatan's promises to supply the English with corn. In a long exchange of bitter words, the two men sidestepped each other's readings of their friendship as distortions and misperceptions. Smith claimed he had "neglected all, to satisfie your desire," to which Powhatan responded with a plain-spoken charge of bad faith: "some doubt I have of your comming hither, that makes me not so kindly seeke to relieve you . . . for many do informe me, your comming is not for trade, but to invade my people and possesse my Country."[65]

Smith and Powhatan continued to do a subtle two-step over the meaning of the corn. Was it tribute coerced by the militarily superior English? Or was it a sign of a father's compassion for a subordinate *werowance* and his hungry people? Powhatan made clear to Smith that he understood the extent of the English dependence upon his people for corn. "What will it availe you, to take that perforce, you may quietly have with love, or to destroy them that provide you food?" he asked Smith. "What can you get by war, when we can hide our provision and flie to the woodes, whereby you must famish by wronging us your friends." He also appreciated the degree to which the English could make him miserable if they did not get what they wanted:

> think you I am so simple not to knowe, it is better to eate good meate, lie well, and sleepe quietly with my women and children, laugh and be merrie with you, have copper, hatchets, or what I want, being your friend; then bee forced to flie from al, to lie cold in the woods, feed upon acorns,

roots, and such trash, and be so hunted by you, that I can neither rest, eat, nor sleepe; but my tired men must watch, and if a twig but breake, everie one crie there comes Captaine Smith, then I must flie I knowe not whether, and thus with miserable feare end my miserable life.[66]

Ultimately, Powhatan attempted to represent his conflict with Smith as the clash of an older, wiser authority with a young upstart. "I knowe the difference of peace and warre, better then any in my Countrie," he reminded Smith, his paternal self-depiction contrasting sharply with what he labeled Smith's youthful and "rash unadvisednesse." Displeased with this rendering of their relationship with its suggestion of childish inexperience, Smith reasserted the English warrior personae with a vengeance. He informed Powhatan that "for your sake only, wee have curbed our thirsting desire of revenge," reminding him that the "advantage we have by our armes" would have allowed the English easily to overpower Powhatan's men "had wee intended you anie hurt."[67]

◆   ◆   ◆

Although we can never know with any certainty what the all-male band of English settlers signified to indigenous peoples, their own organization of gender roles seems to have shaped their responses to the English. Using sexual hospitality to "disarm" the strangers and exploiting English needs for food, Algonquians were drawn into a female role as suppliers of English sexual and subsistence needs. Although Indian women were occasionally successful in manipulating English desires for sexual intimacy and dominance, the English cast these triumphs as the consequence of female seduction, an interpretation that only reinforced discourses about feminized Algonquians. Dependence upon indigenous peoples for corn was potentially emasculating for the English; they thus redefined corn as tribute or booty resulting from English military dominance.

The encounter of English and Indian peoples wrought changes in the gender relations of both societies. Contact bred trade, political reshuffling, sexual intimacy and warfare. On both sides, male roles intensified in ways that appear to have reinforced the patriarchal tendencies of each culture. The very process of confrontation between two groups with male-dominated political and religious systems may initially have strengthened the value of patriarchy for each.

The rapid change in Indian life and culture had a particularly devastating impact upon women. Many women, whose office it was to bury and mourn the dead, may have been relegated to perpetual grieving. Corn was also uniquely the provenance of women; economically it was the source of female authority, and religiously and symbolically they were identified with it. The wanton burning and pillaging of corn supplies, through which the English transformed their dependence into domination, may have represented to tidewater residents an egregious violation of women. Maneuvering to retain patriarchal dominance over the English and invoking cultural roles in which women exercised power, Algonquian Indians may have presented their best defense against the "feminization" of their relationship to the English. But as in Indian society itself, warriors ultimately had the upper hand over agriculturists.[68]

English dominance in the region ultimately led to the decline of the native population and its way of life. As a consequence of war, nutritional deprivation, and disease, Virginia Indians were reduced in numbers from the approximately 14,000 inhabitants of the Chesapeake Bay and tidewater in 1607 to less than 3,000 by the early eighteenth century. White settlement forced tidewater dwellers further west, rupturing the connections between ritual activity, lineage, and geographic place. Priests lost credibility as traditional medicines failed to cure new diseases while confederacies such as Powhatan's declined and disappeared. Uprooted tidewater peoples also encountered opposition from piedmont inhabitants upon whose territory they encroached. The erosion of traditionally male-dominated Indian political institutions eventually created new opportunities for individual women to assume positions of leadership over tribal remnants.[69]

The English, meanwhile, emerged from these early years of settlement with gender roles more explicitly defined in English, Christian, and "middling order" terms. This core of English identity proved remarkably resiliant, persisting through seventy years of wars with neighboring Indians and continuing to evolve as English settlers imported Africans to work the colony's tobacco fields. Initially serving to legitimate the destruction of traditional Indian ways of life, this concept of Englishness ultimately constituted one of the most powerful legacies of the Anglo-Indian gender frontier.

NOTES

1. Spanish literature divided "barbaric" populations into two main categories: one of obedient and child-like laborers, and the other of evil, conniving and dangerous cannibals. The English similarly typed both Gaelic Irish and American Indians. See Anthony Pagden, *The Fall of Natural Man* (Cambridge: Cambridge University Press, 1986); Nicholas P. Canny, *The Elizabethan Conquest of Ireland: A Pattern Established 1565–76* (New York: Barnes and Noble, 1976), 160; Loren E. Pennington, "The Amerindian in English Promotional Literature 1575–1625" in *The Westward Enterprise: English Activities in Ireland, the Atlantic, and America, 1480–1650*, ed. K.R. Andrews, Nicholas P. Canny, and P.E.H. Hair (Detroit: Wayne State University Press, 1979), 184, 188; Anne Laurence, "The Cradle to the Grave: English Observation of Irish Social Customs in the Seventeenth Century," *The Seventeenth Century*, 3 (Spring 1988): 63–84; Nicholas P. Canny, "The Ideology of English Colonization: From Ireland to America," *William and Mary Quarterly*, 3rd ser., 30 (October 1973): 597 (hereafter cited as *WMQ*). Christianity, moreover, allowed the English to maintain the belief that their economic and imperialist motives in the Americas were part of God's work and to distinguish and devalue Indian culture; see John Smith, *The Proceedings of the English Colonies in Virginia* [London, 1612] in *Narratives of Early Virginia 1606–1625*, ed. Lyon Gardiner Tyler (New York: Barnes and Noble, 1907), 178; Karen Kupperman, ed., *Captain John Smith: A Select Edition of His Writings* (Chapel Hill, N.C.: University of North Carolina Press, 1988), 154.

2. For a useful discussion of the performative nature of identity that is especially applicable to the early modern period and the encounter of cultures in the Americas, see Judith Butler, "Gender Trouble," in *Feminism/Postmodernism*, ed. Linda J. Nicholson (New York: Routledge, 1990), 336–339.

3. For the by-now classic account of gender as a means of communicating power, see Joan Scott, "Gender: A Useful Category of Historical Analysis," *American Historical Review*, 91 (December 1986): 1053–1075. For analyses of economic, linguistic, and religious "frontiers," see James Merrell, "'The Customes of Our Country': Indians and Colonists in Early America," in *Strangers Within the Realm: Cultural Margins of the First British Empire*, ed. Bernard Bailyn and Phillip D. Morgan (Chapel Hill, N.C.: University of North Carolina Press, 1991), 117–156. In no way separate or distinct, the gender frontier infiltrated other frontiers we usually describe as economic, social, or cultural; for further elaboration see Kathleen M. Brown, "Brave New Worlds: Women's and Gender History," *WMQ*, 3rd ser., 50 (April 1993): 311–328.

4. On Powhatan's influence over neighboring Algonquian-speaking peoples, see Nancy Lurie, "Indian Cultural Adjustment to European Civilization," in *Seventeenth-Century America*, ed. James Morton Smith (Westport, Ct.: Greenwood Press, 1980), 40–42. Lurie uses the term "Confederacy" to refer to these peoples, although she distinguishes between the "influence" Powhatan wielded and the "undisputed control" he never fully realized. Helen Rountree, *Pocahontas's People* (Norman, Ok.: University of Oklahoma Press, 1990), 3, argues that "Confederacy" is inaccurate, preferring to describe it as a "sophisticated government." See also Peter H. Wood, Gregory Waselkov, and M. Thomas Hatley, eds., *Powhatan's Mantle: Southeastern*

44

Indians in the Colonial Era (Lincoln, Neb.: University of Nebraska Press, 1989), xv, for the use of the term "mantle." The groups under Powhatan's mantle of authority included the Pamunkey, Kecoughtan, Mattaponi, Appamattuck, Rappahannock, Piankatank, Chiskiack, Werowocomoco, Nansemond, and Chesapeake.

5. Lurie, "Indian Cultural Adjustment," 40–41; G. Melvin Herndon, "Indian Agriculture in the Southern Colonies," *The North Carolina Historical Review* 44 (July 1967): 283–297; Charles Hudson, *The Southeastern Indians* (Knoxville, Tenn.: University of Tennessee Press, 1976), 8–9, 23; Timothy Silver, *A New Face on the Countryside: Indians, Colonists, and Slaves in South Atlantic Forests, 1500–1800* (New York, Cambridge University Press, 1990), 39; J. Leitch Wright, *The Only Land They Knew: The Tragic Story of the American Indians in the Old South* (New York: Free Press, 1981), 11.

6. The secondary literature about gender and social order in England during the late sixteenth and early seventeenth centuries is vast. Among the accounts that have influenced me the most are the following: G.R. Quaife, *Wanton Wenches and Wayward Wives: Peasants and Illicit Sex in Early Seventeenth Century England* (London: Croom Helm, 1979); Anthony Fletcher and John Stevenson, eds., *Order and Disorder in Early Modern England* (New York: Cambridge University Press, 1985); Susan Cahn, *Industry of Devotion: The Transformation of Women's Work in England 1500–1660* (New York: Basil Blackwell, 1987); Susan Dwyer Amussen, *An Ordered Society: Gender and Class in Early Modern England* (New York: Columbia University Press, 1988), chapter 2, "Political Households and Domestic Politics"; Martin Ingram, *Church Courts, Sex and Marriage in England, 1570–1640* (New York: Cambridge University Press, 1987); Joan Kelly, *Women, History and Theory* (Chicago: University of Chicago Press, 1984), chapter 4, "Early Feminist Theory and the Querelle des Femmes"; Linda Woodbridge, *Women and the English Renaissance: Literature and the Nature of Womankind, 1540–1620* (Urbana, Ill.: University of Illinois Press, 1984); Constance Jordan, *Renaissance Feminism: Literary Texts and Political Models* (Ithaca, N.Y.: Cornell University Press, 1990). For a useful anthology of reprinted pamphlets and advice books, see Katherine Usher Henderson and Barbara F. McManus, eds., *Half Humankind: Contexts and Texts of the Controversy about Women in England, 1540–1650* (Chicago: University of Illinois Press, 1985).

7. For examples of gendered discourses of difference in the Irish context, see Laurence, "Cradle to the Grave"; for a classic early English account of Africans, see Richard Jobson, *The Golden Trade* [London, 1623].

8. Among the most useful accounts of English agriculture are Joan Thirsk, ed., *The Agrarian History of England and Wales*, 6 vols. (Cambridge: Cambridge University Press, 1967) vol. 4; K.D.M. Snell, *Annals of the Laboring Poor: Social Change and Agrarian England, 1660–1900* (Cambridge: Cambridge University Press, 1985); D. E. Underdown, "Taming of the Scold: the Enforcement of Patriarchal Authority in Early Modern England," in Fletcher and Stevenson, *Order and Disorder in Early Modern England*, 116–136; Ann Kussmaul, *Servants in Husbandry in Early Modern England* (Cambridge: Cambridge University Press, 1981).

9. Cahn, *Industry of Devotion*, 80–90, 158; Amussen, *Ordered Society;* William Gouge, *Domesticall Duties* (London, 1622); Richard Brathwait, *The English Gentlewoman* (London, 1631); Gervase Markham, *Country Contentments or the English Housewife* (London, 1623).

10. For the terms "good wives" and "nasty wenches," see John Hammond, *Leah and Rachel, or the Two Fruitfull Sisters* (London, 1656).

11. Martin Ingram, "Ridings, Rough Music, and the 'Reform of Popular Culture,'" in *Early Modern England*," *Past and Present*, 105 (November 1984): 79–113; Underdown, "The Taming of the Scold."

12. Ramon Gutierrez, *When Jesus Came the Corn Mothers Went Away* (Stanford, Ca.: Stanford University Press, 1991), 3–7; Hudson, *Southeastern Indians*, 148–159; Helen Rountree, *The Powhatan Indians of Virginia: Their Traditional Culture* (Norman, Ok.: University of Oklahoma Press, 1989), 135–138; William Strachey, *The Historie of Travell into Virginia Britania* [London, 1612], 89, 103.

13. Edwin Randolph Turner "An Archaeological and Ethnohistorical Study on the Evolution of Rank Societies in the Virginia Coastal Plain" (Ph.D. diss., The Pennsylvania State University, 1976), 182–187; Rountree, *Powhatan Indians*, 45, finds Turner's estimates perhaps too high.

14. Herndon, "Indian Agriculture in the Southern Colonies," 288, 292–296, especially the reference on 292 to "She-Corn." Hudson, *Southeastern Indians*, 151–156, 259–260; Wright, *Only Land They Knew*, 8–14; Silver, *New Face on the Countryside*, 39–41, 44–52; Colonel Henry Norwood, "A Voyage to Virginia" [London, 1649] in *Tracts and Other Papers, relating principally to the Origin, Settlement and Progress of the North American Colonies*, ed. Peter Force, 4 vols. (New York, 1836; rpt., Cambridge, Mass., Peter Smith, 1947), 3: 36–37. John Smith often rendered invisible or insignificant the work of women; see Kupperman, *John Smith*, 138–139. See also Kupperman, *John Smith*, 151, 156, for Smith's description of women's role as mourners and the passage of property and political power through women.

15. Wright, *Only Land They Knew*, 8–14; Hudson, *Southeastern Indians*, 148–156, 258–260; Kupperman, *John Smith*, 105, 144, 153; Henry Spelman, "Relation of Virginia," in *Travels and Works of Captain John Smith*, ed. Edward Arber and A.G. Bradley, 2 vols. (Edinburgh, John Grant, 1910), 1: cvi.

16. Hudson, *Southeastern Indians*, 259; Kupperman, *John Smith*, 61, 163.

17. Strachey, *Historie*, 83, 74.

18. For Powhatan's clever manipulation of gender customs and symbols of power, see Strachey, *Historie*, 40, 44, 62, 65–69, and Spelman, "Relation," cxiv.

19. For a survey of changing English attitudes toward Indians in the South, see Gary B. Nash, "The Image of the Indian in the Southern Colonial Mind," *WMQ*, 3rd ser., 29 (April 1972): 197–230. See also George Percy, "Observations by Master George Percy, 1607," [London, 1607], in Tyler, *Narratives*, 17–18, and Thomas Hariot, *A Briefe and True Report of the New Found Land of Virginia* (London, 1588; rpt. New York, 1903).

20. See Smith, *Proceedings of the English Colonies*, in Tyler, *Narratives*, 178; William Cronon, *Changes in the Land: Indians, Colonists and the Ecology of New England* (New York: Hill and Wang, 1983), 47–51; Silver, *New Face on the Countryside*. See also Alfred Crosby, *Ecological Imperialism: The Biological Expansion of Europe, 900–1900* (Cambridge: Cambridge University Press, 1986), 280, for his contention that rather than being part of the landscape, Indians acted as the first wave of "shock troops" on the New World environment that cleared the way for the subsequent European migration of peoples, agricultural systems, flora and fauna.

21. Smith, *Proceedings of the English Colonies*, in Tyler, *Narratives*, 178. John Smith,

"Description of Virginia," [London, 1612], in Tyler, *Narratives*, 83; Pennington, "The Amerindians in English Promotional Literature," 189, for her summation of the argument in Robert Gray, *A Good Speed to Virginia* [London, 1609]. For Smith's recognition of native concepts of property, see Kupperman, *John Smith*, 140. Most early English commentators also noted the potential of New World abundance for exploitation by agriculturists and hunters; see for example, Percy, "Observations" in Tyler, *Narratives*, 17–18; Hariot, *A Briefe and True Report*.

22. Strachey, *Historie*, 24, 103; John Smith, "A Map of Virginia," in *The Complete Works of Captain John Smith*, ed. Philip Barbour, 3 vols. (Chapel Hill, N.C.: University of North Carolina Press, 1986), 2: 146.

23. Smith, "Description," in Tyler, *Narratives*, 102; Silver, *New Face on the Countryside*, 67.

24. V.G. Kiernan, "Private Property in History," in *Family and Inheritance: Rural Society in Western Europe, 1200–1800*, ed. Jack Goody, Joan Thirsk and E. P. Thompson (Cambridge: Cambridge University Press, 1976), 361–398; see also E. P. Thompson, *Whigs and Hunters: The Origin of the Black Act* (New York: Random House, 1975). James Axtell, *The European and the Indian: Essays in the Ethnohistory of Colonial North America* (New York: Oxford University Press, 1981), discusses the English view of "civilizing" Indians as a process of making men out of children. Although most voyagers wrote critically of Indian men, others compared them favorably to English men whose overly cultured and effeminate ways had made them weak in character and resolve; Hariot, *A Briefe and True Report*. For a critique of English effeminacy, see *Haec Vir* [London, 1620] in Henderson and MacManus, *Half Humankind*; Richard Brathwait, *The English Gentleman* (London, 1631). Strachey, *Historie*, 18, 24, 25, equated civility with manliness.

25. Kupperman, *John Smith*, 158. Smith, "Description of Virginia," in Tyler, *Narratives*, 98–99.

26. See Kupperman, *John Smith*, 138–139.

27. Kupperman, *John Smith*, 140.

28. Percy, "Observations," in Tyler, *Narratives*, 18. For an extended discussion of this theme for Virginia and elsewhere, see David D. Smits, "'The Squaw Drudge': A Prime Index of Savagism," *Ethnohistory* 29 (1982): 281–306.

29. Smith, "Description," in Tyler, *Narratives*, 101, 96–97, 103; See also John Smith, *Travels and Works*, quoted in Edmund Morgan, *American Slavery, American Freedom: The Ordeal of Colonial Virginia* (New York: W.W. Norton, 1975), 51.

30. Laurence, "The Cradle to the Grave," 66–75; Jo Murphy-Lawless, "Images of Poor Women in the Writings of Irish Men Midwives," in *Women in Early Modern Ireland*, eds. Margaret MacCurtain and Mary O'Dowd (Edinburgh: Edinburgh University Press, 1991), 201–303.

31. "Their women (they say) are easilie delivered of childe, yet doe they love children verie dearly," reported Smith; see Smith, "Description," in Tyler, *Narratives*, 99.

32. See Axtell, *The European and the Indian*, 45, 47–55, 57–60, for the deeper reverberations of different clothing and naming practices; Kupperman, *John Smith*, 100; Strachey, *Historie*, 73.

33. Smith, *Proceedings of the English Colonies*, in Tyler, *Narratives*, 153–154.

34. Hariot, *Briefe and True Report*; Percy, "Observations," in Tyler, *Narratives*, 12; Smith, "Description," in Tyler, *Narratives*, 99–100.

35. Smith, "Description," in Tyler, *Narratives*, 100; Percy, "Observations," in *ibid*, 12. For a reprint of sixteenth-century sketches of American Indians, see Theodore deBry, *Thomas Hariot's Virginia* (Ann Arbor, Mi.: University of Michigan Press, 1966).

36. Smith, *Proceedings of the English Colonies*, in Tyler, *Narratives*, 154. The horns worn by native women may have reinforced this notion of promiscuity because of English associations of horns with cuckoldry.

37. Hariot, *A Briefe and True Report*.

38. Percy, "Observations," in Tyler, *Narratives*, 10.

39. Smith, "Description," in Tyler, *Narratives*, 106. Percy, "Observations," in Tyler, *Narratives*, 6.

40. Percy, "Observations," in Tyler, *Narratives*, 6. For the history of the word cannibalism and its connection to English aspirations in the New World, see Peter Hulme, *Colonial Encounters: Europe and the Native Caribbean, 1492–1797* (London: Routledge, 1986), 45–87.

41. Smith, *True Relation*, in Barbour, *Complete Works*, 1: 59.

42. Spelman, "Relation," cxiv, cviii.

43. Smith, "Description," in Tyler, *Narratives*, 99; Strachey, *Historie*, 70.

44. Smith, *True Relation*, in Barbour, *Complete Works*, 1: 54–55. See also James Axtell, *Beyond 1492: Encounters in Colonial North America* (New York: Oxford University Press, 1992), 66.

45. Smith, *True Relation*, in Barbour, *Complete Works*, 1: 85.

46. "Letter of John Rolfe, 1614," in Tyler, *Narratives*, 241.

47. See Clifford M. Lewis and Albert J. Loomie, *The Spanish Jesuit Mission in Virginia, 1570–1572* (Chapel Hill, N.C.: University of North Carolina Press, 1953); Axtell, *Beyond 1492*; 104; Rountree, *Powhatan Indians*, 142; Rountree, *Pocahantas's People*, 15–18. For Indian investigations of Smith's possible involvement in the killing of the Tappahannock *werowance*, see Smith, *True Relation*, in Barbour, *Complete Works*, 1: 51. Powhatan spoke to Smith of other Europeans and of Roanoake; see *ibid*, 39. C.A. Weslager, *The Nanticoke Indians* (Newark, Del.: University of Delaware Press, 1986), 27, suggests that initial Nanticoke hostility to the English was a result of previous contact.

48. Smith, *True Relation*, in Barbour, *Complete Works*, 1: 39, 91.

49. Axtell, *Beyond 1492*, 101; Strachey, *Historie*, 85. See also *ibid*, 66, for an account of Warroskoyack Indians mocking the English when an Indian hostage escaped from an English ship.

50. Rountree, *Powhatan Indians*, 89; Kupperman, *John Smith*, 173.

51. Kupperman, *John Smith*, 174, for Powhatan's speech to Smith. For a Chickahominy orator's similar comments to Smith, see Kupperman, *John Smith*, 190. See also Kupperman, *John Smith*, 185, for Smith's admission of the English dependence on native corn supplies. For Smith's description of the engagement with the Kecoughtan, see Smith, *General Historie*, in Barbour, *Complete Works*, 2: 144.

52. Smith, *General Historie*, in Barbour, *Complete Works*, 2: 45.

53. Kupperman, *John Smith*, 175.

54. These sexual diplomats may well be the same women Smith claimed "were common whores by profession"; see Kupperman, *John Smith*, 156, 157.

55. Smith, "Description," in Tyler, *Narratives*, 114–115.

56. The provision of women to foreign men was a fairly common Indian diplomatic practice throughout the South as well as in Central and South America; see for example, Gutierrez, *Corn Mothers*, 16–20. This was a highly politicized form of sexual hospitality which stood in sharp contrast to the violent reaction when native women were kidnapped by foreign warriors; see Kupperman, *John Smith*, 100.

57. Axtell, *Beyond 1492*, 39, 45, 102; My interpretation is compatible with Axtell, *Beyond 1492*, 31–33, in which he claims that while Europeans stressed sharp distinctions between Europeans and non-Europeans, Indians stressed the similarities. William Strachey believed that assimilation was Powhatan's strategy for mediating English relations with other Indians outside the paramount chiefdom; see Strachey, *Historie*, 107.

58. Strachey, *Historie*, 60.

59. Strachey, *Historie*, 63; Smith, *True Relation*, in Barbour, *Complete Works*, 1: 71, for a similar tactic by Powhatan.

60. Smith, *True Relation*, in Barbour, *Complete Works*, 39.

61. Spelman, "Relation," cviii.

62. Kupperman, *John Smith*, 62, 65.

63. J.A. Leo Lemay, *Did Pocahantas Save Captain John Smith?* (Athens, Ga.: University of Georgia Press, 1992) is the most recent interpretation of this event. An ardent believer in Smith's veracity, Lemay fails to explore the degree to which Smith may have misunderstood the meaning of the near-death ritual. For primary accounts of the events, see Smith, *True Relation*, in Barbour, *Complete Works*, 1: 45; Smith, *General Historie* in Kupperman, *John Smith*, 64–65.

64. Smith, *True Relation*, in Barbour, *Complete Works*, 1: 61–67.

65. Kupperman, *John Smith*, 173.

66. Kupperman, *John Smith*, 173–175.

67. Kupperman, *John Smith*, 175.

68. Stephen R. Potter, "Early English Effects on Virginia Algonquian Exchange and Tribute," in Wood, *Powhatan's Mantle*, 151–172, especially 151, 160; Martha McCartney, "Cockacoeske, Queen of the Pamunkey: Diplomat and Suzeraine," in Wood, *Powhatan's Mantle*, 173–195; Merrell, "Customes of Our Country," 122–123; Robert Beverley, *The History and Present State of Virginia [1705]*, ed. Louis V. Wright (Chapel Hill, 1947), 232–233.

69. For analyses of the devastation wrought by contact, see Hudson, *Southeastern Indians*, chapter 8; Silver, *New Face on the Countryside*, 74–83, 88, 102; Crosby, *Ecological Imperialism*, chapter 9; Merrell, "'The Customes of Our Country,'" 122–126. Powhatan himself commented upon the devastation he had witnessed in the course of three generations; see Kupperman, *John Smith*, 174. See also Wright, *The Only Land They Knew*, 24–26; Peter Wood, "The Changing Population of the Colonial South: An Overview by Race and Region, 1685–1790," in Wood, *Powhatan's Mantle*, 38, 40–42; Silver, *New Face on the Countryside*, 72, 81, 87–88, 91; Potter, "Early English Effects on Virginia Algonquian Exchange and Tribute"; Robert Steven Grumet, "Sunksquaws, Shamans, and Tradeswomen: Middle Atlantic Coastal Algonkian Women During the 17th and 18th Centuries" in *Women and Colonization: Anthropological Perspectives*, ed. Mona Etienne and Eleanor Leacock, (New York: Praeger, 1980), 43–62.

2

NANCY SHOEMAKER

KATERI TEKAKWITHA'S TORTUOUS PATH TO SAINTHOOD

The Indian village at Kahnawake was perhaps the most successful of Christian "praying towns" in the New World. Founded in the late 1660s by a small group of Iroquois, Hurons, and Eries, the village was formally attached to the Jesuit Mission of St. Francis Xavier. For many Indians, especially the Iroquois, Kahnawake became a refuge from the rise in drinking, violence, and warfare that plagued many Indian villages in the northeast in the seventeenth and eighteenth centuries. Shoemaker's essay focuses on the life of one Christian Indian woman, Kateri Tekakwitha, who lived at Kahnawake during the 1670s, when the Christian fervor within the village reached its peak. Today, the Catholic Church at Kahnawake Reserve in Canada houses Tekakwitha's relics and continues to attract pilgrims who come to pray at her shrine.

Kateri Tekakwitha died at Kahnawake in 1680 in the odor of sanctity (a sweet odor filled the room). Pilgrims from all over New France journeyed to her tomb to ask her to intercede with God on their behalf. In 1683, Tekakwitha's divine intervention saved several Jesuits from certain death when a windstorm caused the mission church at Kahnawake to collapse around them.[1] Ten years later, André Merlot's "inflammation of the eyes" healed after he made a novena to Tekakwitha, rubbing his eyes with a solution of water, earth from Tekakwitha's grave, and ashes from her clothing.[2] Colombière, Canon of the Cathedral of Québec, testified in 1696 that his appeal to Tekakwitha relieved him of "a slow fever, against which all remedies had been tried in vain, and of a diarrhea, which even ipecacuana could not cure."[3] The Roman Catholic Church acknowledged Tekakwitha's holiness by declaring her venerable in 1943. In 1980, Tekakwitha was beatified. Perhaps soon, Tekakwitha will pass the next and final step of canonization and be recognized as a saint. She is the only Native American to rise so far in the saintly canon of the Catholic Church.[4]

Kateri Tekakwitha appears in most historical accounts of missionization in New France except, oddly enough, those that deal explicitly with women and missionization.[5] The now classic research of Eleanor Leacock and two recent books on women and missionization, one written by Karen Anderson and the other by Carol Devens, do not mention Tekakwitha.[6] More surprising is that the historical literature on native women and religion in New France ignores the Iroquois, even though there is a voluminous literature debating the power of Iroquois women before and after European contact.[7] Leacock and Devens confined their studies to the Montagnais (an Algonquian-speaking tribe), while Anderson's research focused on the Montagnais and Huron, who were culturally and linguistically related to the Iroquois but often at war with them.

Tekakwitha's experience does contradict the usual argument that missionaries forced native people to adopt patriarchy along with Christianity and that missionization helped to devalue women's role in native societies. The usual narrative of missionization's impact on native women in New France describes how epidemic disease and progressively deeper involvement in the fur trade created an economic imbalance and a crisis of faith within native communities; the Jesuits' persistent vilifying of native customs, especially marriage customs, eventually led missionized Indians to abandon the old ways and accept the basic tenets of Christianity and Western culture.

The choicest pieces of evidence used to support the argument that native people in New France ultimately conformed to missionary preachings and Western patriarchy come from a 1640 Jesuit account of the Montagnais mission at Sillery, which was recovering from a severe smallpox epidemic. One particular incident figures prominently in the arguments of Leacock, Anderson, and Devens. Several Montagnais women complained to the Jesuits that the men had brought them to a council to reprimand them:

> "It is you women," they [the men] said to us [the women], "who are the
> cause of all our misfortunes,—it is you who keep the demons among us.
> You do not urge to be baptized; you must not be satisfied to ask this
> favor only once from the Fathers, you must importune them. You are lazy
> about going to prayers; when you pass before the cross, you never
> salute it; you wish to be independent. Now know that you will obey your
> husbands."[8]

Leacock and Anderson gave this as evidence of missionized Indian men
dominating women. Devens used this example to show that native
women resisted Christianity, partly because of its patriarchal implications.
However, Devens' argument is weakened by her own discussion of how
some native women eagerly embraced Christianity.

These arguments presume a linear, assimilationist model of change and
seem to come from a Western narrative tradition that depicts people as one
thing, and after a crisis of some sort, they become another thing. However,
it seems more likely that historical change is constantly in motion, perhaps
moving in many different directions at once. Crisis may not lead automatically to permanent change but instead may simply be the moment in time
when competing interests clash in a visible and tangible way. Smallpox
made 1640 an especially stressful year in this Montagnais village, and men
and women may have become embattled as they sought to reassert some
control over their lives. Montagnais men were probably not successfully
dominating women, but they may have been trying to and may have tried
using the symbols of Christianity to do so. Some women may have in similar moments called upon the symbols of Christianity to assert their own
identity and authority within the native community.

This narrative of a decline into patriarchy appeals to those of us with
historical hindsight; however, even though we may view Christianity as
part of a patriarchal, Western tradition that assisted in the conquest of
America, native people may have interpreted it differently. First, Roman
Catholicism, especially in the way the Jesuit missionaries presented it,
paralleled Iroquois religious beliefs, allowing certain aspects of Christianity to be easily incorporated. Second, Roman Catholicism, perhaps more
than any other Christian religion, employs feminine imagery, such as the
Virgin Mary and women saints, which could be coopted by women as
symbols of power. And third, while scholars of missionization in New
France have emphasized Jesuit efforts to enforce monogamous, life-long
marriages on native converts as crucial to women's disempowerment, they
have ignored the Jesuits' even more profound admiration of women who

refused to marry, a novel idea when introduced to the Iroquois and one that some women may have appreciated as an alternative to their pre-scribed role within Iroquois society. The Jesuits preached patriarchy, but also brought to the Iroquois a toolkit of symbols, stories, and rituals that portrayed women as powerful or that gave women access to power. Just as native people transformed Europeans' material toolkit of guns, blan-kets, and glass beads to suit their own needs, Iroquois women and men may have sometimes adopted, sometimes rejected, but continually worked to transform the spiritual and symbolic toolkit of Christianity to meet the needs of the moment.

The Jesuit compulsion to missionize in the Americas was partly the product of a religious revival that swept through elite circles in France in the early 1600s.[9] Jesuits first arrived at the French colonial settlement of Québec in 1625. After briefly losing the colony to an alliance of English colonists and the disaffected French Protestants known as Huguenots, France reestablished Québec in 1632, and within the year the Jesuits arrived again, this time to set up permanent missions. At first, the Jesuits concentrated their missions among the Hurons, Montagnais, and Algo-nquins. They made several attempts to missionize the Iroquois but did not survive long in any of the Iroquois villages. However, some Iroquois, many of them Huron or Algonquin war captives who had been adopted into Iro-quois families, left their villages to form Christian communities. One of the largest and most successful of these "praying towns" was Kahnawake.

Kahnawake (or Caughnawaga) originated at La Prairie de la Madeleine near Montréal in the late 1660s. La Prairie consisted of three distinct, but interacting, communities: the Jesuit Mission of St. Francis Xavier, a village of French colonists, and a growing native village of Algonquins, Hurons, and Iroquois. The first native settlers at La Prairie were Catherine Gandeac-teua, an Erie woman, and her Huron husband, Francois Xavier Tonsahoten. Both of them had previously learned about Christianity at Jesuit missions, but had then been taken captive and adopted into the Oneida tribe, one of the five Iroquois nations. By the early 1670s, Gandeacteua, Tonsahoten, and other members of their family had left their Oneida village and per-manently settled near Montréal. For a variety of reasons, the native village and the mission moved a few miles up the St. Lawrence River to Sault St. Louis in 1677. Although the French usually called this Indian settle-ment "the Sault," the native inhabitants named their village Kahnawake, meaning "at the sault" or falls in Mohawk, a reflection of the growing number of Mohawks who had joined the community. As the easternmost of the Iroquois tribes, the Mohawks were the first to feel most intensely the disruptive consequences of European contact, and many Mohawks came to see Kahnawake, with its strict prohibitions against alcohol, as a haven from the alcohol-induced violence plaguing Iroquois villages in the late 1600s.[10]

According to Tekakwitha's two hagiographers, the Jesuits Pierre Cholenec and Claude Chauchetière, Tekakwitha was one of the many Mohawks who sought refuge at Kahnawake.[11] She was born in 1656 at Gandaouague (now Auriesville, New York) near present-day Albany. Her mother was an Algonquin who had been missionized by the Jesuits at Trois Rivières, and her father was Mohawk and a "heathen." When Tekak-witha was about four years old, a smallpox epidemic killed her immediate family and left Tekakwitha disfigured and with weak eyes that could not bear bright light. She was raised by her aunts and by an uncle who was considered one of the most powerful men in the village as well as a vehe-ment opponent of Christianity.

As a young girl, Tekakwitha did what all Iroquois girls did. (However, she was also "gentle, patient, chaste, innocent, and behaved like a well-bred French child.")[12] She helped gather firewood, worked in the cornfields, and became skilled at various decorative crafts. And although she later "looked back upon it as a great sin" requiring "a severe penance," she arrayed herself in typical Iroquois finery and engaged in other vani-ties.[13] When Tekakwitha reached marriageable age, her relatives began pressuring her to marry. At one point, they even arranged a marriage, but when the intended bridegroom came into the longhouse and seated him-self next to Tekakwitha, by which custom the arranged marriage was revealed to her, she "left the lodge and hid in the fields."[14]

Tekakwitha first encountered the Jesuits as a young girl when Fathers Frémin, Bruyas, and Pierron stayed in her uncle's lodge while arranging to establish missions among the five Iroquois Nations. It was not until several years later, however, that Tekakwitha received her first instruction in Chris-tianity. Jacques de Lamberville, then Jesuit missionary to the Mohawk, visited Tekakwitha's lodge and found her eager to hear more, or at least she was one of the few Iroquois he could get to listen. (Her eye problems and other ailments often kept her confined to the longhouse while other women went to work in the cornfields.) He baptized her in 1676 and gave her the Christian name of Catherine.[15] Harassed by the non-Christian majority, Tekakwitha fled to Kahnawake about a year and a half later, arriv-ing shortly after the village had relocated from La Prairie to Sault St. Louis.

While at Kahnawake, Tekakwitha's enthusiasm for Christianity became more intense. She moved in with her adopted sister and faithfully learned

Christian prayers and the lives of the saints from Anastasia, "one of the most fervent Christians in the place" and the matrilineal head of the family in that longhouse.[16] Her first year there, she went on the winter hunt as was the custom for residents of Kahnawake, but could not bear being deprived of Mass, the Eucharist, and daily prayer. She built her own shrine, a cross, in the woods and prayed to it, but would have preferred to be back in the village. The next winter, she refused to go on the hunt, which meant that she also chose to go without meat for the entire winter.

Once again, Tekakwitha's relatives, including Anastasia, pressured her to marry. They even solicited Cholenec's assistance in convincing Tekakwitha of the importance of marriage. At first Cholenec took the side of the relatives, for he knew that in Iroquois society women were dependent on men for clothing (provided through the hunt and later through the fur trade), and that, without a husband to contribute meat and hides to the longhouse, Tekakwitha was not helping herself or her longhouse family. But Tekakwitha insisted that she could "'have no other spouse but Jesus Christ.'" Finally persuaded that she was "inspired by the Holy Spirit," Cholenec changed sides in the family dispute and began to defend Tekakwitha's decision to remain unmarried.[17]

Meanwhile, Tekakwitha had formed a close friendship with another young woman, Marie Therese. They dedicated themselves to each other, to Christianity, and to leading lives modeled after that of the nuns in Québec and Montréal. Cholenec ascribed their knowledge of the nuns to Tekakwitha, and said that she had for herself seen how the hospital nuns in Montréal lived and had learned of their vows of chastity and penitential practices.[18] However, Chauchetière credited a third young woman, Marie Skarichions, with suggesting to Tekakwitha and Marie Therese that they model themselves after the nuns.[19] Skarichions was from Lorette, a community similar to Kahnawake but located near Québec, and she had once been cared for there by the Sisters de la Hospitalière.

These three women determined to form their own association, in which they dedicated themselves to virginity and helped each other in their self-mortifications. Tekakwitha's penances were many and varied. She walked barefoot in ice and snow, burned her feet "with a hot brand, very much in the same way that the Indians mark their slaves [war captives]," put coals and burning cinders between her toes, whipped her friends and was whipped by them in secret meetings in the woods, fasted, mixed ashes in her food, and slept for three nights on a bed of thorns after hearing the life story of Saint Louis de Gonzague.[20] Tekakwitha's self-mortifications eventually took their toll and she became ill, so ill that

Cholenec, making an exception for her, had to bring all his ritual equipment to her in her lodge to perform the last rites. She died at age 24 on April 17th, 1680.

This narrative of Tekakwitha's life needs to be interpreted from two different perspectives. First, there is the issue of Tekakwitha as a Jesuit construction. Why did they think she might be a saint? How did their own culture shape the narrative of Tekakwitha's life story? Second, what was she really doing? Was she forsaking traditional Iroquois beliefs to become Christian or did her actions make sense within an Iroquois cultural framework?

Undeniably, Tekakwitha was to some extent a Jesuit construction.[21] If you were to strip this narrative of its occasional Iroquois element—the longhouse, women in the cornfields, the winter hunt—it could have taken place in fourteenth-century bourgeois Siena. Her life story follows the hackneyed plot-line typical of women's hagiographies, especially that of Saint Catherine of Siena, except that Tekakwitha did not live long enough to become an advisor to popes and kings.[22] First, there are the unrelenting relatives who try to force Tekakwitha into marriage, purportedly for her own sake but primarily for the economic advantage of the family as a whole. Then, there is her complete devotion to Christian ritual: persistent prayers, a particular emotional intensity expressed for the Holy Eucharist, and her feelings of desperation and longing when deprived of the ritual experience. And finally, like other women who by the seventeenth century had been recognized as saints or likely saints, Tekakwitha's reputation for holiness was based entirely on her dedication to virginity and her proclivity for abusing her own body. Because Tekakwitha's life story follows an established hagiographical model, it could be that Cholenec and Chauchetière fictionalized their narratives to make her life fit the model. However, it is more likely that they thought she might be a saint because her life fit the model so well.

There were other potential saints among the Indians at Kahnawake. There was, for instance, Catherine Gandeacteua, the founder of the native village at La Prairie. The Jesuits praised her effusively, but according to the other model typical for women saints. Instead of being a self-mortifying virgin, Gandeacteua, "like Saint Anne," impoverished herself through her charity to others. She died before the village moved to the Sault, and so her body was buried at La Prairie. When the native village moved, the Indians and the French colonists at La Prairie vied for who should possess her corpse.[23] The Indians probably planned to rebury Gandeacteua's body near the new village. The French at La Prairie, however, must have thought Gandeacteua had virtues worthy of a saint, for they wanted the body, "the relics," presumably so they could have access to her intercessory powers with God. It was the custom in Europe to pray for a saint's intercession at the tomb or to the more portable relics (the saint's bones, clothes, dirt from near the tomb, whatever had physically been the saint or been touched by the saint).[24] French colonists were probably suffering from saint-deprivation, for there were as yet no saints' tombs in New France and most of the more easily transported relics were still in Europe. In this unusual colonial struggle, the French won and Gandeacteua's body remained at La Prairie.

There were even more saintly possibilities among Tekakwitha's peers at Kahnawake. She was merely one of many to join in a penitential fervor that raged through the village in the late 1670s and early 1680s. According to Chauchetière,

> The first who began made her first attempt about Christmas in The year 1676 [the year before Tekakwitha arrived at Kahnawake], when she divested herself of her clothing, and exposed herself to The air at the foot of a large Cross that stands beside our Cemetery. She did so at a time when the snow was falling, although she was pregnant; and the snow that fell upon her back caused her so much suffering that she nearly died from it—as well as her child, whom the cold chilled in its mother's womb. It was her own idea to do this—to do penance for her sins, she said.[25]

Chauchetière then described how four of her friends, all women, followed her example but invented other, more elaborate forms of penance. Tekakwitha learned about penance from other Indians at Kahnawake and did not initiate the practice.[26]

Moreover, penitential practices seem to have reached their peak after Tekakwitha's death. Chauchetière gave the clearest account of this development in his short history of the Mission at the Sault. After referring to how, in 1680, the "mission gave to paradise a treasure which had been sent to it two years before, to wit, the blessed soul of Catherine Tegakwita, who died on the 17th of april," Chauchetière recounted the events that transpired later that year:

> The demon [the devil], who saw the glorious success of this mission, used another kind of battery. Transfiguring himself as an angel of light,

he urged on the devotion of some persons who wished to imitate Catherine, or to do severe penance for their sins. He drove them even into excess,—in order, no doubt, to render christianity hateful even at the start; or in order to impose upon the girls and women of this mission, whose discretion has never equaled that of catherine, whom they tried to imitate. There were Savage women who threw themselves under the ice, in the midst of winter. One had her daughter dipped into it, who was only six years old,—for the purpose, she said, of teaching her penance in good season. The mother stood there on account of her past sins; she kept her innocent daughter there on account of her sins to come, which this child would perhaps commit when grown up. Savages, both men and women, covered themselves with blood by disciplinary stripes with iron, with rods, with thorns, with nettles; they fasted rigorously, passing the entire day without eating,—and what the savages eat during half the year is not sufficient to keep a man alive. These fasting women toiled strenuously all day—in summer, working in the fields; in winter, cutting wood. These austerities were almost continual. They mingled ashes in their portion of Sagamité; they put glowing coals between their toes, where the fire burned a hole in the flesh; they went bare-legged to make a long procession in the snows; they all disfigured themselves by cutting off their hair, in order not to be sought in marriage. . . . But the Holy Ghost soon intervened in this matter, enlightening all these persons, and regulated their conduct without diminishing their fervor."[27]

For the Jesuits, who knew that one saint was rare and ten or twenty completely implausible, the only way to explain this was to distinguish Tekakwitha's self-mortifications as inspired by God and everyone else's as inspired by the devil.

Despite their attempts to isolate Tekakwitha as especially holy, the Jesuit accounts show that the entire village of Kahnawake, both men and women, but especially the women, were taking Christianity to an extreme. The Jesuits frequently mentioned having to intervene to "regulate" penitential practices, and as Chauchetière admitted, "The Savage women sometimes propound to us doubts in spiritual matters, as difficult as those that might be advanced by the most cultured persons in France."[28] The Christian Indians at Kahnawake were inventive and self-motivated, exhibiting an independence and intensity which frightened the Jesuits because they risked being unable to control it. But still, from the Jesuits' perspective, Tekakwitha and the other Indians at Kahnawake were behaving in ways that were comprehensible as Christian.

However, the historical literature on missionization in New France has shown how Christian Indians created a syncretic religion, a new religion that melded traditional native beliefs and Christian rituals.[29] The Jesuits assisted the syncretic process in their accommodationist approach to native cultures. Similarities between Christianity and Iroquois religious beliefs, which the Jesuits rarely admitted to, also made syncretism possible.

The Jesuits' previous missionizing experiences and their scholarly emphasis led them to develop a somewhat sly missionary philosophy. They learned the native language and worldview in order to package Christianity in a conceptual framework that was familiar to the people they were attempting to missionize. In China, the Jesuits had first tried to ease into Chinese society by looking and acting like Buddhist monks. They then switched to the more comfortable role of scholar, and began to dress and act like the Chinese literati.[30] In New France, the Jesuits retained their usual style of dress, which is why the Indians called them "Black Robes," but slid into the only social category that approximated what they were: shamans. And even though the Jesuits saw themselves as superior to the native "conjurors," they did act just like shamans. They performed wondrous miracles by foretelling eclipses.[31] They interpreted "visions," while railing against native shamans who interpreted "dreams."[32] To cure people, they had their own set of mysterious and powerful rituals, such as bleeding, songs and prayers, and strange ritual implements.[33] Since they feared backsliders and usually only baptized adults who were on the verge of death, they were often perceived as either incompetent shamans or shamans who used their powers for evil purposes.[34] But in any case, the Indians were able to view them as people who had access to special powers.

These special powers were most observable in the new rituals which the Jesuits introduced to the Indians. Tangible manifestations of Christianity proved to be more important than theology in assisting the missionizing effort. Visual images and stories about people, either Bible stories or saints' lives, were the most efficacious missionary tools. Chauchetière was especially proud of his collection of religious paintings and drawings, some of which he drew himself or copied from other works. His depiction of "the pains of hell" was "very effective among the savages." The mission church at Kahnawake also had on display "paintings of the four ends of man, along with the moral paintings of M. le Nobletz," and eventually, after Tekakwitha's death, a series of paintings by Chauchetière depicting events in her life.[35]

Although the Jesuits shied away from attempting to explain the abstract principles of Christianity, which could not easily be translated into native languages anyhow, there were conceptual similarities between Iroquois religious beliefs and seventeenth-century Catholicism which also furthered missionization. Christian origin stories, from Adam and Eve to the birth of Jesus Christ, are similar to the Iroquois origin story, which even has an Immaculate Conception.[36] The Holy Family—the somewhat distant and unimportant Joseph, the powerful and virtuous Virgin Mary, her mother, St. Anne, and the son Jesus Christ—was structurally more like the matrilineal Iroquois family than the patriarchal nuclear family of western culture.[37] And the rosary, a string of beads with spiritual significance, resembled Iroquois wampum, belts and necklaces made of shell beads, which had spiritual and political meaning.[38] Indeed, many of the actions of Christianized Indians, which the Jesuits proudly recorded and took credit for, conformed to the cultural norms of traditional Iroquois society. Gandeacteua's Christian virtues—her generosity, especially in giving food and clothing to the poor, and her complete disavowal of all her personal possessions when she heard, mistakenly, that her husband had died—were more than virtues among the Iroquois; they were established customs.[39]

In emphasizing the syncretism of Christianity at Kahnawake, however, I do not want to belittle the significance of becoming Christian as people at the time perceived it. Christian Indians did see themselves as different, and non-Christian Indians ascribed a distinct identity to Christian Indians, even if they lived within the same village and spoke the same language. Also, even though the Indians at Kahnawake maintained many of their traditional beliefs and customs, they agreed to conform to some Jesuit demands, such as their prohibition of divorce.[40] For an Iroquois in the seventeenth century, becoming Christian and choosing to live near the Jesuits would have been a difficult decision, for the Iroquois rightly associated Christian missions with the French, who were, except for brief interludes, their enemies. The tensions arising from such a decision reached their peak in the early 1680s, when the Iroquois at Kahnawake reluctantly joined the French in a war against the main body of Iroquois to their south.[41]

Also, despite the conceptual similarities between Iroquois beliefs and Christianity, those who converted to Christianity do seem to have been already marginal within their communities. As Daniel Richter has observed, many of the residents at Kahnawake were former war captives who had been adopted into Iroquois families.[42] This might also explain the prominence of women in the mission accounts of Kahnawake. Since female war captives were more likely than men to be adopted permanently into the tribe, many Iroquois women had a dual ethnic identity.

Tekakwitha's marginality came from two directions: her mother and her disfigurement from smallpox. The Mohawks in Tekakwitha's original village thought of her as an Algonquin, suggesting that her mother, although presumably formally adopted as Iroquois, still strongly identified as Algonquin or was strongly identified by others as Algonquin.[43] According to her hagiographers, Tekakwitha was also self-conscious about her weak eyes and her smallpox scars. Unlike other Iroquois women, she always tried to keep her face covered with her blanket. Supposedly, some of her fellow villagers ridiculed her and said, after she died, "that God had taken her because men did not want her."[44]

The marginality of Tekakwitha and adopted Iroquois women might explain why they, and not others, chose Christianity, but it does not explain what they saw in Christianity. In Tekakwitha's case, there seem to have been three conceptual similarities between Iroquois beliefs and seventeenth-century Catholicism which make her actions comprehensible from both the Iroquois and Jesuit cultural perspectives. First, the Iroquois Requickening ceremony and the Christian ceremony of baptism, though conducted through different kinds of rituals, achieved the same end of renewal through imitation. Second, the Iroquois and the Jesuits employed voluntary societies as an additional level of social organization beyond the family and the political council. Voluntary societies served as an avenue by which individual women and men could acquire prestige, authority, and kin-like bonds within the larger community. And third, Iroquois and Jesuit beliefs about the body, the soul, and power were similar enough to allow for a syncretic adoption of self-denial and self-mortification as spiritually and physically empowering acts.

Undeniably, the Jesuits favored men in their daily administration of the mission. If given the choice, the Jesuits would have preferred to have more male converts, especially men of influence, than female converts. The Jesuits also granted men more authority and prestige by giving them roles as assistants in church services and by making them "dogiques" (native catechists). However, women turned Christianity to their advantage and incorporated the ritual of baptism, Christian societies, virginity and penance as means to establishing a firmer place for themselves in a changing Iroquois society.

First, the Christian ritual of baptism resembled an Iroquois Requickening ceremony. In both ceremonies, someone assumed the name and the metaphorical identity of an important person who had died. In both ceremonies, water played a purifying role. The Jesuits sprinkled holy water to mark the baptismal moment, whereas the Iroquois drank "water-of-pity" to signify the transition to a new identity. Among the Iroquois, names of important people were passed on within clans. Individuals from later generations assumed these names and were expected to live up to them by imitating the person who had died and by fulfilling the obligations that went along with the name. For instance, when the Jesuit Lafitau arrived as a missionary at Kahnawake in 1712, the Iroquois requickened him in the place of Father Bruyas.[45] Although men and women could be renamed and "requickened," the ceremony was also held as part of the Condolence ceremony, the raising up of a new chief, and therefore was in its most prestigious manifestation held as a ceremony for men.[46]

The Jesuits introduced the Iroquois to new images of women in their stories of the Virgin Mary and women saints, and then provided the ritual, baptism, which encouraged imitation of these seemingly powerful women. When Tekakwitha was baptized, "The spirit of Saint Katherine of Sienna and of other saints of this name, was revived in her."[47] She was at the same time requickened as Saint Catherine of Siena, a woman whom the Jesuits featured prominently in their stories and devotions. Tekakwitha probably was deliberately modeling herself after her namesake. She would have heard the story of Saint Catherine's life many times—the fasting and penitential practices, her refusal to marry and her marriage to Jesus Christ in a vision, and her later role as an adviser to male political leaders. Tekakwitha and the other women at Kahnawake may have sensed the underlying patriarchy of the Jesuit mission, but also heard the Jesuits talk of powerful women, like St. Catherine of Siena, and were urged to imitate them.

Second, the women at Kahnawake used the model of the Christian society to enhance their collective role as the women of the village. One such Christian association was the Confraternity of the Holy Family, an organization of men and women which the Jesuits established at Kahnawake to bind the most devoted Christians together.[48] Women appear to have been among the most active participants in this organization. Perhaps the Jesuits' use of the "holy family" as the model for this society's devotions inspired its members to assume a matrilineal organization for determining members' relationships, mutual obligations, and decision-making powers.

The Jesuits viewed the Confraternity of the Holy Family as a successful operation, but expressed some doubts about the indigenous Christian organizations sprouting at Kahnawake. For example, Tekakwitha and her two friends attempted to form a nunnery. They planned to leave the village and set up a separate community of Christian women on Heron

Island, until Father Frémin talked them out of it.[49] Chauchetière described another women's organization in connection with the penitential practices adopted at Kahnawake:

> The use of these [instruments of penance] Daily becomes more general. And, as The men have found that the women use them, they will not Let themselves be outdone, and ask us to permit them to use these every Day; but we will not allow it. The women, to the number of 8 or 10, Began The practice; and The wife of the dogique—that is to say, of him who Leads the Singing and says The prayers—is among the number. She it is who, in her husband's absence, also causes The prayers to be said aloud, and Leads The Singing; and in this capacity she assembles the devout women of whom we have spoken, who call themselves sisters. They tell One another their faults, and deliberate together upon what must be done for The relief of the poor in the Village—whose number is so great that there are almost as many poor as there are Savages. The sort of monastery that they maintain here has its rules. They have promised God never to put on their gala-dress. . . . They assist One another in the fields; They meet together to incite one another to virtue; and one of them has been received as a nun in The hospital of monreal.[50]

Chauchetière's account suggests that women deliberately formed these societies as an alternative to the gender-mixed Confraternity of the Holy Family and that the men at Kahnawake viewed women's societies as a challenge to their own authority and status.

However, "confraternities" were fundamental, well-established components of Iroquois village life. Iroquois women used similar "confraternities" to organize their work and acknowledge women's achievements.[51] The Iroquois also had healing societies, like the False-Faces, which possessed a specialized knowledge and their own healing rituals.[52] The women at Kahnawake added to this familiar kind of social institution the newly-introduced, Christian example of the nunnery, of which several existed in New France. In Québec in 1639, the Ursulines arrived to start a mission school for Indian girls and the Sisters de la Hospitalière opened a hospital. Later, Montréal also had some hospital sisters.[53] Although the Catholic Church restricted the authority of women's religious orders by making them ultimately subject to a male director, the women at Kahnawake were more likely to be aware of how these women, because of their unusual lifestyle and their healing activities, appeared to be powerful and respected members of French colonial society. As their husbands became the Jesuits' "dogiques," women may have refashioned their work-oriented organization after the Christian model to reassert a traditional balance of power, which the Jesuits were disrupting by appointing men to positions of power and high status. The women's dedication to penance, and the envy among the men which this inspired, further suggests that both men and women at Kahnawake came to view penance as an empowering ritual.

Iroquois and Jesuit philosophies about the relationship between the body, the soul, and power illuminate why Tekakwitha and the other residents of Kahnawake accepted the Christian ideals of virginity and penance. In Catholic and Iroquois religious traditions, there was an ambivalence about the connection between the body and the soul. Both belief systems characterized the soul as a separate entity from the body, but elaborate funerary rites and the homage paid to soulless corpses show that they were reluctant to disavow all connections between the soul and the body. In Catholic theology, the soul left the body upon death and, in the case of saints and other holy people, resided in heaven. The Iroquois believed the soul left the body at death and lived an afterlife that would be like life on earth, but better.[54] The Iroquois also believed that the soul left living bodies while they were asleep. Dreamers made trips to this other world and brought back important messages needing interpretation. Shamans' skills included diagnosing these dreams so that they could be acted upon for the good of the individual and the community.[55] Although Iroquois dream interpretation was from the Jesuit point of view one of the most despicable and pagan aspects of Iroquois culture, in the Catholic tradition, holy people also bridged these two worlds. In their lifetime, they might have visions which connected them to the Virgin Mary or Jesus Christ, and after their death, they became the intercessors for others.

Saints functioned like guardian spirits, which in Iroquois culture were not people who had died but instead were animals or some other being that was part of the natural world.[56] In Iroquois tradition, a token (which might be a feather, a pebble, or a piece of oddly-shaped wood) was the physical key to the spiritual world, just as Catholics prayed to the saint's physical remains, to a relic, or at the tomb to reach guardian angels and saints.[57] Since the Iroquois believed everything in nature had a soul, unlike Christians who believed only people did, their range of possible guardian spirits was broader. However, the idea of appealing to a guardian spirit for miraculous cures, success in hunting and warfare, for love and happiness, or for special powers was part of both religions. Among the Iroquois, everyone and everything had some power, or "orenda," but some had more than others.[58] This power could be called upon by appeals to guardian spirits, and could be used for either good or bad. The Jesuits believed that only a few were graced with divine power. And even though they had earthly authority as administrators of Christianity, it was a rare Jesuit who was also graced with divine authority, as a martyr or as someone who exhibited such extreme devotion to Christian ideals that they had to be a saint.

Within the Christian tradition, it was difficult for women to acquire authority on earth, but mystical experiences and Christian virtue carried to extremes produced saints. Self-mortification, virginity, and especially fasting appear in most hagiographies but especially dominate in the stories of women saints' lives. Refuting other scholars' claims that bodily abuse was an expression of women's hatred of their bodies, Rudolph Bell in *Holy Anorexia* and Caroline Walker Bynum in *Holy Feast and Holy Famine* argued that women seeking a sense of identity and self-assertion tried to control their world through the only means available, by controlling their own bodies and by controlling the symbols of women's domestic authority, such as food distribution. By fasting, making a vow of chastity, and engaging in penitential self-abuse, Catherine of Siena and other women saints revealed that they were among the select few graced with divine authority. As in the case of Catherine of Siena, a woman saint's divine authority could bring her some earthly authority as well, authority over her own life as well as over the lives of others. Saint Catherine of Siena's marriage to Jesus Christ in a vision partly explained why she could not marry on earth and also gave her the authority to tell kings and popes what to do.

In Iroquois society, one could similarly acquire power by controlling one's own body through fasting and sexual abstinence. Although lifelong celibacy struck the Iroquois as odd, virginity and sexual abstinence were conceived of as sources of power.[59] Virgins had certain ceremonial roles, and Iroquois legends told of there having once been a society of virgins.[60] The Iroquois viewed sexual abstinence as an avenue to physical and spiritual strength and as essential to men's preparations for war and the hunt. Fasting and tests of physical endurance also could be used as a means to acquire power. The Iroquois coming-of-age ritual for young men and women was a vision quest.[61] They went into the woods by themselves, fasted, and hoped to receive a vision or token from a guardian spirit. Those with especially powerful visions might become shamans (professional healers and visionaries).[62] Since some Indian residents at Kahnawake accused Tekakwitha of being a "sorceress," apparently the same acts that inspired the Jesuits to think of her as holy also gave her access to "orenda."[63]

Bell and Bynum revealed how virginity and fasting had a special meaning for women saints in medieval Europe. In contrast, among the Iroquois, virginity and fasting seem to have been equally available to men and women as sources of individual empowerment. Still, Bell's and Bynum's analyses of the relationship between food and control can shed light on why the Iroquois had a more democratic understanding of who could acquire "orenda" and how. Although Iroquois women controlled the distribution of food, both men and women made important, complementary contributions to food production. Women grew corn, and men hunted meat. Moreover, both men and women equally shared in their fear of starvation during winter. Iroquois rituals—many of which involved fasting, feasting, or cannibalism—all show an obsession with food, which may have been a cultural expression of their daily anxieties about an uncertain supply of food in the future.

Virginity and fasting resonated with Iroquois traditions. Penance was an entirely new ritual, but one that paralleled Iroquois ritual torture of war captives. The Iroquois adopted all war captives into the place of deceased clan members, and clans then chose whether the adoptee would live or die in the spirit of their namesake. Those consigned to die in the place of a mourned relative were put through a lengthy and painful series of tortures, after which parts of their body might be eaten. If the captive had died an especially brave death, he (usually it was a he) was more likely to be eaten because his body parts were seen as possessing that strength and courage. Through ritual torture, war captives became the repositories for violent emotions; by directing anxiety, stress, and grief for dead relatives outward, the Iroquois kept peace among themselves.[64]

Although the Jesuits condemned Iroquois torture, they recognized awkward similarities between Iroquois cannibalism and the Eucharist. The Eucharist is a metaphoric ritual in which participants eat the body of Christ and drink his blood, a reference to the theological notion that Christ sacrificed himself so that others might live. Fearing that the Iroquois might think they condoned cannibalism, the Jesuits translated the Eucharist to mean a feast and did not tell the Iroquois about its sacrificial connotations.[65] If it had not been so uncomfortably reminiscent of Iroquois ritual cannibalism, the Eucharist might have been a useful missionizing tool, with which the Jesuits could have offered the Iroquois a ritual to replace the torture of war captives.

However, David Blanchard has argued that the Indians at Kahnawake replaced the ritual torture of war captives with ritual self-torture. They called their penitential practices "hotouongannandi," which Chauchetière translated to mean "public penance."[66] According to Blanchard, a better translation of the term would be "They are making magic," suggesting that the Iroquois saw penitential practices as a ritual source of power. Blanchard emphasizes the importance of this ritual in helping the Iroquois, as in their dreams, to leave the world on earth and visit "the sky world."[67] It is also important to emphasize, however, that they used visits to "the sky world" to control and improve life on earth.

The Indians at Kahnawake probably saw penance as a powerful healing and prophylactic ritual. Since the penitential practices at Kahnawake began at about the same time as a 1678 smallpox epidemic, which ebbed quickly and caused little damage, penitents at Kahnawake may even have viewed penance as an especially effective ritual to counter new diseases like smallpox.[68] The rise of penitential practices in Europe, evident in such movements as the Flagellants, which emerged after the Bubonic Plague, suggests that Christians in fourteenth-century Europe also thought that self-induced abuse of the body was a means to control the uncontrollable.[69] Also, the Iroquois at Kahnawake may have viewed penance as a prophylactic ritual to prevent torture and death at the hands of one's enemies. The Jesuits deliberately drew analogies between Christian hell and the torture of war captives practiced by northeastern Indians, and promised that Christian devotion would save one from an eternity in hell.[70]

In conclusion, the Iroquois who adopted Christianity did so for reasons that made sense within an Iroquois cultural framework. Certain Christian rituals fit easily into traditional Iroquois beliefs, while the new ritual practices, like penance, offered a special power lacking in traditional Iroquois rituals. Whereas the Jesuits emphasized the importance of Christian ritual in determining one's place in the afterlife, Tekakwitha and other Christian Iroquois had new and pressing needs for empowering rituals to control the increasingly uncertain, earthly present. Smallpox, increased warfare, alcohol, and the economic and political assaults on traditional gender roles did create a growing sense of crisis in Iroquois communities. To deal with that crisis and control their changing world, many Iroquois women and men turned to Christianity. However, they did not become Christian in the way the Jesuits intended; instead, they transformed Christianity into an Iroquois religion.

During one particular moment of crisis, at Kahnawake in the 1670s and 1680s, Iroquois women and men struggled to reshape the Jesuits' preachings into something meaningful for them. Part of the struggle had to do with the patriarchal structure of Christianity. The Jesuits supported male authority in the village by promoting men as administers of Christianity and church activities. Women responded by using Christian symbols to assert their authority and identity within the community. Through a syncretic transformation of the ritual of baptism, the Christian society, virginity, and self-mortification, Tekakwitha appeared holy and Christian to the Jesuits while pursuing status and a firmer sense of her own identity within Iroquois society. The Jesuits tried to implement patriarchy at their missions, but they also brought the symbols, imagery, and rituals women needed to subvert patriarchy.

NOTES

The author thanks Deborah Sommer and Louis Dupont for their help with this article.

1. Claude Chauchetière, "Annual Narrative of the Mission of the Sault, From its Foundation Until the Year 1686," in *The Jesuit Relations and Allied Documents: Travels and Explorations of the Jesuit Missionaries in New France, 1610–1791 (JR)*, ed. Reuben Gold Thwaites (NY: Pageant, 1959), 63: 229; Pierre Cholenec more elaborately tells how Tekakwitha appeared to Chauchetière in a vision and prophesied the destruction of the church in "The Life of Katharine Tegakoüita, First Iroquois Virgin" (1696), Document X, in *The Positio of the Historical Section of the Sacred Congregation of Rites on the Introduction of the Cause for Beatification and Canonization and on the Virtues of the Servant of God Katharine Tekakwitha, the Lily of the Mohawks*, ed. Robert E. Holland (NY: Fordham University Press, 1940), 312.

2. Peter Rémy to Father Cholenec, 12 March 1696, Document IX, in *The Positio*, 227.

3. Colombière is quoted in "Letter from Father Cholonec, Missionary of the Society of Jesus, to Father Augustin Le Blanc of the Same Society, Procurator of Missions in Canada," in *The Early Jesuit Missions in North America: Compiled and Translated From the Letters of the French Jesuits, with Notes*, ed. William Ingraham Kip (Albany: Joel Munsell, 1873), 115.

4. "'Lily of the Mohawks'", *Newsweek* 12 (1 August 1938), 27–28; "The Long Road To Sainthood," *Time* 116 (7 July 1980), 42–43. At about the time of Tekakwitha's beatification, the Catholic Church undertook a major reform of the saint-making process and reduced the number of miracles required for beatification and canonization. Under the old rules, Tekakwitha needed two documented miracles to be beatified or declared "blessed." Under the new rules, she only needed one. However, even though Tekakwitha is credited with many miracles, not one was able to meet the documentation standards required by the Catholic Church. Pope John Paul II waived this requirement for her, perhaps to give American Indians a saint of their own. To be canonized, and thereby declared a "saint," she would need two miracles according to the new rules, but since the documentation standards have already been waived for her, it is not clear whether there are any remaining obstacles to her canonization. Kenneth L. Woodward, *Making Saints: How the Catholic Church Determines Who Becomes a Saint, Who Doesn't, and Why* (NY: Simon and Schuster, 1990), 99, 117–188, 208, 217.

5. James Axtell, *The Invasion Within: The Contest of Cultures in Colonial North America* (NY: Oxford University Press, 1985), 23–127; Cornelius J. Jaenen, *Friend and*

Foe: Aspects of French-Amerindian Cultural Contact in the Sixteenth and Seventeenth Centuries (NY: Columbia University Press, 1976); Daniel K. Richter, *The Ordeal of the Longhouse: The Peoples of the Iroquois League in the Era of European Colonization* (Chapel Hill: University of North Carolina Press, 1992), 105–132.

6. Eleanor Burke Leacock, "Montagnais Women and the Jesuit Program for Colonization," *Myths of Male Dominance: Collected Articles on Women Cross-Culturally* (NY: Monthly Review Press, 1981), 43–62; Karen Anderson, *Chain Her By One Foot: The Subjugation of Women in Seventeenth-Century New France* (NY: Routledge, 1991); Carol Devens, *Countering Colonization: Native American Women and Great Lakes Missions, 1630–1900* (Berkeley: University of California Press, 1992), 7–30. An exception is Natalie Zemon Davis' article "Iroquois Women, European Women," which argues that Christianity may have given Indian women in New France access to a public voice denied them in traditional Iroquois oratory. This article is in *Women, "Race," and Writing in the Early Modern Period*, eds. Margo Hendricks and Patricia Parker (NY: Routledge, 1994), 243–258, 350–361.

7. W.G. Spittal, *Iroquois Women: An Anthology* (Ohsweken, Ontario: Iroqrafts, 1990).

8. *JR* 18 (1640), 105–107; Leacock, 52; Anderson, 219; Devens, 7.

9. W.J. Eccles, *France in America* (NY: Harper and Row, 1972); Cornelius J. Jaenen, *The Role of the Church in New France* (Toronto: McGraw-Hill Ryerson, 1976); J. H. Kennedy, *Jesuit and Savage in New France* (New Haven: Yale University Press, 1950).

10. Chauchetière, *JR* 63 (1686), 141–245; *JR* 61 (1679), 239–241; Henri Béchard, *The Original Caughnawaga Indians* (Montréal: International Publishers, 1976); E.J. Devine, *Historic Caughnawaga* (Montréal: Messenger Press, 1922); Gretchen Lynn Green, "A New Peole in an Age of War: The Kahnawake Iroquois, 1667–1760" (Ph.D. diss., College of William and Mary, 1991).

11. The historical documents on Tekakwitha are conveniently available in *The Positio*, the compendium of materials used by the Vatican to determine whether she was worthy of Veneration. Cholenec, who headed the mission at Caughnawaga during Tekakwitha's stay there, wrote at least four versions of her life, which are usually but not entirely consistent. The 1696 "Life" (Document X in *The Positio*) is the most elaborate in describing Tekakwitha's virtues, trials, and posthumous miracles. Document XII, which also appears in Kip, is Cholenec's 1715 letter to Augustin Le Blanc and is a more straightforward account. Chauchetière's "The Life of the Good Katharine Tegakoüita, Now Known as the Holy Savage," probably first drafted in 1685 and revised or amended in 1695, is Document VIII in *The Positio*. Cholenec, Chauchetière, and Frémin (who apparently chose not to write a life of Tekakwitha) were the Jesuits stationed at Kahnawake during the time Tekakwitha lived there.

12. Chauchetière, *The Positio*, 121.

13. Cholenec, in Kip, 83.

14. Chauchetière, *The Positio*, 125.

15. Catharine, Katharine, Katherine, Catherine, Kateri ("gadeli" as it is pronounced among the Mohawks), Katerei all appear in the records; Kateri seems to be the more accepted, contemporary term.

16. Cholenec, in Kip, 95.

17. Cholenec, in Kip, 105

18. Cholenec, in Kip, 108.

19. Chauchetière, *The Positio*, 175.

20. Cholenec, in Kip, 111; Cholenec, *The Positio,* 295.

21. K.I. Koppedrayer, "The Making of the First Iroquois Virgin: Early Jesuit Biographies of the Blessed Kateri Tekakwitha," *Ethnohistory* 40 (1993): 277–306.

22. Rudolph M. Bell, *Holy Anorexia* (Chicago: University of Chicago Press, 1985); Caroline Walker Bynum, *Holy Feast and Holy Fast: The Religious Significance of Food to Medieval Women* (Berkeley: University of California Press, 1987); Donald Weinstein and Rudolph M. Bell, *Saints and Society: The Two Worlds of Western Christendom, 1000–1700* (Chicago: University of Chicago Press, 1982).

23. Chauchetière, *The Positio,* 161, 165.

24. Peter Brown, *The Cult of the Saints: Its Rise and Function in Latin Christianity* (Chicago: University of Chicago Press, 1981).

25. Chauchetière, *JR* 62 (1682), 175.

26. Cholenec, in Kip, 98–99.

27. Chauchetière, *JR* 63 (1686), 215–219; also see Cholenec, in Kip, 106–108.

28. Chauchetière, *JR* 62 (1682), 187.

29. See Axtell; Jaenen, *Friend and Foe;* David Blanchard, ". . . To the Other Side of the Sky: Catholicism at Kahnawake, 1667–1700," *Anthropologica* XXIV (1982), 77–102. Also see Henry Warner Bowden's discussion of the Hurons and the Jesuits in *American Indians and Christian Missions: Studies in Cultural Conflict* (Chicago: University of Chicago Press, 1981), 59–95; James P. Ronda and James Axtell, *Indian Missions: A Critical Bibliography* (Bloomington: Indiana University Press, 1978).

30. Jacques Gernet, *China and the Christian Impact: A Conflict of Cultures* (NY: Cambridge University Press, 1985); Charles E. Ronan and Bonnie B.C. Oh, *East Meets West: The Jesuits in China, 1582–1773* (Chicago: Loyola University Press, 1988).

31. *JR* 58 (1673–74), 181–183; *JR* 62 (1683), 199.

32. *JR* 60 (1675), 61–63.

33. Le Jeune's 1634 *Relation* of his mission among the Montagnais, in *JR* 7, shows in great detail how Jesuits deliberately competed with shamans to prove their superior access to supernatural authority.

34. *JR* 6 (1634), 139; *JR* 58 (1673–74), 191, 219–221; *JR* 61 (1679), 229.

35. Chauchetière, *The Positio,* 115–116, 146. See also *JR* 5 (1633), 257–259. François-Marc Gagnon, *La Conversion Par L'Image: Un Aspect de la Mission des Jésuites Auprès des Indiéns du Canada au XVIIe Siècle* (Montréal: Les Éditions Bellarmin, 1975).

36. Hazel W. Hertzberg, *The Great Tree and the Longhouse: The Culture of the Iroquois* (NY: Macmillan, 1966); J.N.B. Hewitt, "Iroquoian Cosmology," Part Two, *Annual Report, Bureau of American Ethnology,* 1925–1926 (Washington, D.C.: 1928), 465.

37. For example, see Pamela Sheingorn, "The Holy Kinship: The Ascendency of Matriliny in Sacred Genealogy of the Fifteenth Century," *Thought* 64 (1989), 268–86. Also, for a fascinating discussion of how the Jesuits responded to Iroquoian matrilineality and their own need for a patriarchal authority structure to justify their role as "fathers," see John Steckley, "The Warrior and the Lineage: Jesuit Use of Iroquoian Images to Communicate Christianity," *Ethnohistory* 39 (1992), 478–509.

38. *JR* 58 (1673–74), 185–189; Blanchard's ". . . To the other side of the Sky" discusses the rosary-wampum syncretism at length.

39. Chauchetière, *The Positio,* 162.

40. *JR* 58 (1672–73), 77.

41. Daniel K. Richter, "Iroquois versus Iroquois: Jesuit Missions and Christianity in Village Politics, 1642–1686," *Ethnohistory* 32 (1985), 1–16.

42. Richter, *The Ordeal of the Longhouse*, 124–128.

43. Cholenec, in Kip, 87.

44. Chauchetière, *The Positio*, 123.

45. Lafitau, Volume II, 240; Volume I, xxxi; J.N.B. Hewitt, "The Requickening Address of the Condolence Council," ed. William N. Fenton, *Journal of the Washington Academy of Sciences* 34 (1944), 65–85.

46. Lafitau, Volume I, 71; *JR* 60 (1675), 37.

47. Chauchetière, *The Positio*, 169, 137.

48. *JR* 58 (1672–73), 77; Cholenec, *JR* 60 (1677), 281.

49. Chauchetière, *The Positio*, 176.

50. Chauchetière, *JR* 62 (1681–83), 179. See also Chauchetière, *JR* 63 (1686), 203–205.

51. Arthur C. Parker, "Secret Medicine Societies of the Seneca," *American Anthropologist*, n.s., vol. 11 (1909), 161–185; Lafitau, Volume II, 54–55.

52. William N. Fenton, *The False Faces of the Iroquois* (Norman: University of Oklahoma Press, 1987).

53. Joyce Marshall, ed., *Word From New France: The Selected Letters of Marie De L'Incarnation* (Toronto: Oxford University Press, 1967).

54. Lafitau, Volume II, 230–231, 237–238; for a comparison of Huron (Iroquoian) and Christian conceptions of the soul, see *JR* 7 (1635), 293; *JR* 10 (1636), 287. Also see John Steckley's linguistic analysis of these concepts in Huron in "Brébeuf's Presentation of Catholicism in the Huron Language: A Descriptive Overview," *Revue de l'Université d'Ottawa/University of Ottawa Quarterly* 48 (1978), 93–115. Much of my perspective on Christian beliefs about the soul and body is based on Caroline Walker Bynum's work, especially the articles collected in *Fragmentation and Redemption: Essays on Gender and the Human Body in Medieval Religion* (NY: Zone Books, 1991). Although her discussion refers to medieval Europe, she could just as easily have been describing the beliefs of seventeenth-century Jesuits, as revealed by their self-reflexive remarks on Iroquois differences in the *Jesuit Relations*.

55. Lafitau, Volume I, 231–234; *JR* 54 (1669–70), 65–73; Anthony F.C. Wallace, "Dreams and the Wishes of the Soul: A Type of Psychoanalytic Theory among the Seventeenth Century Iroquois," *American Anthropologist* 60 (1958), 234–248.

56. Lafitau, Volume I, 230.

57. Lafitau, Volume I, 236, 243; "Narrative of a Journey into the Mohawk and Oneida Country, 1634–1635," in *Narratives of New Netherland, 1609–1664*, ed. J. Franklin Jameson (NY: Charles Scribner's Sons, 1909), 137–162.

58. J.N.B. Hewitt, "Orenda and a Definition of Religion," *American Anthropologist*, n. s., 4 (1902), 33–46; Hope L. Isaacs, "*Orenda* and the Concept of Power among the Tonawanda Senecas," in *The Anthropology of Power: Ethnographic Studies from Asia, Oceania, and the New World*, ed. Raymond D. Fogelson and Richard N. Adams, eds. (NY: Academic Press, 1977), 167–184.

59. Lafitau, Volume I, 218. Also see Marina Warner, *Alone of All Her Sex: The Myth and the Cult of the Virgin Mary* (NY: Alfred A. Knopf, 1976), 48–49, for a

discussion of how the Christian ideal of virginity has roots in classical beliefs about virginity as a magic source of power.

60. Lafitau, Volume I, 129–130.
61. Lafitau, Volume I, p. 217.
62. Lafitau, Volume I, 230–240.
63. Chauchetière, *The Positio,* 208.
64. Lafitau, Volume II, 148–172; *JR* 54 (1669–70), 25–35; Daniel K. Richter, "War and Culture: The Iroquois Experience," *William and Mary Quarterly* 40 (1983), 528–559; Thomas S. Abler and Michael H. Logan, "The Florescence and Demise of Iroquoian Cannibalism: Human Sacrifice and Malinowski's Hypothesis," *Man in the Northeast* 35 (1988), 1–26.
65. See Jaenen, *Friend and Foe*, 145; Steckley, "Brébeuf's Presentation of Catholicism in the Huron Language," 113.
66. Chauchetière, *JR* 64 (1695), 125.
67. Blanchard, 97.
68. Chauchetière, *JR* 63 (1686), 205.
69. Philip Ziegler, *The Black Death* (NY: John Day Company, 1969), 86–98; also see Andrew E. Barnes, "Religious Anxiety and Devotional Change in the Sixteenth Century French Penitential Confraternities," *Sixteenth Century Journal* 19 (1988), 389–406, which is about a resurgence of penance during the crisis of the Protestant Reformation and simultaneous with Catholic-Huguenot violence.
70. See Axtell's discussion of the Jesuits' conflating hell and torture as a way to attract converts in *The Invasion Within*, 114–115; Steckley, in "The Warrior and the Lineage," shows how the Jesuits described hell as worse than the ritual torture practiced by Northeastern tribes.

3

LUCY ELDERSVELD MURPHY

AUTONOMY AND THE ECONOMIC ROLES OF INDIAN WOMEN OF THE FOX-WISCONSIN RIVER REGION, 1763–1832

Murphy's article on Indian and white interactions in the Fox-Wisconsin river-way region (what is now southern Wisconsin, northern Illinois, and eastern Iowa) deals with the history of primarily three Indian groups: the Mesquakies (Fox), Sauks, and Winnebagos. The native people of the Fox-Wisconsin riverway became heavily involved in trading with the French in the eighteenth century and then were colonized by the British who defeated the French in the French and Indian War (1754–1763). After the American Revolution, their lands fell within territorial claims of the United States, and under pressure from white settlers and miners, the United States arranged a series of treaties with the Indians calling for land cessions. Rising tension and violence between Indians and whites culminated in an 1832 war led by a Sauk leader, Black Hawk. Although the Mesquakies, Winnebagos, and most of the Sauks remained neutral during the Black Hawk War, when the war ended, the U.S. forced all three tribes to sign treaties that arranged for the Indians to retain small reservations while ceding most of their lands to the United States.

On September 25, 1766, the Winnebago chief of a village near Green Bay, a woman named Ho-po-ko-e-kaw, or Glory of the Morning, welcomed a Connecticut Yankee explorer named Jonathan Carver to her community. Carver recorded: "Here the queen who presided over this tribe instead of a Sachem, received me with great civility, and entertained me in a very distinguished manner during the four days I continued with her."[1] Carver held a council with her and with the other, male chiefs, and received permission to pass through the Winnebago country. He gave Glory of the Morning a number of gifts, and noted that the young women who attended her "seemed greatly pleased whenever I showed any tokens of respect to their queen, particularly when I saluted her, which I frequently did to acquire her favour. . . . [T]he good old lady . . . by her smiles showed she was equally pleased with the attention I paid her."[2]

Sixty-five years later and two hundred miles to the southwest, a delegation of women from the village of Saukenuk called on Major General Edmund Gaines at Rock Island in the Mississippi River to protest their people's removal from their homes. It was June 7, 1831, and they were members of the "British Band" of Sauk Indians, followers of Black Hawk. For years, their people had been quarreling with the agents of the U.S. government, refusing to move to the west of the Mississippi. On June 4 and 5, the Sauk men had attended meetings with Gaines, and had protested removal. Formal diplomacy with Euro-Americans was traditionally left to Indian men in this region, but on this occasion, in the middle of the growing season, the issue of relocation directly affected the women's most important domains: their cornfields.

Black Hawk introduced the group's spokeswoman, explaining, (according to minutes of the meeting), "that their women having worked their fields till they had become easy of cultivation, were now unwilling to leave them; & that they had decided not to move."[3]

The minutes of the meeting do not name the woman who spoke, but Black Hawk's autobiography identified her as "the daughter of Mat-ta-tas, the old chief of the village."[4] Her speech is paraphrased in the transcript as follows: "One of the women then rose & said that the land was theirs & had never been sold & so forth."[5]

Quashquame, a male Sauk leader, then spoke, saying,

> that, the woman who had spoken was the daughter of a great chief—
> that she had a right to know of any bargains, & never having heard of
> the sale of the lands, she had come with her women to say that they
> had never consented to such a measure.[6]

According to Black Hawk's memoir, Gaines first dismissed the woman's remarks with the disdainful comment "that the president did not send him here to make treaties with the women, nor to hold council with them!" Then, addressing the spokeswoman in what may have been a subtle, suggestive insult, Gaines said that the Sauk "young men must leave the fort, but she might remain if she wished!"[7]

Under threat of force, the Saukenuk villagers crossed the Mississippi under an agreement that Gaines would, in Black Hawk's words, "give us corn in place of that we had left growing in our fields."[8] But, Black Hawk recalled,

> The corn that had been given us, was soon found to be inadequate to our wants; when loud lamentations were heard in the camp, by our women and children, for their *roasting-ears, beans,* and *squashes.* To satisfy them, a small party of braves went over, in the night, to steal corn from their own fields.[9]

These two contrasting events, sixty-five years apart, illustrate some of the dynamics and consequences of economic change which took place during the late eighteenth and early nineteenth centuries. Carver's visit among Glory of the Morning's people took place in the context of the tradition of trade established by French-Canadian predecessors, which involved Indian women and men as producers for local, regional, and international markets, while white and métis people served as consumers and traders. As the regional economy developed during the following half-century, however, Indian women accelerated their market production and developed local resources until white U.S. settler men seized the resources and forcibly took over the Indian women's roles as lead miners and farmers.

The response of Major General Gaines, a white Virginian, to the insubordinate Sauk women, presents an important contrast to both the respect Glory of the Morning had received, and to the Sauks' acknowledgement of the women's rights and prerogatives. These women clearly had substantial influence within their own communities. As a group, Indian women of a given village might exert considerable power. Black Hawk's support, for example, owed a great deal to the Sauk women and the issue of the cornfields. Individual women in this region could achieve authority, depending on age, family connections, talent, and inclination. Glory of the Morning was "a very ancient woman"; she and the Sauk spokeswoman were both the daughters of chiefs.[10] Younger women might be subject to the authority of their parents and brothers. On the whole, in both the eighteenth and early nineteenth centuries, Indian women acted with considerable independence of Indian men generally and of their husbands in particular. But the autonomy of their people had been eroded by the greed of white men, miners and farmers, who coveted the resources which the Indian women themselves had so successfully developed during the previous half century.

This essay will examine the economic roles and productive organization of native women during the late eighteenth and early nineteenth centuries in the region bounded by the Fox-Wisconsin and Rock riverways in what is now southern Wisconsin, northwestern Illinois, and a small section of eastern Iowa. This region was of crucial importance because of its central location as the main transportation link between the Great Lakes and the Mississippi River, as part of a borderland between Canada, the U.S., and French and Spanish Louisiana, and as an area of unusually rich and varied natural resources.

The majority of the people of this region were Sauk, Mesquakie (often called Fox), and Winnebago, although there were some Menominees, Potawatomies, and others, including biracial communities and increasing numbers of whites of various ethnic backgrounds. This essay will focus on the Sauk, Mesquakie, and Winnebago villagers. The Sauk and Mesquakie people, Algonkian-speakers, were very similar culturally, intermarried extensively, and were almost considered one tribe by many outsiders. The Winnebagos were Siouan-speakers who had become somewhat "Algonkianized," according to Nancy Lurie, due primarily to extensive intermarriage with neighboring groups following demographic catastrophes of the seventeenth century.[11] Although they were often at odds with the Sauks and Mesquakies, the Winnebagos' village economies were very similar to those of their neighbors.

An issue which scholars have begun to consider is the extent to which Indian women's roles and status were affected by contact with whites, and particularly by market participation. Native women responded to increased market access and to white immigration in a variety of ways. One response was marriage of Indian women to the white traders. A number of scholars, such as Sylvia Van Kirk, Jennifer S. H. Brown, Jacqueline Peterson, and Tanis Chapman Thorne, have examined the experiences of these women and their families in extremely interesting ways.[12]

Another of the many responses to market participation was the continuation of traditional village economies with the addition of increased production by women for local, regional, and international markets. The women who chose this latter alternative are the subjects of this essay.

A number of studies have argued that market participation altered women's economic roles in ways that resulted in their subordination to men. For example, Kathryn Holland Braund, in a study of eighteenth-century Creek women, suggested that although the deerskin trade made commercial hunting a team effort for Creek couples, kinship patterns were somewhat disrupted and wives became "dependent on hunter husbands for cotton and woolen textiles and metal agricultural tools."[13] Mary C. Wright argued that in the nineteenth-century Pacific Northwest, "Since Indian women's subsistence activities faded and those with a cash value did not correspondingly grow, they gradually became trapped . . . into a sphere labeled domestic, with limited access to public arenas."[14] Others, such as Karen Anderson, noted that economic changes resulting from white contact often made Indian communities susceptible to religious influences and related gender-role changes.[15]

In an essay on late-nineteenth-century Seneca women, Nancy Shoemaker suggested that although Seneca women did not become increasingly subordinate to Seneca men during a period when "[a]ll Senecas lost power as they were confined to ever-smaller reservations," the women's economic and political roles and activities changed in important and complex ways.[16] Nancy Bonvillain argued that the fur trade "lessened the social valuation of female labor," except in instances where women maintained control of resources, such as among the Iroquois.[17]

The present study suggests that during the late eighteenth and early nineteenth centuries, the experiences of Native American women in the Fox-Wisconsin region differed from those analyzed by Anderson, Braund, and Wright. During this period, Sauk, Mesquakie, and Winnebago women came to produce large quantities of products for local, regional, and international markets, and continued to produce food, clothing, shelter, and other items for their families and communities. At the same time they appear, in general, to have maintained kinship structures, independence relative to men, and access to the public arena *within their own communities.* They were able to do this by continuing subsistence production, producing for the market, maintaining control of resources and the means of production, and adapting traditional gender work roles to a new commercial commodity, lead. Like the Seneca women in Shoemaker's study in a later period, these women avoided increased subordination to their own men at a time when all of their people were losing autonomy in the face of pressure from white Americans.

As elsewhere, during the late eighteenth century a system of clearly delineated work roles characterized indigenous gender relations in the Fox-Wisconsin region. Men were in charge of hunting, fishing, warfare, and diplomacy. Besides preparing the family's meals and clothing, the women managed agricultural production and maple sugar making, were the primary producers of crafts, and towards the turn of the century took a very active role in lead mining.

The Indian peoples of this region had long enjoyed relatively egalitarian gender relations. One traveller who visited the Sauks during the 1770s noted the women's independence, writing, "In General the Women find Meanes to Grattafy them Selves without Consent of the Men."[18] In 1827, Thomas Forsyth, who had traded with the Sauk and Mesquakie people and served as their U.S. Indian Agent over the course of nearly thirty years, noted that women had substantial claims on resources, and tended not to be particularly subordinate to their husbands:

> It is a maxim among the Indians that every thing belong[s] to the woman or women except the Indian's hunting and war implements, even the game, the Indians bring home on his back. . . . [P]roperly speaking, the husband is master, the wife the slave, but it is in most cases voluntary slavery as the Indians seldom make their wives feel their authority, by words or deeds, they generally live very happy together, they on both sides make due allowances.[19]

Winnebago husbands were also said to be "kind and affectionate," and to be less than domineering, particularly in private.[20]

These people were villagers who organized their economies seasonally, and migrated during specific parts of the year in order to maximize use of the area's abundant natural resources. Thus, in the spring, the women planted fields of corn, beans, squash, melons, and other crops and tended them until they had a good start (when the corn was knee-high). Then the villagers split up into smaller groups, with the younger men departing for summer hunts or fishing, and women, elderly men, and children to gather rushes, herbs, roots, and so forth. By the end of the eighteenth century, some groups of women and old men would go to the lead mines during this summer migration. After about six weeks, during early August, the groups reunited at their villages, in anticipation of the harvest, and exchanged the commodities they had collected. "This is a happy season of the year—" Black Hawk explained, "having plenty of provisions, such as beans, squashes, and other produce, with our dried meat and fish, we continue to make feasts and visit each other, until our corn is ripe."[21]

After the harvest, families dispersed to their winter hunting camps until March, when they moved to their maple sugar camps. After a month

of sugar making, they returned to their village to prepare for spring planting, and began the cycle anew.[22]

Indian women, like Indian men, had long been active in producing
for trade in the Great Lakes Region. Before white contact, indigenous
people had traded across ecological zones, items including agricultural
products, crafts, and medicinal herbs grown, manufactured, and gathered
by women.[23] As early as the seventeenth century, a few European traders
provided both men and women with limited access to international markets. Nicolas Perrot, who came into this region in 1667, wrote that, while
men provided furs, the Indian women "fabricate many curious little articles which are much in demand by our French people, and which they
even send to France as rarities."[24]

An eighteenth-century trader noted the high quality of the Winnebago
women's crafts: "Their squaws in general are very industrious . . . they also
make handsome mats, and garnish mocasins, shot pouches &c with porcupine quills, with great neatness and ingenuity."[25]

During the second half of the eighteenth century, Winnebago, Sauk,
and Mesquakie women not only produced food, clothing, mats, and other
craft items for their own families and friends, but also traded increasing quantities of these products to provision the mixed-race trade centers
such as Prairie du Chien. They also traded outside the region, for goods
such as blankets, other textiles, kettles, and knives. During the early nineteenth century, many of these women came to the homes of white
"settlers" and to the Mississippi rapids when keelboats passed, to trade
craft items, feathers, and food.[26]

In 1820, Morrill Marston, a U.S. army officer stationed at Ft. Arm-
strong near present-day Rock Island, reported that the Sauk and
Mesquakie women living in villages near the east bank of the Mississippi
cultivated three hundred acres of land. He wrote, "They usually raise from
seven to eight thousand bushels of corn, besides beans, pumpkins, mel-
lons, &c. &c. About one thousand bushels of the corn they annually sell
to traders & others."[27] The women of these villages (with an estimated
local population of about two thousand), also traded three thousand
pounds of feathers, and one thousand pounds of beeswax.[28] U.S. factors
in the Fox-Wisconsin-Rock region, who did only a small percentage of the
region's trade, took in for the year 1819 nearly two thousand pounds of
maple sugar, 980 pounds of feathers, 680 pounds of tallow, 343 pounds
of beeswax, and 216 mats.[29]

Marston was particularly impressed with the mats, observing, "The
women usually make about three hundred floor mats every summer;

these mats are as handsome & as durable as those made abroad. The twine which connects the rushes together is made either of bass wood bark after being boiled and hammered or the bark of the nettle; the women twist or spin it by rolling it on the leg with the hand."[30] Women manufactured such mats, not only for flooring, but as the external coverings for their wigwams, and they might be up to six feet long. These mats were apparently the specialty of elderly women.[31]

Juliette Kinzie, wife of the Indian agent at Portage, Wisconsin, recalled that in 1830 the Indians traded not only furs but "maple-sugar in abundance, considerable quantities of both [fresh and dried, parboiled] Indian corn . . . , beans and the *folles avoines*, or wild-rice, while the squaws added to their quota of merchandize a contribution in the form of moccasins, hunting pouches, mococks, or little boxes of birch-bark embroidered with porcupine quills and filled with maple-sugar, mats of a neat and durable fabric, and toy-models of Indian cradles, snow shoes, canoes, &c., &c."[32]

The month of sugar making in early spring was a special event at which women managed the boiling of maple tree-sap, which continued day and night, while children helped or played nearby and men, in an auxiliary role, chopped wood for the fires, and hunted to provide meat for the whole party.[33] By the early nineteenth century, when the native population of this region was around twelve thousand, maple sugar was a commodity of major importance.[34] The Indians of northern Illinois and southern Wisconsin sold seventy thousand pounds of it in 1816, not counting what they made for their own consumption. The Indian women around Green Bay alone produced 25,000 pounds of this amount in one season.[35]

Besides trading with merchants and government agents, Indians bartered with private individuals, often their neighbors. The reminiscences of early white settlers in this region reveal some of the dynamics of this type of trade. Exchanges might be negotiated formally, or they might take the form of gifts with implied obligations of reciprocity.

An example of a formal trade took place during the 1830s in a newly-built tavern near Lake Winnebago. An Indian woman called on the tavern's white landlady, Mrs. Pier, and arranged to exchange feathers— which were highly-valued components of Euro-American bedding—for flour. The native woman apparently left well satisfied with her bargain, and broadcast news of it in her own community. An early chronicler of the region reported that "soon after [the trade,] the room was filled with squaws anxious to barter feathers for either flour or pork."[36]

Sometimes gift exchanges were graceful and satisfying to all parties. A memoir of John B. Parkinson's childhood in LaFayette County, Wisconsin, recalled that during the 1830s his family had established friendly relations with their Winnebago neighbors:

> . . . a girl about the size of my sister came to the house. My sister had on some shoes which were worn out at the toes. The next day the Indian girl came back and presented her with a pair of beautiful moccasins. Mother then made a cake, and we took it over to the girl. They made much of our visit to the tent, and spread some skins on the ground for us to sit on.[37]

Kinzie recalled that "it was always expected that a present would be received graciously, and returned with something twice its value." Her description of the exchange process at the Portage Indian Agency House suggests that protocol was enforced by the native women (who gave Kinzie the honorary title of "mother" because her husband represented the U.S. government):

> The Indian women were very constant in their visits and their presents. Sometimes it was venison—sometimes ducks or pigeons—whortleberries, wild plums, or cranberries, according to the season—neat pretty mats for the floor or the table—wooden bowls or ladles, fancy work of deer-skin or porcupine quills. These they would bring in and throw at my feet. If through inattention I failed to look pleased, to raise the articles from the floor and lay them carefully aside, a look of mortification and the observation, "Our mother hates our gifts," showed how much their feelings were wounded.[38]

Not all gift exchanges were understood nor gracefully received. Early settler Lydia Dow Flanders developed a strong dislike for Washington Woman, the Winnebago wife of her friend Yellow Thunder. In a brief essay about him, she wrote "when wishing to return the value of some favor[,] it was sent by the hand of his wife, who, I grieve to say, often tried to bargain his generosity by the gain of something for herself."[39] These occasions clearly lacked the gracious mutuality expected of gift exchanges.

Before European contact, Native Americans had used and traded minerals such as lead in small quantities for religious purposes and ornamentation. Three thousand years ago lead from this region was traded as far away as present-day Ohio, Alabama, Georgia, Louisiana, and Ontario.[40] The demand for lead increased dramatically with the introduction of firearms by Europeans because it could be fashioned into ammunition, but most mining in the upper Mississippi Valley during the eighteenth century seems to have been for local use.

Indian lead miners were generally women, according to contemporary accounts. For example, Henry Rowe Schoolcraft, on a journey of exploration for the U.S. government in 1820, arrived August 6th at the Mesquakie village known by the name of its principal chief, Kettle, near the site of the present city of Dubuque, Iowa. Traders and interpreters from nearby trading posts accompanied him as he asked permission to explore the local Mesquakie lead mines. According to Schoolcraft, the village leaders (evidently male), "manifested a great jealousy of the whites—were afraid they would encroach upon their rights . . . and did not make it a practice even to allow strangers to view their diggings."[41] At length, however, permission was reluctantly granted and two Mesquakie men accompanied Schoolcraft on his tour. He recorded:

> The lead ore at these mines is now exclusively dug by the Fox [Mesquakie] Indians, and as is usual among savage tribes, the chief labour devolves upon the women. The old and superannuated men also partake in these labours, but the warriors and young men, hold themselves above it. They employ the hoe, shovel, pick-axe, and crow-bar, in taking up the ore.[42]

Indians were mining at three other locations within twenty-one miles, east of the Mississippi River.[43] Winnebagos and Sauks also mined lead in this region.[44]

In view of current knowledge that exposure to lead can be dangerous to health, it would be tempting to accept Schoolcraft's implications, and those of other white observers, that the Indian women were oppressed victims of lazy and arrogant men who forced them to work in the mines.[45] However, there are a number of factors which suggest that Indian lead mining may have been an adaptation of indigenous gender roles in which women had at least some say in the management of production and perhaps even the allocation of resources. Clearly the Sauk women mentioned in the introduction to this paper had a proprietary attitude toward their cornfields, and both Sauk men and women indicated that the women ought to have a say in the fields' disposition. Maple sugar production seems to have been considered an arena of female management; the sugar was considered to belong to them. Similarly, women seem to have had some influence in determining mining techniques and access to the mines.

Although there had been some small efforts at lead mining by Frenchmen beforehand, sustained commercial development began only with Julien Dubuque. Dubuque, a Canadian, moved to Prairie du Chien to trade during the early 1780s. In 1788 he married a Mesquakie woman and obtained permission from her people to engage in lead mining. His French-language permit signed by Mesquakie leaders allowed him to work the mine "trouve par le femme Peosta" (found by the woman Peosta).[46] From then until his death in 1810, Dubuque promoted prospecting and mining among the Indians on both sides of the Mississippi, traded the lead to St. Louis, and was regarded with great respect and affection by his wife's nation.[47] After Dubuque's death, however, as Schoolcraft found out, the Sauks, Mesquakies, and Winnebagos tried to keep all whites out of the lead mining region, and drove off or killed all intending to settle there, with the exception of three men—two traders and a smelter—who married Indian women.[48] Men who could be accepted as bridegrooms by the local women and their families could gain access to the mines and to the region as they established kinship with the native community.

The organization of the lead mining operations apparently resembled the organization of maple sugar production. Like sugar-making, lead mining was for the Indians a seasonal occupation, of relatively short duration.[49] Like sugar-making, in which men chopped wood and kept the fires going, men were probably in charge of chopping wood for the smelting fires, and may have been in charge of the smelting process until white traders began to process the ore themselves.[50]

Indian and Euro-American mining techniques seem to have differed markedly. Schoolcraft noted that,

> . . . no shafts are sunk, not even of the simplest kind, and the windlass and bucket are unknown among them—They run drifts into the hills so far as they can conveniently go, without the use of gun-powder, and if a trench caves in, it is abandoned. They always dig down at such an angle that they can walk in and out of the pits. . . . When a quantity of ore has been got out, it is carried in baskets, by the women, to the banks of the Mississippi, and there ferried over in canoes to the traders. . . .[51]

These miners seem to have organized the process to suit themselves.

During the first two decades of the nineteenth century, Indian lead production became an important part of villagers' seasonal economy. Nicholas

Boilvin, U.S. agent for the Winnebagos, wrote in 1811, the year after Dubuque's death, that the Sauks and Mesquakies had given up hunting except to provide their families with meat, and instead of trading furs, had turned to lead production to acquire trade goods.[52] No doubt this was an exaggeration, but the Mesquakies were said to have produced four hundred thousand pounds of lead, sold to Canadian traders, the previous year. In 1818, Indians traded to U.S. factors alone, at Prairie du Chien, nearly two hundred thousand pounds of lead.[53]

This production, reported by men like Schoolcraft and Zebulon Pike, drew the attention both of U.S. federal policy makers, who wanted a reliable supply of lead for ammunition, and of whites casting about for opportunities for investment or adventure. In 1822, the U.S. government ordered troops into the Indian lead mining region to protect James Johnson and his eight male miners, four black and four white. About four dozen others came in that year.[54] At least some of the early blacks in the lead region were slaves: twenty-one black slaves were enumerated in the 1830 federal census, twelve of them female. Twenty-seven free blacks also appeared in this census.[55]

During the first year or two, the Indian, white, and black miners worked side by side rather amicably, according to a smelter who moved there in 1823. He remembered:

> The Indian women proved themselves to be the best as well as the shrewdest miners. While Col. Johnson's men were sinking their holes or shafts, in some instances the squaws would drift under them and take out all the mineral or ore they could find. When the men got down into the drift made by the women, the latter would have a hearty laugh at the white men's expense.[56]

Unfortunately, the friendly competition soon turned bitter. Thousands of white miners, most of them restless, young, and single men, flooded into the area during the following decade. By August of 1826, the U.S. government had licensed 453 white and black miners; two years later the Indian agent complained that eight hundred whites were mining illegally on Indian lands.[57]

Soon there were violent encounters between the white men and Indians of both genders. For example, white boatmen kidnapped six Winnebago women and took them on a keelboat journey up the Mississippi River in 1827, prompting a Winnebago attack on the boats, one of several acts of

Winnebago violent defiance that year.[58] The Winnebagos complained to the Indian agent the following year that hundreds of whites were settling illegally on their lands, and that "some of the white people are insulting to the Indians and take liberties with their women, which the Indians do not like."[59] In the Galena/Fever River mining area, a white man knocked down an Indian woman and stamped on her head, killing her. This incident was ignored by local white authorities.[60]

Before long, the Indians were also battling whites who wanted the cornfields. For example, Forsyth reported in May of 1829 that "sometime early in the spring a number of settlers came to the Sauk village on Rocky River and enclosed nearly all the Sauk Indians cornfields."[61] Shortly after, "a young Indian went to a whiteman, to enquire what his mother had done that he should have struck her, when about planting her corn, the whiteman presented his rifle to the Indian's breast to shoot him."[62]

What this mother had done, was to carry on in her role as tiller of the cornfield, when a white man wanted that field and that role. As tillers of the soil and miners of lead, Indian women might have substantial independence and exert considerable influence within their own communities, but they could not maintain their resources when white men and their families wanted them, and the U.S. government was willing to back these men up with force.

Market participation had not subordinated women villagers within their own communities in the Fox-Wisconsin region. The Sauk, Mesquakie, and Winnebago people there had adapted traditional gender roles in ways that maintained gender balance for those who remained within the village economy. This was probably supported by the frequent absences of men in their roles of warriors, guides, messengers, interpreters, hunters, and diplomats as they increasingly provided such services to outsiders. The rich natural environment provided both a variety of resources and a climate warm enough for the agriculture that women used in providing for their own people's needs and in producing marketable surpluses. Unlike the situation in other regions which scholars have studied, here few missionaries or other agents of "civilization" mounted concerted efforts to force gender role changes, and those few met with resistance. Of course, the Indian women who married white and métis men and lived outside the native villages *did* experience changes in economic and social roles, experiences which are outside the scope of this essay. As in other regions, the Sauk, Mesquakie, and Winnebago men hunted for furs which women processed for trade, but by the 1830s the fur trade was only one part of a diverse economy, in which Indian women were active producers. It was a sad irony that the resources these women had used and developed as participants in the market economy, and which assisted in maintaining their "social valuation" among their own, attracted the attention of men like Major General Gaines and Col. James Johnson.

In 1832, a year after the Sauk women's protest to Gaines, they and roughly one thousand other Indian men, women, and children recrossed to the east side of the Mississippi and attempted to resettle on their own lands. Most of them were slaughtered in a debacle commonly called the Black Hawk War. United States officials used this as an excuse to force land cessions from other Indians in the region, including the Winnebagos, some of whom had aided the Sauks.

Following the Black Hawk War, the Sauk and Mesquakie people were finally forced west of the Mississippi, and they spent a miserable thirteen years confined to Iowa, their population reduced by malaria, smallpox, alcoholism, starvation, and violence from about six thousand in 1833 to 2,478 in 1845, when they were removed to Kansas. During the early 1850s, a group of about one hundred Mesquakies, fed up with Kansas, returned to Iowa and established a community at Tama which is still in existence. By 1869, another two hundred had joined them. In that year, the remaining members of the Sac and Fox Tribe (as they were officially known) were moved to Indian Territory. Only about seven hundred of them had survived the cholera, smallpox, measles, alcoholism, and poverty of their twenty-four years in Kansas.[63]

Between 1827 and 1862, the Winnebago people were victims of multiple treaties and forced land cessions, and of removals to a series of five reservations in Iowa, Minnesota, and North Dakota. In 1865 their present reservation in Nebraska was established. But over the years, many Winnebagos resisted removal, hiding out or returning to Wisconsin, and many took homesteads during the late nineteenth century under the Indian Homestead Act of 1875. As of 1978, they owned 3,673 acres of homestead land and about 554 acres of tribal community land in Wisconsin.[64]

In an oral history given in 1887, Spoon Decorah, an elderly Winnebago man descended from Glory of the Morning, discussed the lead mines:

> Our people once owned the lead mines in Southwestern Wisconsin. . . .
> When the whites began to come among the mines, the Big Father said
> to his Winnebago children: "I want this land and will have my own peo-
> ple to work it, and whenever you go out hunting come by this way, and
> you will be supplied with lead." But this agreement was never carried
> out by the Big Father or his agents. . . . For many years there was much

sorrowful talk among the Winnebagoes, at the manner in which the Big Father had treated them, with regard to the mines. No, we never saw any of our lead again, except what we paid dearly for; and we never will have any given to us, unless it be fired at us out of white men's guns, to kill us off.[65]

NOTES

An earlier version of this paper was presented at the Ninth Berkshire Conference on the History of Women at Vassar College, June 12, 1993. The author would like to thank the following people for their helpful advice on previous drafts of this article: Allan Kulikoff, Barbara Posadas, Simon Newman, Winifred Creamer, Terry Sheahan, Rebecca Kugel, Nancy Shoemaker, Helen Tanner, Ellen Whitney, Mary Young, Mike Fraga, and Tanis Thorne. Thomas, Colin, and Bethany Murphy and Patricia Gleason Stevenson deserve special credit for their crucial support of this project in the form of creative domestic management.

1. Jonathan Carver, *Travels through the Interior Parts of North-America, in the Years 1766, 1767, and 1768* (Dublin: 1779), 29; Daniel Steel Durrie, "Captain Jonathan Carver, and 'Carver's Grant,'" in *Collections of the State Historical Society of Wisconsin* 6 (1872), 224n.
2. Carver, *Travels*, 30.
3. "Memorandum of Talks between Edmund P. Gaines and the Sauk" in *The Black Hawk War, 1831–1832*, ed. and comp. Ellen M. Whitney (Springfield: Illinois State Historical Library, 1973), 2: 30.
4. Donald Jackson, ed., *Black Hawk, An Autobiography* (Urbana: University of Illinois Press, 1955, 1990), 112.
5. Whitney, *Black Hawk War*, 2: 30.
6. Whitney, *Black Hawk War*, 2: 30.
7. Jackson, *Black Hawk*, 112.
8. Jackson, *Black Hawk*, 114.
9. Jackson, *Black Hawk*, 114.
10. Carver, *Travels*, 29.
11. Nancy Oestreich Lurie, *Wisconsin Indians* (Madison: State Historical Society of Wisconsin, 1987), 13–14.
12. Sylvia Van Kirk, *Many Tender Ties; Women in Fur-Trade Society, 1670–1870* (Norman: University of Oklahoma Press, 1980); Jennifer S. H. Brown, Strangers in *Blood; Fur Trade Company Families in Indian Country* (Vancouver: University of British Columbia Press, 1980); Jacqueline Peterson, "The People in Between: Indian-White Marriage and the Genesis of a Métis Society and Culture in the Great Lakes Region, 1680–1830" (Ph.D. diss., University of Illinois at Chicago Circle, 1981); Tanis Chapman Thorne, "People of the River: Mixed-Blood Families on the Lower Missouri" (Ph.D. diss., University of California, Los Angeles, 1987).
13. Kathryn E. Holland Braund, "Guardians of Tradition and Handmaidens to

Change: Women's Roles in Creek Economic and Social Life During the Eighteenth Century," *American Indian Quarterly* 14 (1990): 239–258.

14. Mary C. Wright, "Economic Development and Native American Women in the Early 19th Century," *American Quarterly* 33 (1981): 526.

15. Karen Anderson, "Commodity Exchange and Subordination: Montagnais-Naskapi and Huron Women, 1600–1650," *Signs: Journal of Women in Culture and Society* 11 (1985), 48–62; Karen Anderson, *Chain Her By One Foot: The Subjugation of Women in Seventeenth-Century New France* (New York: Routledge, 1991); see also Carol Devens, *Countering Colonization: Native American Women and Great Lakes Missions, 1630–1900* (Berkeley: University of California Press, 1992).

16. Nancy Shoemaker, "The Rise or Fall of Iroquois Women," *Journal of Women's History* 2 (1991): 39–57, quoted on p. 40.

17. Nancy Bonvillain, "Gender Relations in Native North America," *American Indian Culture and Research Journal* 13 (1989): 1–28, quoted on pp. 6–7.

18. "Journal of Peter Pond," in *Collections of the State Historical Society of Wisconsin* 18 (1908), 335.

19. Emma Helen Blair, *The Indian Tribes of the Upper Mississippi Valley and Region of the Great Lakes* (Cleveland: Arthur H. Clark, 1911), 2: 218.

20. Juliette M. Kinzie, *Wau-Bun; The "Early Day" in the North-West* [1856] (Urbana: University of Illinois Press, 1992) 194, 48; Lydia A. Flanders, "Personal Recollections of Yellow Thunder (Mi-ja-jin-a-ka); The Last War Chief of the Winnebago Tribe of Indians," typescript, SC 493, State Historical Society of Wisconsin, Madison, Wisconsin.

21. Jackson, *Black Hawk*, 93.

22. Jackson, *Black Hawk*, 89–95; Morrill Marston, Draper Manuscripts, Forsyth Papers, 1T: 58, State Historical Society of Wisconsin (microfilm); "Journal of Peter Pond," 335.

23. Gary A. Wright, "Some Aspects of Early and Mid-Seventeenth Century Exchange Networks in the Western Great Lakes," *Michigan Archaeologist* 13 (1967): 181–97.

24. Blair, *The Indian Tribes* 1:76; Louise Phelps Kellogg, *The French Regime in Wisconsin and the Northwest* [1925] (New York: Cooper Square, 1968), 123.

25. William Arundell, "Indian History," *The Miner's Journal*, 30 October 1830, typescript, p. 2, State Historical Society of Wisconsin. According to this piece, Arundell was a trader before 1809.

26. Jacqueline Peterson, "Many Roads to Red River: Métis genesis in the Great Lakes region, 1680–1815," in *The New Peoples: Being and Becoming Métis in North America*, eds. Jacqueline Peterson and Jennifer S.H. Brown (Lincoln: University of Nebraska Press, 1985); "Journal of Peter Pond," 340; Harry Ellsworth Cole, *Stagecoach and Tavern Tales of the Old Northwest* (Cleveland: Arthur H. Clark, 1930) 102; *Galena Advertiser*, 21 September 1829, 3.

27. Morrill Marston, Draper Manuscripts, 1T: 58.

28. Marston, Draper Manuscripts, 1T: 58; Helen Hornbeck Tanner,ed., *Atlas of Great Lakes Indian History* (Norman: University of Oklahoma Press, 1987) 139.

29. *New American State Papers: Indian Affairs, 1789–1860* (Wilmington, Del.: Scholarly Resources, 1972), vol. 3, 308.

30. Morrill Marston, Draper Manuscripts, 1T: 58a.

31. Kinzie, *Wau-Bun*, 42.

32. Kinzie, *Wau-Bun*, 9–10.

33. Margaret Holman and Kathryn C. Egan, "Maple Sugaring," *Michigan History* 74 (1990): 30–35; George Irving Quimby, *Indian Culture and European Trade Goods* (Madison: University of Wisconsin Press, 1966), 173; Thomas Ridout, "An Account of my Capture by the Shawanese Indians" *Western Pennsylvania Historical Magazine* 12 (January 1929): 18.

34. Tanner, *Atlas of Great Lakes Indian History*, 139–41.

35. Thomas Forsyth Papers, Draper Manuscripts, 3T: 63. As late as the 1890s, Indians in east-central Wisconsin were still selling maple sugar to their white neighbors. Mary Maples Dunn, letter to the author, 29 June 1993.

36. Cole, *Stagecoach and Tavern Tales*, 102.

37. John B. Parkinson, *Memories of Early Wisconsin and the Gold Mines* reprinted from the *Wisconsin Magazine of History* 5 (December 1921), 8. A discussion of gift exchange related to trade appears in Richard White, *The Middle Ground: Indians, Empires, and Republics in the Great Lakes Region, 1650–1815* (New York: Cambridge University Press, 1991) ch. 3.

38. Kinzie, *Wau-Bun*, 192.

39. Flanders, "Personal Recollections," 4.

40. Ronald M. Farquhar and Ian R. Fletcher, "The Provenience of Galena from Archaic/Woodland Sites in Northeastern North America: Lead Isotope Evidence," *American Antiquity* 49 (1984): 774–785.

41. Henry Rowe Schoolcraft, *Travels through the Northwestern Regions of the United States* [1821] (Ann Arbor, Michigan: University Microfilms, 1966), 343.

42. Schoolcraft, *Travels*, 344–45.

43. Schoolcraft, *Travels*, 346.

44. Thomas Forsyth, Draper Manuscripts, 4T: 133, 258; Jackson, *Black Hawk*, 92.

45. A similar assessment to Schoolcraft's appeared in M.M. Ham, "Who was Peosta?": ". . . the working of the lead mines in after years was given over almost entirely to the squaws, for the Indians consider it beneath their dignity to labor at mining or any thing else. All manual labor was cast upon the women. . . ." *Annals of Iowa* 3rd ser. 2, no. 6 (July 1896): 470–472.

46. Thomas Auge, "The Life and Times of Julien Dubuque," *The Palimpsest* 57 (1976), 2–13; M.M. Hoffmann, *Antique Dubuque, 1673–1833* (Dubuque: Telegraph Herald Press, 1930), 80.

47. William E. Wilkie, *Dubuque on the Mississippi, 1788–1988* (Dubuque: Loras College Press, 1988); Reuben Gold Thwaites, "Notes on Early Lead Mining in the Fever (or Galena) River Region," in *Collections of the State Historical Society of Wisconsin* 13 (1895), 271–292; Joseph Schafer, *The Wisconsin Lead Region* (Madison: State Historical Society of Wisconsin, 1932). Indian esteem for Dubuque was far-reaching enough that Black Hawk, a Sauk, referred to him as "our relation." Jackson, *Black Hawk*, 150.

48. Thwaites, "Notes on Early Lead Mining," 287.

49. Jackson, *Black Hawk*, 92; Thomas Forsyth to J.C. Calhoun, 24 June 1822, Draper Manuscripts 4T: 133.

50. Thwaites, "Notes on Early Lead Mining," 282.

51. Schoolcraft, *Travels*, 44.

52. Thwaites, "Notes on Early Lead Mining," 285.

53. *New American State Papers*, 3: 308.

54. Schafer, *Wisconsin Lead Region*, chapters 3,4; Thwaites, "Notes on Early Lead Mining"; Moses Meeker, "Early History of the Lead Region of Wisconsin," *Collections of the State Historical Society of Wisconsin* 6 (1872), 271–96.

55. U.S. Census, 1830, Jo Daviess County, Illinois. Typescript in the Historical Collection, Galena Public Library, Galena, Illinois.

56. Meeker, "Early History," 282.

57. Thwaites, "Notes on Early Lead Mining," 291; Thomas Forsyth to William Clark, 25 June 1828, Draper Manuscripts, 6T: 89.

58. Whitney, *Black Hawk War*, 2: 793n3; Wisconsin Writers' Program, *The Story of Mineral Point* (Mineral Point: Mineral Point Historical Society, 1979), 18.

59. Forsyth to Clark, 10 June 1828, Draper Manuscripts, 6T: 84.

60. Joseph M. Street to the Secretary of War, 15 November 1827, typescript in the State Historical Society of Wisconsin.

61. Forsyth to Clark, 17 May 1829, Draper Manuscripts, 6T: 97.

62. Forsyth to Clark, 17 June 1829, Draper Manuscripts, 6: 105.

63. William T. Hagan, *The Sac and Fox Indians* (Norman: University of Oklahoma Press, 1958), 205–232, 261.

64. Lurie, *Wisconsin Indians*, 10, 18–20.

65. Reuben Gold Thwaites, ed., "Narrative of Spoon Decorah," *Collections of the State Historical Society of Wisconsin* 13 (1895), 458–59.

4

THEDA PERDUE

WOMEN, MEN AND AMERICAN INDIAN POLICY
THE CHEROKEE RESPONSE TO "CIVILIZATION"

The Cherokees originally resided in what is now northern Georgia, Tennessee, and the western Carolinas. In the seventeenth and eighteenth centuries, they became active in the deerskin trade introduced into the Southeast by Europeans, but by the late 1700s, Euro-Americans were more interested in land than in trading for hides. From the end of the Revolutionary War through the 1830s, the U.S. pressured the Cherokees to cede more of their land. As Perdue discusses, the Cherokees were at the same time subjected to a "benevolent" effort on the part of the U.S. to "civilize" them; that is, to remake them in its image. The Cherokees willingly accommodated certain aspects of American culture, but were still forced to cede their lands in the Southeast and remove to Indian Territory in the winter of 1838–39. The Cherokees built a new nation in the West, in what is now Oklahoma, while a small number of Cherokees who had avoided removal also reorganized as a tribe and today have a reservation in western North Carolina.

The implementation of a policy, conceived by whites and promulgated in Washington, among a Native American people often brought surprises and frustrations to those who saw United States Indian policy as the key to culture change. Even the Cherokees, widely regarded by contemporaries and subsequent scholars as the Native people most adept at cultural transformation, attempted to rewrite policy. They sought to transform Washington's schemes into solutions for their own problems, as they defined them, and to use Indian policy to strengthen, rather than destroy, their cultural traditions. At the end of the eighteenth century, the Cherokees, who had participated in European colonial expansion as allies and trading partners, found themselves with an economy geared to trade and a government shaped by warriors. Invigorated by its political reorganization in 1789, the United States had little use for such anachronistic native societies, and so the federal government took on the task of "civilizing" the Indians, that is, converting them culturally into Anglo-Americans. Guided by an idealized view of men and women in their own society, the founding fathers sought to turn Native men into industrious, republican farmers and women into chaste, orderly housewives. The traditional Cherokee economy of male hunters and female farmers was anathema to "civilization," and so the "civilizers" turned to an economic restructuring of Cherokee life. Since hunting was no longer a viable enterprise, they expected men to replace women as farmers. These expectations, however, failed to take into account the durability of gender conventions and the adaptability of Cherokee culture.

The idea of Indians becoming "civilized" was not a new one. Eighteenth-century writers usually attributed differences between Indians and Europeans to European cultural, not racial, superiority and held out hope that Native peoples could progress to Europe's elevated position. Thomas Jefferson suggested that with time, literacy, and an increase in population, the American Indians might even produce an individual comparable to Isaac Newton.[1] Scottish social theorists largely shaped North American interpretations of culture, including that of Jefferson, and provided a framework for understanding Native peoples. Native peoples were "savages" whose cultures were less complex than "civilized" ones. "Savage" peoples lived off the bounty of the land without investing their labor while "civilized" peoples were busy, as Robert Berkhofer has phrased it, "transforming nature into property."[2] "Savage" peoples, according to the learned academicians revered by the early republic, did not farm. Benjamin Rush echoed the Scottish school when he divided all mankind into three groups: "The savage lives by fishing and hunting, the barbarian by pasturage, and the civilized man by agriculture." Agriculture, he believed, was "the true basis of national health, riches and populousness."[3] For Native people to become "civilized," they must shift from hunting to farming.

Henry Knox, George Washington's Secretary of War, introduced the concept of the federal government as "civilizing" agent. Earlier attempts at "civilization" had rested primarily on converting and educating Indians, but Knox suggested a novel approach: "Were it possible to introduce among the Indian tribes a love for exclusive property, it would be a happy commencement of the business." In order to instill in Native peoples a sense of private property, Knox proposed making gifts of livestock to chiefs or their wives.[4] While "civilization" involved a radical transformation of Native societies, including their government and religion, economic change was the first order of business on Knox's agenda. The "civilization" program became an official part of Cherokee relations with the federal government in 1791 when the Cherokees signed the Treaty of Holston. The treaty provided that the federal government furnish the Cherokees with "implements of husbandry" and send residential agents to give instruction in their use. As a result of this aid, "the Cherokee nation may be led to a greater degree of civilization, and to become herdsmen and cultivators, instead of remaining in a state of hunters."[5]

The Cherokees, devastated by invasion and impoverished by the decline of the deerskin trade, welcomed assistance. Yet they must have been somewhat bemused by the preferred lessons in agriculture. Not only had Cherokee women been farming for centuries, many of the crops and techniques used by Euro-Americans came from Native peoples.[6] Most Europeans, however, assumed that the Native economy rested on hunting. Lieutenant Timberlake, who purchased corn from Native women, described the Cherokees in his *Memoirs* as hunters.[7] James Hall wrote in his history of the West that "the Indians subsist entirely by hunting," and Samuel Stanhope Smith described hunting as "the necessary means of their subsistence."[8] Others simply belittled the economic importance of agriculture or blurred the distinction between gathering wild foods and farming. Robert Beverley described "the natural Production of that Country, which the Native *Indians* enjoy'd, without the Curse of Industry, their Diversion alone, and not the Labour, supplying their Necessities. . . . But none of the Toils of Husbandry were exercised by this happy People; except the bare planting a little Corn, and Melons, which took up only a few Days in the Summer, the rest being wholly spent in the Pursuit of their Pleasures."[9] Virtually all observers discounted cultivation by women: if only women farmed, then agriculture could not be very important in the Cherokee economy. Yet agriculture was the basis of "civilized" life, and so Native peoples must be taught to rely on its bounty.

A letter to the Cherokees from George Washington in 1796 outlined the key provisions of the "civilization" program, particularly the economic changes required of the Cherokees:

Some of you already experience the advantage of keeping cattle and hogs: let all keep them and increase their numbers, and you will have plenty of meat. To these add sheep, and they will give you clothing as well as food. Your lands are good and of great extent. By proper management you can raise live stock not only for your own wants, but to sell to the White people. By using the plow you can vastly increase your crops of corn. You can also grow wheat (which makes the best bread) as well as other useful grain. To these you will easily add flax and cotton which you may dispose of to the White people; or have it made up by your own women into clothing for yourselves. Your wives and daughters can soon learn to spin and weave.[10]

Washington's instructions did not bode well for Cherokee women. Directly addressing Cherokee men, the President implied that animal husbandry and farming were male responsibilities in a "civilized" society. Spinning, weaving, and sewing were women's work. Such expectations threatened the traditional division of labor in Cherokee society and whatever remnants of female autonomy remained. The President assumed that Cherokee men would take up the tasks and adopt the work habits common in the United States while women would become help-mates, mere auxiliaries. Beyond the economic message, however, was an even more ominous one for Cherokee women: in a "civilized" society women belonged to men. The President addressed Cherokee women only through men: "*your own* women;" "*your* wives and daughters."

The person charged with delivering and implementing the President's message was Benjamin Hawkins, the superintendent for Indian affairs south of the Ohio.[11] Hawkins resided permanently with the Creeks, but he visited the Cherokees in the fall of 1796. Although the President had addressed his letter to the men, Hawkins spent his time primarily with women. One of his hostesses, a Mrs. Gagg, invited a group of women over to meet him: "They informed me that the men were all in the woods hunting, that they alone were at home to receive me, that they rejoiced much at what they had heard and hoped it would prove true, that they had made some cotton, and would make more and follow the instruction of the agent and the advise of the President."[12] Because "civilization" rested on agriculture and domestic manufactures, tasks women traditionally performed, the women believed that the "civilization" program validated what they did.

Women's level of production became apparent to Hawkins when he visited women in the town of Etowah: "They informed me they performed most of the labour, the men assisted but little and that in the corn. They generally made a plenty of corn and sweet potatoes and pumpkins. They made beans, ground peas, cymblins, gourds, watermelons, collards and onions." Furthermore, these women kept livestock. One group of women told Hawkins that they raised "hogs, some cattle, and a great many poultry," and he encountered other women driving cattle to market. Women also had primary responsibility for domestic manufactures. They told Hawkins that "they made sugar, had raised some cotton, and manufactured their baskets, sifters, pots and earthen pans." Again and again they indicated to him their support for "the plan contemplated by the government for the bettering of the condition of the Red people" because they understood the concrete ways in which support for agriculture, animal husbandry, and domestic manufactures could improve their lives.[13]

Women envisioned "civilization" bringing improvement, not profound change. The matters Hawkins discussed with them were perfectly comprehensible because farming, tending livestock, and making utilitarian items had long been part of their world. In some ways, surprisingly little had changed during the preceding century: they continued to farm as their ancestors had for centuries. Metal hoes made the job easier, but the work remained the same. Agricultural production had expanded to include a number of crops introduced by Europeans, including watermelons, onions, collards, fruit trees, and even a little cotton,[14] but farming remained women's work.

Cherokee women viewed animal husbandry as an extension of their role as farmers. The Cherokees traditionally did not fence their fields, and so the horses, cows, and pigs that eighteenth-century traders brought into the Nation presented a genuine threat to the crops. Although men complained to whites about damage done by roaming livestock, women actually had the responsibility for keeping the animals out of the fields. This led to a growing familiarity with the animals' habits and needs. By the end of the eighteenth century Cherokee women were well acquainted with the principles of animal husbandry. They also knew how to use such animals. Nancy Ward, the War Woman of Chota, supposedly introduced the keeping of milk cows, and a white woman whom she rescued during the Revolution taught her to make butter. When Hawkins asked "what they wished, in aid of their own exertions," they answered "salt." This request demonstrates that women owned not only milk cows and laying hens but also animals used for meat: "Where they were able to supply themselves plentifully with meat, they were unable to preserve it for the want of salt."[15] Keeping livestock and preserving domesticated meat expanded women's role but only within the context developed in the eighteenth-century deerskin trade.

Spinning, weaving, and sewing conformed to women's practice of making clothing, household utensils, mats, and baskets and of dressing deerskins, and it too promised to free them from dependence on the declining deerskin trade. Fabric had been part of Cherokee material culture throughout most of the eighteenth century because men exchanged their deerskins for calico, strouds, duffels and even finished petticoats and blouses. Although leggings and hunting shirts remained popular with men well into the nineteenth century, women dressed almost exclusively in the woven cloth for which men traded.[16] The demise of the deerskin trade, therefore, inflicted a particular hardship on women who no longer could obtain clothing. As a result, they seized the opportunity to manufacture their own clothes. While a few women already planted cotton, spinning and weaving were new skills for most of them. Lah-to-tau-yie had learned to card, spin, and weave from her English husband, who ordered a wheel from England and made her a loom himself.[17] A few women such as Sally Waters, who served as Hawkins' interpreter, had learned how to spin and weave while living in white settlements, but they normally had not been able to acquire wheels and looms. One woman told Hawkins that "once she had made as much cotton as purchased a petticoat, that she would gladly make more and learn how to spin it, if she had the opportunity."[18] As soon as their agent Silas Dinsmoor, who served as Hawkins's subordinate in the Nation, made cards, wheels, and looms available in 1797, Cherokee women began adopting them. In 1809 a Cherokee man reminisced with Major John Norton about the women's response: "He [Dinsmoor] then addressed our women, and presented them with cotton seeds for planting; and afterwards with cards, wheels and looms to work it. They acquired the use of them with great facility, and now the most of the clothes we wear are of their manufacture."[19]

Moravian missionaries, who visited the Cherokees in 1799 to request permission to open a school, provide a good description of the Cherokees' domestic life three years after Hawkins's initial visit. One of the Cherokees they visited was John Watts whose "family is supported mainly by his mother-in-law, the widow of the former chief, Hanging Maw. This old woman is called Grandmother Maw by the whites and is respected as a very sensible and industrious woman." When the Moravians arrived, Grandmother Maw "was breaking corn in a field not far off and putting it in fine baskets woven of reed." At the homestead "there were only women and children" since the men were hunting. At Hiwasee, which was in the process of being abandoned, Kulsathee showed Moravian missionaries "his cotton carding-combs, spinning wheel and, also yarn that his daughter had spun." The Moravians visited the plantation of Betty Martin, the Cherokee wife of a white man. She lived in a hewn-log house with plastered walls and a stone fireplace which she had furnished with "two bedsteads with bedding, a table of walnut-wood and a closet with tin and china ware." In addition to cotton cards, Mrs. Martin also had a loom. Her fenced corn fields "were plowed and cleared of grass; the wheat had been sown." Mrs. Martin and her neighbors kept "horses, cattle, hogs, fowl, dogs and cats." Their hostess also had "negro slaves that were well clothed." Although Washington's plan had not fully taken hold when the Moravians visited, there were promising signs.[20] Women apparently had embraced its major tenets.

The prosperous farms and industrious work habits described by the Moravians, according to "civilizers," represented the Cherokees' hope for the future while hunting deer and trading skins reflected the past. Hawkins described the poverty which reliance on hunting had brought: "Their men hunted in their proper season and aided them with the skins in providing cloaths and blankets, such as I saw, but this was not sufficient to make them comfortable and the poor old men, women and children were under the necessity of sleeping as I saw them in their town house."[21] Nevertheless, many men persisted in their hunting economy. When resident agent Return J. Meigs arrived in 1801, he had to settle a hunting party's claim for 123 deerskins, forty bearskins, five small furs, and a buffalo skin that its eight members had left in the hunting grounds the previous year when a group of whites threatened them.[22] Like Hawkins, Meigs discovered that by November the chiefs had "gone to their hunting grounds & will not return for two or three months."[23] Yet hunting days were numbered. By 1808, claims which the agent paid for losses from hunting camps were more likely to be compensation for half a bear and some deermeat than a substantial pile of skins.[24] Hunting, however, was one of the things that defined masculinity, and few Cherokee men were willing to forego it. When a twenty-four-year-old man applied for admission to the school at Brainerd, he requested permission to hunt to clothe himself: instead, missionaries gave him a job on the farm.[25]

The persistence of hunting and the Cherokees' attachment to hunting grounds troubled "civilizers." Thomas Jefferson instructed Hawkins in 1803 "to promote among the Indians a sense of the superior value of a little land, well cultivated, over a great deal, unimproved." Eventually, he hoped, their hunting grounds "will be found useless, and even disadvantageous."[26] When

Cherokee men's devotion to the chase momentarily thwarted Meigs's attempt to secure a cession of the Cumberland Mountain region in 1805, he complained: "That land is of no use to them. There is not a single family on it, & the hunting is very poor. Yet those of idle dispositions spend much time in rambling there & often return with a stolen horse which they have afterwards to pay for. In fact it is only a nursery of savage habits and operates against civilization which is much impeded by their holding such immense tracts of wilderness."[27] Meigs summarized the "civilizers'" major concerns. First of all, hunting promoted idleness rather than the industriousness on which "civilization" was based. Secondly, the common ground encouraged a disregard for private property. And finally, "wilderness" stood in direct opposition to "civilized" towns, pastures, and fields. Meigs, Hawkins, Jefferson and other "civilizers" linked the cession of hunting grounds with the "civilizing" process. Herdsmen and farmers presumably no longer needed vast forests, and so the United States looked forward to the acquisition of the Indians' "surplus & waste lands."[28]

Most Cherokee men, long familiar with the machinations of Euro-Americans, viewed "civilization" with suspicion from the very start. One Cherokee man revealed to John Norton that upon hearing the President's plan, "many of us thought it was only some refined scheme calculated to gain an influence over us, rather than ameliorate our situation; and slighted his advice and proposals." The fact that the President of the United States who normally sent messages about war and trade now wanted to talk about farming was enough to make the most gullible Cherokee man suspicious. Consequently, Cherokee men at first chose to ignore the "civilization" program. As a result, men suffered by comparison to women. John McDonald, an intermarried white man, told Norton that "the females have however made much greater advances in industry than the males, they now manufacture a great quantity of cloth; but the latter have not made proportionate progress in Agriculture."[29] The men's initial lack of enthusiasm and relative failure may well have derived from their assumption that because farming was women's work, "civilization" had little to do with them.[30] For the "civilization" program to succeed among men, they had to adapt it to Cherokee culture.

Washington and Knox provided an avenue for just such an adaptation: they suggested that the transition to farming be eased by the Cherokees' first becoming herdsmen. Spanish explorers had introduced livestock into the southeast in the sixteenth century (the Cherokees borrowed their word for "cow," *wa'ka*, from the Spanish *vaca*). By the eighteenth century, traders had made livestock familiar, but Cherokee men exhibited little interest in keeping hogs, cattle, or sheep.[31] Instead, they commonly regarded such animals as game. At the abandoned encampment of a hunting party in 1751, colonists found five sheepskins and some beef bones.[32] White backcountry farmers as well as the garrison at Fort Loudoun complained constantly about the loss of livestock to hunting parties.[33] Because livestock usually foraged in the forest until late fall, the Native assumption that these animals were game was not implausible. The Cherokees had no tradition of domesticated animals other than the dog, which they apparently did not eat, and so the distinction between foraging animals that one could kill freely and those that belonged to an individual may well have appeared artificial. Even in the towns, domestic animals belonging to traders were not safe. Adair complained that "Indian youth are as destructive to the pigs and poultry, as so many young wolves or foxes" and that their parents did little to control their behavior.[34] Such an attitude did not bode well for the keeping of livestock by men.

By the end of the eighteenth century, Cherokees certainly knew the difference between livestock and game even though their behavior sometimes belied that knowledge. A vegetarian German pietist, who fled ridicule in Pennsylvania in 1795 and took refuge among the tolerant Cherokees, fretted constantly about the Cherokees lack of regard for God's creatures. He offered to loan one of his milk cows to Cherokee neighbors on the condition that they would not kill it, but according to Moravian missionaries who met him, "the Indians could not agree to the condition." His compassion finally compelled him to provide a cow to an infirm elderly man despite his failure to exact the promise. Upon the old man's death, however, the heirs slaughtered the cow.[35] As late as 1818, visitors to the Cherokees expressed amazement at the way men treated livestock:

> It was near sunset when we arrived. When he [the Cherokee host] learned who we were, and saw the obligation he was under to entertain us for the night, he took his rifle as I supposed to shoot some wild game which might be near. But while we were standing in a sort of porch attached to his hut, he discharged it at a cow which was eating grass immediately before our eyes; he only wounded the poor animal, which ran bellowing and frantic about the yard. In this situation, two or three half naked negroes, who stood at the corner of the house to enjoy the bloody spectacle, fell upon the cow with axes; cleaved it to the ground; butchered it immediately, and in two hours after our arrival, part of the very cow which we had found browsing happily on the grass, was stewed for our supper.[36]

Clearly Cherokee culture did not readily equip men to care for livestock.

Nevertheless, by the time of Hawkins's visit some men were beginning to raise livestock and their numbers increased steadily in the
nineteenth century. Among the first herdsmen in the Cherokee Nation
were white men or the sons of white men. John Candy, who had come
to the Cherokee Nation from East Florida in 1783, for example, owned
"some fine cattle." But native Cherokee men, even traditionalists, also
kept stock. The Terrapin, who spoke only his Native tongue, "had raised
some cattle of 1,200 lbs."[37] Deer were still fairly plentiful, however, and
livestock remained relatively scarce at the turn of the nineteenth century.
In 1802 when the Agent Return J. Meigs surveyed the boundary
between North Carolina and the Cherokee Nation, he paid a dollar
apiece for deer while hogs cost between $3.25 and $6.00 each and a
single beef brought $16.00.[38]

The Cherokees ceded their last expanse of hunting grounds in a series
of treaties in 1805–06. The remaining forests near their towns could not
sustain a hunting economy, and so they acquired more cattle and hogs.
These domesticated animals competed for food with the dwindling supply of game. White intruders further strained resources by grazing their
herds on Cherokee land. In one part of the Cherokee Nation in 1805,
over one thousand head of cattle belonging to intruders grazed on Cherokee land.[39] After a decade of rapidly expanding herds in the Cherokee
country, one visitor observed: "Since they have become graziers, the game
has nearly disappeared from their country."[40] Cherokee men had found a
new use for their "hunting grounds," that is, land they did not cultivate.
They simply restocked hunting grounds with cattle and hogs. By 1810,
the Cherokees owned 19,500 cattle and 19,600 hogs as well as 6,100
horses and 1,037 sheep, and all accounts suggest that the number was
growing rapidly.[41] The male approach to raising livestock, however, can
hardly be called animal husbandry.

The work pattern of Cherokee herding did not differ dramatically from
that of hunting. The Cherokees, like most southerners, did not pen their
livestock during the summer nor put them in barns in winter. Major John
Norton observed that "people raise cattle with the greatest facility, and without any further trouble or expence than that of giving them *salt*. In the
winter, they feed in cane brakes, and in summer, they are dispersed in herds
in the vicinity of little Salt Licks."[42] In the late fall and winter, the herdsmen
simply shot the animals they intended to butcher. The practice appalled visitors accustomed to abattoirs or slaughter pens, but American Board
missionaries requested a gun soon after their arrival "on account of the

beeves we kill being so very wild that we cannot catch them without shoot-ing."[43] The process of capturing those animals which they hoped to take to market could be nearly as time-consuming as hunting. In November 1802, the chief Doublehead delayed his journey to purchase supplies, he explained, because "I am so engaged hunting and gathering my beef cattle that I expect it will be a moon or two before I can come."[44] This "hunting and gathering" sometimes involved a mad chase through the woods. Daniel S. Butrick, an American Board missionary, could easily have been writing about game in 1818 when he noted that the congregation was "soon a little enlarged by the arrival of a number of men in pursuit of cattle."[45]

If we consider the grazing of cattle analogous to hunting, it is not too farfetched to regard horse-stealing as a substitute for war. Horse-stealing was not confined to the Cherokees in the late eighteenth and early nine-teenth century, but the border between the Cherokee Nation and the states proved attractive to Indian and white horse-thieves alike. The con-fusion over jurisdiction, the readiness of the federal government to settle claims for stolen horses, and the mountainous terrain made the frontier ideal territory for the illicit traffic in horses.[46] By the first decade in the nineteenth century, horses had replaced deerskins as a medium of ex-change: Meigs described them as "a kind of currency."[47] As such, horses helped soften the economic blow from the demise of warfare and trade. Horse-stealing fit well into a male culture that expected men to distin-guish themselves on forays against the enemy. After the Chickamaugans made peace in 1794, young men had few other ways in which to demon-strate martial skills, prove their valor, and become men in the traditional sense.[48] Horse-stealing, however, provided men with some of the same rewards as warfare—it demonstrated prowess and brought profit—and horses became a kind of substitute for the war captives who previously had been sold as slaves. In one episode in 1797, the Cherokees literally equated the two: a Virginia man traded a horse for his brother who had been taken prisoner by the Cherokees some years earlier.[49] With the open-ing of a road through the Cherokee Nation, opportunities for theft became more numerous, and thieves became more brazen and less discriminating. Although horses remained the preferred prize, travelers lost hogs, cows, salt, clothing, boats, and slaves.[50] The Cherokee Council ultimately had to order return of property "detained" along the road.[51] When Cherokee men adapted male imperatives to horse-stealing, they confronted a host of neg-ative European attitudes. White settlers were understandably reluctant to regard the theft of their property as an acceptable alternative to raids by war parties. Horse-stealing seemed particularly despicable because it inflicted enormous hardship on subsistence-level families and embodied a European folklore of nightriders and highwaymen.

The Euro-American response to hunting was less visceral but equally negative. "Civilizers" believed that hunting was at the very heart of Native "savagery" because it permitted men to engage in "sport and pastimes" instead of labor.[52] Benjamin Franklin attributed the failure of colonial efforts to "civilize" Indians to "The Proneness of Human Nature to a Life of Ease" provided by "the Spontaneous Productions of Nature, with the additions of very little Labour, if Hunting and Fishing may indeed be called Labour when Game is so plenty."[53] Thomas McKenney later suggested that a major obstacle to "civilizing" the Indian was "the preference he cherishes for sport and pastimes," that is, hunting.[54]

The adaptation of livestock herding to traditional labor patterns and land use left the "civilizers" in dismay. The Indians seemed to be reversing the process of domesticating animals by releasing them into the forest to forage. Although most whites in the South and on the frontier did the same, early proponents of selective breeding objected to the practice and decried its extension to Indians. The Indians' half-wild beasts hardly represented progress or reform. Furthermore, this approach to animal husbandry deprived the Cherokees of the refined products—milk, butter, and cheese—that derived from domesticated animals. The only milk available came from those cows who decided, of their own free will, to come home.[55] Yet missionaries who later tried to set a good example by penning their livestock complained that the animals starved in winter.[56]

John McDonald, an intermarried white man, told John Norton why livestock raising was the only part of the "civilization" program most Cherokee men had accepted: "They raise great herds of cattle, which can be done with little exertion; and the sale of these brings much wealth into the Nation."[57] That is, herding demanded the same kind of "exertion" as hunting and provided the same kind of return. Cherokee herding methods required little of what Europeans considered labor and failed to promote the industrious habits associated with "civilization." Meigs pointed out with some disgust that "the raising & manufacturing of cotton is all done by the Indian women. . . . The Indian men attend to the raising of cattle and swine—this costs them no labour, a thing they will avoid as long as possible."[58] In the eyes of Meigs and other "civilizers," farming constituted labor but herding, like hunting, did not. In their attempt to avoid women's work—farming—men seemed to be avoiding any sort of labor at all.

Men found ways to contribute to agricultural productivity and compensate for the women's labor lost to spinning and weaving without actually farming themselves. In the first decade of the nineteenth century, many of them began to lease or rent land to white families on shares.[59] The Council had grave misgivings about the practice since it brought large numbers of white people into the Nation and expelling them at the end of the year was difficult. In 1808 the Council considered banning the practice, but Agent Meigs protested: "I wish you to weigh this matter well before you act because I think you will find that you will again want the help of poor [white] people to raise corn & do other work for you & in a year or two you will do it. All People that ever I know hire poor people to work for them. Some families don't want to hire because they have help enough of their own; but other families have not hands of their own & they ought not to be deprived of having help when they can find it."[60] Meigs clearly saw share-cropping as a way for Cherokees to increase agricultural productivity, but by 1811 he had changed his mind. Instead, cropping was a way for men to avoid work: "They have no need for white men as croppers because it encourages idleness in Indians."[61] As concern over intruders grew, the practice of cropping declined.

Cherokees found another form of labor in African slaves.[62] Traders had brought their own slaves into the Cherokee country in the eighteenth century, and Cherokee warriors had participated in a frontier slave trade. Like horse-stealing, the theft of slaves presented men with an opportunity to remain warriors, and so an illicit traffic in slaves continued well into the nineteenth century.[63] By the early nineteenth century, however, Cherokees also were acquiring slaves for their own use. The transition to slave labor, like that to livestock herding, seems to have been one in which Cherokees invested little thought. When Young Wolf wrote his will in 1814, he explained how he managed to accumulate his estate: "From herding my brother's cattle I recevd one calf which I took my start from, except my own industry, & with cow & calf which I sold, I bought two sows & thirteen piggs sometime after I was abel to purchase three mares & the increase of them since is amounted to thirty more or less & from that start I gathered money enough to purchase a negro woman named Tabb, also a negro man named Ceasar."[64] By 1809 slaves numbered 583.[65] While some of these probably belonged to whites employed by or married to Cherokees, most belonged to Indians. According to a census taken in 1825, the number had increased to 1,277, and by 1835 had reached nearly sixteen hundred. Instead of becoming the yeoman farmers so admired by Washington and Jefferson, most Cherokee men (like Washington and Jefferson) seemed more inclined to adopt the aristocratic planter as a role model. Only a very few ever achieved this goal, but those who did dominated Cherokee economic and political life.[66]

The extent to which Cherokee men took up the plow themselves is difficult to determine. As early as 1796, Hawkins discovered the Terrapin plowing.[67] Furthermore, men normally requested plows from the agent, but these petitioners were headmen who spoke for their towns rather than themselves.[68] Other evidence in the agent's records is contradictory: Meigs's assistant requested a plow for Arthur Burns, "one of the most indefatigable and industrious men," while Bartlet Robbins "was sent by Nancy Falling to the Blacksmith's to have some plough irons sharpened."[69] The novelty of the plow, its status as a gift of the federal government, the example of white men, and the association of the plow with horses, however, may have led increasing numbers of Cherokee men to become directly involved in farming. Men probably adopted the new technology of plow agriculture while women continued to perform their normal tasks, such as hoeing, traditionally associated with farming. Lists of goods being sent from the agency to various Cherokee towns included hoes, women's traditional farming implement, as well as the more innovative plow.[70] Often hoes substantially outnumbered plows, but plows cost four times as much and required the services of a blacksmith to remain useable.[71] By 1811 there were about five hundred plows in the Nation, perhaps one for every four families.[72]

Horses provided an obvious link between men and farming, and by the 1820s, most Cherokees had hitched horses to their plows.[73] Missionary Daniel Butrick wrote that "a horse is their chief dependence for raising support for their families," and when his own mount ran away, he had difficulty borrowing one because the Cherokees had all of theirs in the fields.[74] In 1821, missionaries introduced oxen, which seem to have been common elsewhere in the South, but horses remained the draft animal of choice.[75] Men probably held the reins. Men always had helped women prepare fields and plant corn; then women took over the care of the crops. The plow does not seem to have altered this arrangement substantially, and as a result, men appeared idle during much of the year. As late as 1828, over thirty years after the inauguration of the "civilization" program, missionaries complained that men did not fully occupy themselves with farming:

> Every family has a corn field, plough & horse or horses, to till it. They keep cows & hogs—raise horses & beeves—The women spin & weave—In general old & young are decently clad in cotton cloth of their

own making—especially on the Sabbath. The season of raising corn is a time of general industry with both men & women & perhaps we may say with most of the women, the year round. But as agriculture is extended only to raising corn, potatoes, & cotton (except with a very few, lately, a little wheat) the men have not a sufficient stimulous to keep up their exertions after the corn is laid by—This is a very great evil, both as it tends to demoralize, & also to keep them poor. The women are evidently going before the men; & we think this (at least in a great degree) is owing to their being more constantly employed.[76]

As long as men confined themselves to merely plowing the fields, little hope existed for keeping them "constantly employed." Albert Gallatin complained that "although the men may to some extent have assisted the women in the cultivation of the ground, the greater part of the labors still fell upon the latter."[77] He did concede that the Cherokees had, in a limited way, "become an agricultural nation, meaning thereby that state of society, in which the men themselves do actually perform agricultural labor." But even among the Cherokees, he estimated, only one third of the men farmed.[78]

Nineteenth-century observers agreed that men lagged behind women in adapting to the new economic order, perhaps because "civilized" occupations conformed more nearly to traditional roles of women than of men. But a market economy underlay the "civilization" program as surely as it had the deerskin trade and made the Cherokees no more likely to create the agrarian republic of yeomen farmers than the Jeffersonians and their successors. The economic expansion of the United States drew the Cherokees and other Americans into a maelstrom from which they could not have escaped even if they had been so inclined. As it was, the Cherokees had long ago adapted their political and economic institutions to the demands of an international market. The vast majority of Cherokee men and women had little desire to withdraw.

The women with whom Hawkins spoke had a sophisticated understanding of their own economic subservience. They knew that male ascendancy derived largely from the eighteenth-century market in deerskins. Consequently, they shifted the conversations with Hawkins from production to marketing. The women who told Hawkins about their agricultural production added that "if they could be directed how to turn their labour to account like the white people, they should be contented."[79]

Cherokee women had no complaints about their role as farmers. What they wanted was an opportunity "to turn their labor to account," that is, to profit from what they produced. The obstacles confronting these erstwhile entrepreneurs were considerable. Hawkins heard their complaints: "I was here informed of some of the difficulties and hardships which these poor people are subject to. They sell the fowls grown, 2 for 2½ yards of binding worth 2 cents, a bushel of corn for a quart of salt and sometimes a pint, and the woman had just returned from the [white] settlements, a journey of 17 days. She carried a bushel and a half of chestnuts on her back and gave them for a petticoat."[80] This woman, like most Cherokees, needed to buy salt, clothing, and other goods, and so she had to sell at whatever price she could get. Often Cherokees could find no market at all for what they produced. A group of women complained "that they would make corn enough but that they never could sell it."[81] One of their difficulties was the absence of a substantial internal market. Since most Cherokee households farmed, corn had little market value. Those Cherokees who had no corn usually had no means by which to pay for it.[82] Drought tended to touch all Cherokees equally so that when Cherokees needed to buy corn, no one had corn to sell.[83] Scattered white farmsteads near the Nation's borders offered poor markets, and the distance to larger white settlements coupled with the hardships of travel posed problems for women who had to tend house and mind children as well as farm.[84] The Creeks briefly offered women an opportunity to enter the market: by 1809, Cherokee women were swapping them cloth for cattle.[85] War soon interrupted the trade, however, and Creeks acquired their own spinning wheels and looms.

A broader trade in textiles illustrates the problem women had with marketing. Cherokee women produced a prodigious amount of cloth. By 1809 the Cherokees had sixteen hundred spinning wheels and 467 looms in a total population of just over twelve thousand. Gideon Blackburn, a Presbyterian missionary, estimated that women could produce 584,684 yards of cloth a year if they kept their machines operating constantly.[86] Cherokee women, of course, spent many hours engaged in activities other than textile manufacturing. While the potential is staggering, the more modest actual production of perhaps half Blackburn's estimate was still substantial.[87] Cherokee women did not, however, control the market in textiles. During the eighteenth century, participation in commerce had come to define masculinity as much as war or hunting, and factory-made textiles had become part of the material culture dominated by men and non-Cherokees. In the nineteenth century, textiles became a trophy for young men no longer permitted to go to war, and whites along the frontier complained bitterly about the loss of their best bedding.[88] Furthermore, textiles played a major role in diplomacy. In 1801 the chiefs notified their new agent, Return J. Meigs, that they no longer wanted their annuity paid in goods "not of substantial use," that is, silk stockings, gold lace, damask tablecloths, morocco shoes, and ostrich feathers. Instead, they wanted "blankets, strouds & coating." Meigs added in his instructions to the supplier, "Some fine Cloth is always expected for the Chiefs."[89] Furthermore, the government factory at Tellico Blockhouse in eastern Tennessee stocked a substantial array of textiles and supplied those Cherokees who had money to spend or credit to command. In 1804, the federal government completed a road across the Cherokee Nation which reduced shipping costs by almost one half, and presumably the cost of textiles declined. The government factory closed in 1811, but Cherokee merchants filled that commercial vacuum and continued to market fabric made outside the Nation. Competition to women's manufactures also came from unlikely sources. Missionaries, who arrived in large numbers in the decade following the closing of the government factory, competed with both domestic producers and local purveyors of fabrics. Ann Paine, a New Englander who visited missionaries in 1820, noted that

> many of the Cherokee women are skillful in spinning cotton which they manufacture into cloth, but the Mission is much benefitted by the sale of cloth and garments from the charity boxes. For these the Cherokees give money and articles of produce; and they are sold with considerable proffit as it would not do for the Missionaries to undersell the Cherokee Merchants, at whose stores common shirt factory is sold at 50 cts per yard—A common factory shirt from the boxes is sold for two dollars.[90]

In addition to marketing textiles, the mission also participated in production, although on a more limited basis. The girls at one mission school made quilts from old cloth. The quilts brought six or seven dollars each from the Cherokees and "please them very much."[91]

Women's difficulty in participating in the market stemmed from far more than the industrial and market revolutions. Cherokees had well-established mechanisms for commerce that proved remarkably persistent. Rooted in part in ancient cultural traditions that entrusted men with foreign relations and women with domestic ones, these mechanisms had adapted to an international market economy in the eighteenth century. Men were in the forefront of the deerskin trade in part because men obtained the skins, but also because men dealt with outsiders, that is, with European traders and emissaries. For women suddenly to have entered this world would have disrupted a long-established protocol. Women certainly sold corn, livestock, and even textiles, but the primary responsibility for marketing rested with men. The Cherokees simply adapted established patterns of behavior to new circumstances. Women continued to be women according to old definitions, and men continued to be men.

Within the context of the "civilization" program, men served as the intermediaries between women and the federal government and served as conduits for most of the tools and implements that the agent made available to the Nation. Requests for cotton cards, spinning wheels, looms, and corn hoes normally came from men.[92] Sometimes women directly instigated these requests. Pathkiller and Toochalee prefaced their application for wheels and cards with the words, "These women came to me to write them a few lines to you."[93] Doublehead made a particularly poignant plea when he wrote Meigs: "I have to solicit of you in behalf of two poor middle aged women living here, who have begged me to make the application having large families composed entirely of girls, that you will be so good as to forward them by me three small wheels and three pairs of cards, the familys are very poor and have no other means but their industry to cloth themselves and show much anxiety to learn the usefull arts, they are deprived of the aid of any man in their family having no man in either."[94] One of the things these women needed a man for was to appeal to the agent for tools.

As intermediaries, men also often marketed commodities associated with women. When Meigs participated in surveying the boundary line between North Carolina and the Cherokee Nation in 1802, he purchased sweet potatoes, cabbage, corn and even "Indian bread" from men.[95] Of the eighty-seven receipts Meigs issued to his suppliers, only three—for two chickens, forage, and "provision"—were to women. Women's total direct income from the survey was only $3.75.[96] This does not mean, of course, that women did not produce some of the commodities that Meigs bought from men or profit indirectly, but women did not sell the product of their labor, at least not to Meigs. A new symbiotic relationship between men and women, reminiscent of traditional roles, seemed to be emerging: women, joined by white share-croppers and black slaves, became the primary producers in Cherokee society while men became the entrepreneurs.

In 1801 several headmen from towns along the Tennessee River visited Hawkins: "They stated the improvements made in the products of the country; that a total change had taken place in the habits of the nation since the introduction of the plan for their civilization." Even more significantly, these men requested Hawkins's aid. They told him "that a desire for individual property was very prevalent, and that the current of conversation now was how to acquire it, by attention to stock, to farming and to manufactures."[97] These men viewed "civilization" in strictly material terms: it was a way to obtain "individual property." With the end of the deerskin trade and colonial wars, men had lost an acceptable way to express the aggressive, competitive, individualistic male culture that had shaped their lives. Similarly, the lustre faded on symbols of that lifestyle— guns, war trophies, items of personal adornment. Now they saw an opportunity to reorient male culture toward the acquisition of "individual property," and property became an emblem of success. In the first decade of the nineteenth century, business opportunities abounded in the Cherokee Nation, and intermarried white men and their sons as well as native Cherokees eagerly took advantage of them. The Agent employed a blacksmith to repair tools, but the demand for his services was such that several Cherokees went into partnerships with smiths. Similarly, the demand on the public miller led individual Cherokees to construct their own grist and saw mills and employ skilled white men to run them.[98] By 1804 the business of the National Council was business. The Council granted five-year leases for "houses of entertainment" along the Cumberland Road through Cherokee territory and issued permits to blacksmiths, wheelwrights, millers, a cooper, and saltpetre makers. Apparently agreeing with Meigs on the importance of education in transacting "the ordinary business required in civilized life," the headmen also issued permits to a schoolmaster and Moravian missionaries on the condition that the latter focus on education.[99]

The completion of the 220 mile long road between Augusta, Georgia and Nashville, Tennessee opened other possibilities for men to profit. Individual Cherokee men, in partnership with whites, obtained contracts for taverns and ferries, a turnpike company organized for the maintenance of the road and then sub-contracted its obligations, and a Cherokee applied for the mail contract.[100] The Georgia road proved so successful in facilitating commerce that the Cherokees built another 300 miles of wagon roads at their own expense.[101] In addition to their income from these enterprises, according to Meigs, "they have no inconsiderable quantity of cash in circulation which they receive annually for the sale of cattle and swine."[102] James Vann, in fact, had sufficient cash in 1805 to be robbed of $3,500.[103]

Just as many Cherokee men failed to become great warriors, all Cherokees did not share equally in the spoils of economic expansion. In 1809

Meigs wrote the Secretary of War: "A spirit of industry does by no means pervade the general population. The greatest number are extremely poor from want of industry. The hunting life is here at an end: but a predeliction for the hunter state pervades a great part of the Cherokees."[104] These Cherokees, he believed, should move west of the Mississippi. Meigs defined "want of industry" as the refusal of "the men to labour in the Fields with their own hands."[105] But even wealthy Cherokee men did not "labour." They merely had the capital, inherited from white fathers or acquired through trade, horse-stealing, or official position, to invest in other kinds of labor. As town chiefs and members of the National Council, prominent men had the power to award themselves contracts and permits or to receive gifts, bribes, and private reservations from the federal government.[106] These men adroitly used their capital and political positions to increase wealth and the symbol of success, individual property.

The statistical table Agent Meigs sent to the Secretary of War in 1809 indicated a remarkable change in Cherokee material culture. "The Cherokees," he asserted, "[have] prospered by the pastoral life and by domestic manufactures." Livestock abounded and spinning wheels whirred throughout the Nations.[107] In more fundamental ways, however, Cherokee lives remained remarkably untouched: the Cherokees had adapted "civilization" to their own expectations of men and women. Cherokee women used the "civilization" program to embellish their culture, but they did not transform it. Certainly, women added new crops, cotton in particular, and new skills such as spinning and weaving, but they continued to farm, keep house, and tend children just as they always had done. Similarly, men's culture retained the basic ethic that traditionally governed hunting and warfare, but aggression and competition found expression in the rapidly expanding market economy. Rather than simply embracing the tenets of "civilization" or imitating Anglo-American society, Cherokee men and women restructured United States Indian policy to conform to their own cultural imperatives.

NOTES

1. Thomas Jefferson, *Notes on the State of Virginia* (Boston, 1832), 6, 63, 143, 145.

2. Roy Harvey Pearce, *Savagism and Civilization: A Study of the Indian and the American Mind* (1953; rev. ed., Berkeley: University of California Press, 1988), 66, 83–90; Robert F. Berkhofer, Jr., *The White Man's Indian: Images of the American Indian from Columbus to the Present* (New York: Alfred A. Knopf, 1978), 138.

3. George W. Corner, ed., *The Autobiography of Benjamin Rush: His "Travels Through Life" Together with His Commonplace Book for 1789–1813,* Memoirs of the American Philosophical Society, vol. 25, (Princeton: Princeton University Press, 1948), 71; Benjamin Rush, "Medicine Among the Indians," in *Essays Literary, Moral, and Philosophical* (Philadelphia: Thomas and Samuel F. Bradford, 1798), 290.

4. Henry Knox to George Washington, 7 July 1789, *American State Papers: Indian Affairs (ASP),* 2 vols. (Washington, D.C., 1832), 1: 53.

5. *ASP,* 1: 125.

6. G. Melvin Herndon, "Indian Agriculture in the Southern Colonies," *North Carolina Historical Review* 44 (1967): 283–97.

7. Henry Timberlake, *Lieut. Henry Timberlake's Memoirs, 1756–1765,* ed. Samuel Cole Williams (Johnson City, TN: The Watauga Press, 1927), 99.

8. James Hall, *Sketches of History, Life, and Manners in the West,* 2 vols. (Philadelphia: H. Hall, 1835), 1: 92; Samuel Stanhope Smith, *An Essay on the Causes of the Variety of Complexion and Figure in the Human Species,* ed. Winthrop Jordan (1810; reprint ed., Cambridge: Harvard University Press, 1965), 216.

9. Robert Beverley, *The History and Present State of Virginia,* ed. Louis B. Wright (1705; reprint ed., Chapel Hill, 1947), 156.

10. George Washington to the Cherokees, 1796, *Cherokee Phoenix,* 20 March 1828.

11. See Merritt B. Pound, *Benjamin Hawkins—Indian Agent* (Athens: University of Goergia Press, 1951); Frank L. Owsley, Jr., "Benjamin Hawkins, the First Modern Indian Agent," *Alabama Historical Quarterly* 30 (1968), 7–13; Florette Henri, *The Southern Indians and Benjamin Hawkins, 1796–1816* (Norman: University of Oklahoma Press, 1986).

12. Benjamin Hawkins, *Letters of Benjamin Hawkins, 1796–1806, Georgia Historical Society Collections* 9 (1916), 20. Hawkins also called on one family in which both father and mother were away hunting, and the daughters entertained him (pp. 22–23).

13. *Hawkins,* 18, 21–22.

14. Gary C. Goodwin, *Cherokees in Transition: A Study of Changing Culture and Environment Prior to 1775* (Research Paper No. 181; Chicago: The University of Chicago Department of Geography, 1977), 126–31.

15. *Hawkins,* 16, 21–22.

16. John Norton, *The Journal of Major John Norton, 1816,* ed. Carl F. Klinck and James J. Talman (Toronto: The Champlain Society, 1970), 36, 51; Samuel Cole Williams, ed., *Early Travels in the Tennessee Country, 1540–1800* (Johnson City, TN: The Watauga Press, 1928), 477.

17. Jack Kilpatrick, ed., "The Wahnenauhi Manuscript: Historical Sketches of the Cherokees," *Bureau of American Ethnology Bulletin* 196, 195.

18. *Hawkins,* 18.

19. Norton, 36.
20. Williams, *Early Travels*, 469–471, 485, 490.
21. Hawkins, 21–22.
22. Charles Hicks to Return J. Meigs, 7 Sept. 1801, Records of the Cherokee Agency in Tennessee, 1801–35, U.S. Bureau of Indian Affairs, Record Group 75, National Archives, Washington, D.C., Microcopy M–208 (henceforth M–208).
23. Meigs to Henry Dearborn, 30 Nov. 1801, M–208.
24. Charles Rogers to Meigs, 1 February 1808, M–208.
25. Brainerd Journal, 2 June 1818, Papers of the American Board of Commissioners for Foreign Missions (ABCFM), Houghton Library, Harvard University, Cambridge, MA.
26. Jefferson to Hawkins, 18 February 1803, in *The Writings of Thomas Jefferson*, ed. Paul Leicester Ford, 10 vols. (New York: G. P. Putnam's Sons, 1892–99), 8: 213–14.
27. Meigs to Hawkins, 13 Feb. 1805, M–208.
28. Draft of Jefferson's Fifth Annual Message, Ford, 8: 394.
29. Norton, 36, 59–60.
30. Yet some men treasured the President's advice even if, perhaps, they did not follow it. One of the headmen of Chota treasured a copy of Washington's letter which agent Dinsmore had bound and given him. Williams, *Early Travels*, 469–471, 485, 490.
31. Goodwin (p. 135) suggests that the Cherokees did not keep livestock because they believed that by consuming beef and pork, they would acquire the slow, slovenly characteristics of the animals.
32. William L. McDowell, ed., *Documents Relating to Indian Affairs, May 21, 1750–Aug. 7, 1754* (Columbia: South Carolina Archives, 1958), 82.
33. McDowell, *Documents, 1750–1754*, 29; William L. McDowell, ed., *Documents Relating to Indian Affairs, 1754–1765* (Columbia: South Carolina Archives, 1970), 127, 144, 168; Williams, *Early Travels*, 140n; Timberlake, 72.
34. James Adair, *Adair's History of the American Indians* (Johnson City, TN: Watauga Press, 1930), 443.
35. Williams, *Early Travels*, 481–83.
36. "Reflections on the Institutions of the Cherokee Indians," *The Analectic Magazine* (July 1818), 39.
37. Hawkins, 18, 24.
38. Receipts to Samuel Eckridge, 19 Oct. 1802, M–208.
39. Daniel Alexander to Meigs, 22 Feb 1805, M–208.
40. "Reflections," 41.
41. Jedidiah Morse, *The American Universal Geography; or a View of the Present State of All the Kingdoms, States and Colonies in the Known World* (Boston: Thomas and Andrews, 1812), 574.
42. Norton, 57.
43. Daniel S. Butrick to Samuel Austin Worcester, 2 July 1818; Ard Hoyt to Jeremiah Evarts, 8 January 1819; ABCFM.
44. Doublehead to J. D. Chilsolm, 20 November 1802, M–208.
45. Butrick to Worcester, 2 July 1818, ABCFM.
46. For example, see Abstract of Indemnification for Horses Stolen, 27 Oct. 1801, Meigs to Dearborn, 22 Feb. 1802, and List of Claims, 25 Oct. 1811, M–208. The

Indians enjoyed sovereignty under the supervision of the federal government, but their lack of jurisdiction over whites and the absence of formal laws meant that the prosecution of whites was unlikely. The states, on the other hand, usually refused to admit Native testimony, and so the federal government attempted to intercede to prevent Indians' being tried in state courts.

47. Meigs to Dearborn, 19 Dec. 1807, M–208.

48. William G. McLoughlin, "Cherokee Anomie, 1794–1810," in *The Cherokee Ghost Dance: Essays on the Southeastern Indians, 1789–1861* (Macon, GA: Mercer University Press, 1984), 3–37.

49. Williams, *Early Travels*, 460; Hawkins, 133.

50. Meigs to Cherokee Nation, 14 Aug. 1807; J. D. Chilsolm to Meigs, 19 Aug 1807; James Lusk to Gov. Sevier, 9 Dec. 1807; List of Claims, 25 Oct. 1811; M–208.

51. Black Fox & other chiefs to George Parris & Killachulla, 23 Aug. 1807, M–208.

52. Thomas McKenney, *Memoirs Official and Personal; with Sketches of Travels among the Northern and Southern Indians*, 2 vols. (New York: Paine and Burgess, 1846), 1: 232–33.

53. A.O. Aldridge, "Franklin's Letter on Indians and Germans [1753]," *Proceedings of the American Philosophical Society* 94 (1950): 392.

54. McKenney, *Memoirs*, 1: 232–33.

55. Ann Paine to Evarts, 8 November 1821, ABCFM.

56. Moody Hall's Journal, 17 April 1822, 17 April 1823, ABCFM.

57. Norton, 36, 59–60.

58. Journal of Occurences in the Cherokee Agency in 1802, M–208.

59. John Lowry to Meigs, 20 Oct. 1818; Names of Persons who are on land in Sequchee Valley, 22 April 1809; William Schrimsher and Richard Martins recommendation as croppers for Jn. Boggs, a Cherokee, 21 April 1808; M–208. All people mentioned as employers of sharecroppers were men except for Granny Maw and Nancy. Meigs to Chiefs, 27 March 1810, M–208.

60. Meigs to Chulisa & Sour Mush, 14 March 1808, M–208.

61. Meigs to William Eustis, 27 February 1811, M–208.

62. See R. Halliburton, Jr., *Red Over Black: Black Slavery among the Cherokee Indians* (Westport, CT: Greenwood Press, 1977) and Theda Perdue, *Slavery and the Evolution of Cherokee Society, 1540–1866* (Knoxville: University of Tennessee Press, 1979).

63. Joseph Phillips to Meigs, 12 Aug. 1807; Complaint of Griffin Minor, 5 May 1809; M–208.

64. John Howard Payne Papers, Newberry Library, Chicago, IL, 7: 58–59.

65. Morse, *Geography*, 574.

66. By 1835 nearly sixteen hundred residents of the Cherokee Nation were slaves, but less than eight percent of the heads of household listed on this census owned slaves. Those who did were wealthy in every category listed on the census: they farmed more acres, raised more corn and wheat per acre, sold more of their produce, and owned a disproportionate number of mills and ferries. Twenty of the 209 slaveholders listed on the census (slightly over one tenth) were women, but they were not as wealthy as the men. Women slaveholders averaged slightly over six slaves each while men averaged slightly over seven. Unlike their male counterparts, women slaveholders concentrated their assets in farming: none

owned a mill or ferry, and almost all had only one farm. Cherokee Census of
1835 (Henderson Roll), Record Group 75, U.S. Bureau of Indian Affairs, National
Archives, Washington, D.C., Microcopy T–496.

67. Hawkins, 22–23.
68. Little Turkey to Meigs, 10 Dec. 1801; Upper Town Chiefs to the President, 25
    April 1806; The Glass to Meigs, 8 Feb. 1808; M–208.
69. Bartlet Robbins was a white man "living in the Cherokee Nation with Nancy
    Falling," and Burns, who was married to Cherokee Aky Lowry, may well have
    been white because Lovely suggests that he would be "a good example to the
    Indians." William L. Lovely to Meigs, 30 Jan. 1804; Statement of Bartlett Robbins,
    25 Oct. 1808; M–208.
70. Little Turkey to Meigs, 10 Dec. 1801; Journal of Occurences in the Cherokee
    Agency, 1802; List of Tools, etc., 28 May 1806; Dearborn to Meigs, 24 April
    1807; Meigs to Eustis, 15 Dec. 1810; M–208.
71. Meigs to John Cocke, 7 April 1803; Meigs to Eustis, 15 Dec. 1810; M–208.
72. Meigs to Eustis, 10 May 1811, M–208. Plows were not evenly distributed
    throughout the Nation. Lower towns in Georgia and Alabama received more than
    the Upper Towns in eastern Tennessee or the' Valley Towns in western North
    Carolina. John Tinsley complained to Meigs that only one family in seven in his
    neighborhood had a plow. 10 June 1811, M–208.
73. The Church at Willstown, 10 Oct. 1828, ABCFM.
74. Butrick's Journal, 19 February 1824; Butrick to Evarts, 9 May 1827; ABCFM.
75. Brainerd Journal, 22 April 1820, 5 November 1821, ABCFM.
76. Journal of the Church at Willstown, 10 October 1828, ABCFM.
77. Albert Gallatin, "Synopsis of the Indian Tribes Within the United States East of
    the Rocky Mountains, and in the British and Russian Possessions," *Archaeologia
    Americana: Transactions and Collections of the American Antiquarian Society*, vol. 2
    (Cambridge: Folsom, Wells, and Thurston, 1836), 108.
78. Gallatin, 157.
79. Hawkins, 21–22.
80. Hawkins, 18.
81. Hawkins, 21.
82. Meigs to Black Fox, 29 August 1808, M–208.
83. Muscle Shoals Chiefs to Return J. Meigs, 27 March 1804, M–208.
84. Non-Indians living west of the continental divide had similar problems marketing
    their produce. Some resorted to making whiskey from their grain in order to
    simplify transport to market. The Cherokees, however, had no tradition of
    fermenting and distilling grain.
85. Williams, *Early Travels*, 464; Norton, 125.
86. Morse, *Geography*, 574.
87. Meigs reported that in 1801 weavers produced six hundred yards of cloth on one
    loom at Hiwassee. If weavers averaged that level of productivity, the total yards
    produced would be 280,200. Journal of Occurrences &c. relating to the
    Cherokee Nation [1801], M–208.
88. Thomas Johnson to Genl. Winchester, 20 April 1801, M–208.
89. Meigs to Israel Wheeler, 21 Nov. 1801, M–208. By the 1820s, those ostrich
    feathers at which the chiefs had sneered in 1801 had become so desirable that a

114

case contesting ownership of them reached the Cherokee Supreme Court. Betsey Walker vs. Chekayoue, 24 Oct. 1827, Cherokee Supreme Court Docket, Tennessee State Archives, Nashville, TN.

90. Ann Paine, Notebook II, 20 Dec. 1820, ABCFM.

91. Brainerd Journal, 14 Dec. 1822, ABCFM.

92. Little Turkey to Meigs, 10 Dec. 1807; Black Foxes Speech, 25 Feb. 1804; James Davis, Chief of Tusquitee, to Meigs 29 July 1804; M–208. One man, the Bold Hunter, learned to make looms. Journal of Occurences &c. relating to the Cherokee Nation [1801], M–208.

93. Pathkiller and Toochalee to Meigs, 14 Sept. 1812, M–208.

94. Doublehead to Meigs, 8 June 1804, M–208.

95. Receipts to Samuel Eckridge, 19 Oct. 1802, M–208.

96. Receipt to Nancy Lin, 22 Aug. 1802; Receipt to Susannah Trembel, 23 July 1802; Receipt to Nancy Davis, 8 Sept. 1802; M–208.

97. Hawkins, 360.

98. List of white men permitted to assist the Cherokees in 1811, An agreement between Doublehead & John Smith, Jr., 16 Nov. 1805. M–208.

99. Meigs to Hawkins, 28 Dec. 1802; Resolutions of the National Council, 10 April 1804, M–208.

100. Resolutions of the National Council, 10 April 1804; Lovely to Meigs 4 Nov. 1803; Meigs to Col Walter, 10 Jan 1804; Charles Hicks to Meigs, 19 Aug. 1806; John Lowry to Meigs, 22 March 1807; M–208.

101. Meigs to Eustis, 1 Dec. 1809, M–208.

102. Meigs to Eustis, 1 Dec. 1809, M–208.

103. Nicholas Byers to Meigs, 28 Aug. 1805, M–208.

104. Meigs to Eustis, 1 Dec. 1809, M–208.

105. Meigs to Lovely [1801], M–208.

106. Dearborn to Meigs, 9 July 1801; Meigs to Dearborn, 8 June 1802; Meigs to Dearborn, 31 May 1804; Lovely to Chiefs, June 1805; M–208.

107. Meigs to Eustis, 1 Dec. 1809, M–208.

5

CLARA SUE KIDWELL

CHOCTAW WOMEN AND CULTURAL PERSISTENCE IN MISSISSIPPI

Like the Cherokees, the Choctaws were a southeastern tribe pressured into removing to west of the Mississippi. In the winter of 1831–32, the majority of Choctaws reluctantly relocated to the new Choctaw Nation in Indian Territory. A small group of Choctaws chose to remain in Mississippi, where under a provision of the 1830 removal treaty, individual Choctaws were able to take small allotments of land and become citizens of the state of Mississippi. They later organized as the Mississippi Band of Choctaw Indians, a tribe politically separate from the Choctaw Nation in Oklahoma and consisting of seven reservation communities. Kidwell's paper focuses on the Mississippi Choctaws before and after the removal period.

In a classic case of sexual stereotyping, Joseph Gilfillan, an Episcopalian missionary, described the Chippewa Indians in Minnesota, the tall, graceful male bounding through the forest, unburdened except for his bow and arrow, while behind him plodded the "short, stodgy, rotund" female, bearing a tremendous burden on her back, atop of which rode a small papoose. In Gilfillan's mind, the woman's stature was exemplar of her destiny since women over generations had been squashed down by burden bearing.[1]

Although feminists might deny this equation of anatomy and destiny, the fact is that the female reproductive function is a crucial factor in determining a woman's social role in tribal societies.[2] Women's roles as gatherers, and their contributions to tribal subsistence, were also important in defining status.[3]

In the course of contact between Indian tribes and European colonists, the gender roles in Indian societies changed under pressures of changing subsistence patterns and European ideas about women. Since women's roles were in the domestic sphere, as Rosaldo noted, the effects of cultural contact were less for them than they were for men. Women's roles as child bearers and contributors to subsistence were not threatening to white society and were less affected than those of men. In situations of contact, women become the custodians of traditional cultural values.[4]

If anthropologists build models of culture, historians can show the effects of cultural contact over time. They can give life to the models, in this case by providing the detail of the lives of Choctaw women in Mississippi over a period from the initial European contact through the establishment of the Choctaw reservation in 1918. Since Choctaw women have not left the written records that are the usual stuff of history, however, the recreation of their lives must rely on descriptions by ethnographers and white, male observers, which must be filtered through a lens of cultural understanding based on experience and on anthropological models.

The Choctaw tribe in Mississippi presents an excellent case study of the effects of European contact on women's roles. The experience of proto-Choctaw communities with Europeans began early in recorded history of the Americas, and their southeastern homeland has been subject to the longest historical impact of European exploration and colonization of any part of the country. The records of European observers and later ethnographers about the Choctaw people are extensive.[5]

The seven reservation communities in central Mississippi that constitute the contemporary Mississippi Band of Choctaw Indians have survived vagaries of European contact and policies of the United States government and remain as a distinctive cultural group which has preserved its language to a remarkable degree. The contrast between their survival as strongly knit reservation communities and the relative acculturation of the Choctaw Nation in Oklahoma is evidence of the persistence of a matrilineal culture base.

Indian women in the southeast encountered European men soon after Hernando de Soto and his *entrada* arrived in 1539, landing probably somewhere on Tampa Bay, although the actual landfall is still a matter of debate. From this first major encounter, Indian women became intermediaries between their people and European males. De Soto encountered the Lady of Cofitchaqui in what is now northwestern Georgia in 1541. Accounts vary. In one, she arrived in a litter born on the shoulders of men; in another, in a canoe. In one, she gave de Soto a gift of pearls. In another, she was taken captive, along with casks of fresh-water pearls that represented her wealth. The varying accounts indicate a certain ambivalence in the minds of European men toward Indian women—met as equals, or as potential subjects willing to give gifts, or as enemies to be captured.[6]

The historic Choctaws had no such dramatic female leader as the Lady of Cofitchaqui. The first major European account of their social structure identified four male statuses—*Mingos*, chiefs of the nation, of villages, and war chiefs; *atacoulitoupa*, Beloved Men, a council of old, wise men; *tasca*, warriors; and *atac emittla*, young men who had not "struck a blow in battle" or who had killed only women and children.[7]

Choctaw men reportedly did not want to attack enemy villages for fear the males would flee and leave only women and children to be killed. Young warriors would thus have to remain in this lowest category.[8]

The categories served to define men in their public roles. This seeming disparagement of women as objects of killing actually reveals the basic complementarity of male and female roles in Choctaw society. Men did not demean women but rather expressed what was proper male behavior—to kill other men. War allowed Choctaw men to establish their honor, bravery, endurance, and status by their exploits against enemies. It was not shameful for women to be women; it was rather of low status for men to act in less than manly ways. Women had their roles and expected behaviors in life, and they complemented those of men.

Stickball games are an excellent example of this complementary aspect of role definition and its public display. Choctaw communities challenged each other, and tens, and sometimes hundreds of men, naked except for a belt or loincloth with a horsehair tail behind, flailed wildly with sticks as they chased the deerskin ball toward the goals.[9] The games posed a crucial test of Choctaw manhood because they subjected men to the judgment of the women of the tribe. If a man did not perform according to the standards of the society, women would rush forward to throw a skirt around him. The Choctaw male thus suffered a supreme insult, because he was not acting as a man. Such an insult led to conflict between tribes in about 1790 when the Creeks and the Choctaws played a game. During its course a Creek warrior threw a petticoat on a Choctaw, an insult that led to a vicious combat.[10]

Wives of the losing players staged their own version of the game to avenge the loss. According to one account, they played naked except "for the parts which modesty dictates they shall cover."[11] The stakes on the outcome were equally high. The parallels between men's and women's games emphasize the separate but equal status of Choctaw women.

Men's games had two significant outcomes. They established the superiority of one group of men over another, a superiority based on the power of the medicine men of each group as much as the skill and bravery of the players. They also demonstrated a cultural system (non-capitalist) of property-exchange through gambling. Women and men both gambled on the outcomes of the men's games. Women controlled their own property, and they felt free to dispose of it on the outcome of male prowess. They might, however, find themselves the stakes in a game when their husbands wagered them, and themselves in extreme circumstances. "When they [men] have lost all, they wager their wives for a certain time, and after that wager themselves for a limited time." The stake may have been labor, sexuality, or both. For men, it was undoubtedly labor. The willingness of men to subject themselves to temporary servitude indicates that human labor was part of the medium of exchange in Choctaw society for both men and women.[12]

Women controlled property in another way. Although men were hunters, women controlled the distribution and preparation of the meat that men killed. A man who killed a deer would leave the carcass and walk home to tell his wife where it was. She would take the family horse to carry home the meat, and she thus assumed the right to distribute it as she saw fit.[13]

Finally, women were farmers. Although a French observer characterized them as "slaves to their husbands" because they "work the ground, sow, and harvest the crop," such activity gave them control over a significant part of the Choctaw subsistence base.[14]

Women were the center of Choctaw society. Descent and rights to use property passed through the female line. Society was structured in matrilineages. A Choctaw origin story told how the Great Spirit divided the people who emerged from *Nanih Waiya*, the mother mound within which he had created them. He placed one group on the north side of the mound, and one on the east, thus establishing the two *iksas* (moieties). He then gave them the law of marriage. Children were to take the *iksa* of their mother, and a person must always marry into the opposite *iksa*.[15]

These matrilineal structures regulated marriage and social relationships. In keeping with the matrilineal kinship system, women were accorded a fair degree of latitude in the choice of a husband. Marriages were essentially arranged by families through exchange of gifts, but the marriage ceremony consisted of a ritualized pursuit in which the young man chased the young woman. If she allowed herself to be caught, the marriage was confirmed. If not, the disappointed suitor withdrew.[16]

Women were recognized because of the achievements of their children. They stood in special relationship to the brother's children, and their brothers had special relationships with their children. Women controlled political power in that a chief's nephew, his sister's son, generally inherited his power.[17] After a death, the *iksa* of the widow or widower piled up the bones of the dead and thus acknowledged the opposite moiety.

Iksas cut across town lines, and the towns were scattered among the three major geographical and political divisions of the nation in the 18th century. A man could travel throughout the Choctaw country and find himself accepted by members of his *iksa* in every village.[18] Matrilineal ties of kinship thus bound villages and divisions of the Choctaw nation together. Although women did not have voices in tribal government, they were the audience who determined the standards of male behavior. They controlled property and were certainly individuals in their own rights.

THE EFFECTS OF TRADE AND TREATIES

Choctaw society existed by virtue of carefully defined systems of kinship and male/female power. European colonizing disrupted those systems. Deerskins became a medium of trade with English entrepreneurs in Charleston and Augusta. Women's status because of their power to distribute food diminished when the hides of the animals became more important than the meat. Deerskins went increasingly to the trade market, and women's labor was thus commodified in economic terms rather than subsistence terms. The Choctaws produced more skins for the Louisiana trade than did any other nation throughout the 1750s.[19] But even hides became increasingly scarce during the early nineteenth century. When the Choctaws abandoned villages on the eastern edge of their territory along the Tombigbee River as a result of warfare with the Creeks during the late

Revolutionary War period, much of the deer population had already been hunted out. The Choctaw subsistence base was shrinking.[20]

After 1789, the Choctaws confronted a new colonial government, the United States. They found themselves under pressure to sign treaties of peace and friendship with the new government, but also to cede land so that the United States could consolidate territory against the possible threat of French and Spanish invasion from the west and the south. In 1803, 1805, and 1816, Choctaw men signed treaties ceding lands on the edges of the homeland.[21]

The ceded lands were hunting territories which were becoming increasingly unproductive. Their loss did not affect the status of Choctaw women whose control of land depended on farming. It did affect the ability of the Choctaw nation to be self-sufficient, and dependency on trade goods increased. Domesticated cattle were introduced into the nation by Louis Durant, Hardy Perry, and Louis and Michael LeFlore, white settlers, in the late 1790s.[22] Subsistence shifted from hunting to agriculture and husbandry as the deer herds dwindled in the eastern territory. Shifts in population and changes in subsistence undermined the traditional village/clan structure of Choctaw society. Villages were abandoned as people dispersed to find new grazing lands for cattle. A group of about one hundred people, described as having no clan affiliation, settled near David Folsom's home because he promised them a share of tribal annuities from the Treaty of 1816. His power as a mixed-blood leader replaced traditional maternal clan ties.[23]

By the second decade of the nineteenth century, cloth became the commodity for which Choctaws would trade food and labor.[24] As cloth became part of the fabric of Choctaw life, Choctaw women took on a new role. In 1814, John Schermerhorn reported that Indian women were weaving and knitting large quantities of cloth. By 1820, Jedidiah Morse could report that Choctaw women spun and wove ten thousand yards of cloth in one year, and that the Indians (one must assume he referred to both men and women) were raising large crops of corn. There is ample evidence that women continued to farm throughout the early 1800s. Crops now included, beside corn, "beans, melons, and cotton." Domesticated cattle had now replaced deer as a source of subsistence, and men raised large herds of cattle and had "laid aside hunting, as a business," though some still hunted "for amusement." [25]

Although subsistence patterns were changing, marriage customs persisted. Polygamy was common, marriage ceremonies non-existent, and Morse declared Choctaw morals, "very loose and corrupt."[26] If polygamy was still practiced in the nation, it was a practice adopted by white men as well. Indeed, it played an important role in Indian-white relationships. The influx of white traders and settlers into Choctaw territory in the late eighteenth century led to a new role for some Choctaw women—wives to white men. These intermarriages produced a new element in the society.

Greenwood Leflore (b. June 3, 1800), who would become chief of the Choctaws in 1829, was of mixed French and Choctaw descent. His father, Louis, was a trader who married Rebecca and Nancy Cravat, granddaughters of an English trader and his Choctaw wife, and daughters of a French trader and a mixed-blood Choctaw mother. On their mother's side, they were nieces of Pushmataha, chief of the southern district of the nation.[27]

David Folsom (b. January 25, 1791) was the son of Nathaniel Folsom, one of three sons of a Scotch-Irish couple who settled in the Choctaw country in the late 1700s. Nathaniel and his brother Ebenezer both married Choctaw women and raised large families. Nathaniel had two Choctaw wives, Aiahnichih Ohoyoh (David's mother) and her sister, who were cousins of Mushulatubbee, chief of the northeast district of the nation. By them he had twenty-four children.[28]

A number of white men became politically influential during the latter part of the 18th century because of their trading activities and their connections with the U.S. government and with Choctaw women of prominent families. Their mixed-blood offspring in turn intermarried. David Folsom, Nathaniel's son, married Rhoda Nail, daughter of Henry Nail, a Revolutionary War hero, and his Choctaw wife. John Pitchlynn, an Englishman who lived in the nation and became the primary translator in the negotiations between its leaders and agents of the American government, married Sophia Folsom, daughter of Ebenezer Folsom, and fathered a son, Peter, who later played an important role in the politics of the Choctaw after their removal west of the Mississippi.[29]

These complex relationships of blood and marriage served to create a group of leaders who stood at the crux of two worlds. Although intermarriage is generally perceived as a dilution of cultural identity, in Choctaw country, given the relatively small number of white men and the matrilineal structure of society, women drew men into their spheres of family influence. White men were certainly agents of change in Choctaw society, but their offspring considered themselves Choctaws, spoke the language, and grew up with Choctaw customs.

White fathers raised their children in the Choctaw nation, but they wanted them to be educated in the white man's way. It is here that Choctaw women began to lose influence over their offspring. Nathaniel Folsom sent his son David to school in Kentucky, although he remained

that women controlled their own lands and passed them on to their children at least until 1830.[41]

Other laws passed by Choctaw leaders also affected women's roles. In the Six Towns district, Mingo Hwoolatahoomah and his captains passed a number of laws, including ones against infanticide, polygamy and adultery. It is ironic that the law against polygamy, if adopted by the Choctaw leadership during the late 1700s, could well have prevented the births of Greenwood Leflore and David Folsom, both of whose fathers entered polygamous marriages with Choctaw women. The power of the law against infanticide, which the missionary Cyrus Kingsbury characterized as a "horrid practice," was demonstrated when a woman and her husband were publicly whipped in Hwoolatahoomah's district for killing their baby.[42]

Education and laws, however, affected a relatively small number of the Choctaws in Mississippi. By 1830 most retained traditional customs, including matrilineal residence and female control of property and children. When a woman married, it was common for her husband to build a cabin joined to that of his mother-in-law by a covered porch. A few double cabins still exist in some contemporary Choctaw communities. Men might also maintain homes near their mothers. Tomalachah, whose wife was dead, lived with his children in a cabin about forty yards from that of his mother, who was a widow living alone. Sometimes a father-in-law and his son-in-law might share land and a double cabin when a mother-in-law had died.[43]

Men who shared a relationship through the female line might live in a double cabin and maintain separate households. Ishtahka and his "nephew" (a term implying the relationship of mother's brother to child) Cubbee lived in a double house and farmed their fields and stored their crops separately. Hochefo and Ahpototubbee lived near each other and cultivated separate fields, although under a common fence, because their wives were sisters. They were, however, considered as separate families.[44]

When a marriage ended, the mother took the children. Depending on her situation, she might return to her family or remain on the land as head of her own household.[45] Polygamy persisted, despite missionary injunctions and laws. Tuskahmahah had two wives, of which Ioola, a woman of about forty, with two children, was one. He also had many mistresses. Every month he made a circuit of the wives and mistresses, and he was welcome at each house. None of the women ever complained of neglect because he was willing to do whatever work was needed around the cabin while he visited. He finally moved west in the Choctaw removal of 1831–32, leaving Ioola in Mississippi and perhaps seeking new conquests in the western territory. Tuskahmahah gives a new meaning to the term "circuit rider" among the Choctaws in Mississippi.[46]

Although it might appear that men were becoming settled farmers, the evidence is colored by the fact that it was given before commissioners attempting to determine Choctaw rights to individual land claims. It is probably true that men and women both were tilling the fields because of the scarcity of deer, but men continued to hunt. Male and female roles were changing in some respects by 1830, but for the majority of Choctaws, subsistence farming and hunting meant that the core of gender identity still remained.

THE TREATY OF DANCING RABBIT CREEK

The persistence of Choctaw customs, despite the effects of constitution, laws, and education, led to continuing pressure on the nation to give up its claims to its lands in Mississippi and move to the lands west of the Mississippi River that had been guaranteed to it in the Treaty of Doaks' Stand in 1820. In January of 1830, the Mississippi State legislature forced the issue of removal by extending its laws over the Choctaw Nation. Mississippi law now made it a crime for a man to declare himself the chief of an Indian tribe.[47]

This presumption of jurisdiction compelled the leaders of the nation to confront the fact that Andrew Jackson was committed to a policy of removing all Indians from lands east of the Mississippi. White settlers wanted cheap land, and the sale of public land was the major source of revenue for an economically fragile federal government.

Faced with the inevitable, a small group of Choctaws signed the Treaty of Dancing Rabbit Creek on September 27, 1830. There had been no outspoken Choctaw women to resist pressure toward land cessions in the past, as Nancy Ward had done among the Cherokees.[48] But if there is no evidence that women spoke out in councils, their influence was nonetheless felt at the negotiations for the Treaty of Dancing Rabbit Creek in 1830. The United States commissioner occupied one side of the ground, and the Choctaw representatives sat in a semicircle opposite them, but in the center of this assemblage sat "seven of the oldest women in the Choctaw camp." The government interpreter, John McKee, promised them that he would interpret accurately the words of the commissioners "And if I tell a lie, you may cut my neck off." Although it is unlikely that the old women would have cut off McKee's head, they certainly served to keep him honest.[49]

The decline of deer, the introduction of cattle, and shifting subsistence patterns had changed Choctaw culture, but the land had still been tribal land. The Treaty of Dancing Rabbit Creek, the first removal treaty signed in the southeast, offered Choctaws the opportunity to remain in Mississippi, but as citizens of the state and as individual land owners. The fourteenth article provided that Choctaw individuals who wanted to remain in Mississippi could take 640 acre allotments from the ceded land and remain on them as citizens of the state.

The Choctaws who chose to remain in Mississippi escaped the hardships of those who moved in the winter of 1831–32. Removal was marked by extraordinary hardships—bitterly cold weather, cholera, lack of food and medical supplies, and physical danger. A steamboat transporting Choctaws along the Arkansas River had a boiler explode, with the loss of approximately three hundred Choctaw lives.[50]

Those who remained behind in Mississippi escaped the physical suffering of those who were forced to emigrate, but they were subjected to an oppressive legal process and often forced removal of a different kind as they were driven from their lands by white men. When they tried to take allotments guaranteed by the treaty, the overwhelming majority were denied those rights. Although they lost land rights, they maintained their communities and identity in Mississippi. Women held families together and took on new roles to contribute to economic survival. Their traditional rights to property, however, were redefined within the American legal system. Women could claim the property of deceased husbands, a system contradicting traditional matrilineal property rights but affirming the laws that Choctaw leaders had passed in 1826. Women gained rights to individual property as inheritors of husbands' claims.

The Fourteenth Article of the Treaty of Dancing Rabbit Creek laid out very specific procedures for individual claimants. They must register with the government agent, William Ward, within six months of the ratification of the treaty, and they would receive land for themselves and their dependent children. If they remained on the land for five years thereafter they would receive a title in fee simple.[51]

Ward, the Choctaw agent, sent two lists of claimants to the Office of Indian Affairs. One contained sixty-eight names, and the other seventy-one. The largest number of claimants were white men with Choctaw wives and children (twenty-two) or mixed-blood men (twenty-four). Ten mixed-blood women were listed. These figures are either striking evidence of the extent to which control of land was passing into the hands of white men and their mixed-blood offspring, or evidence that these people were most conversant with the American legal system. In either case, they stood to benefit from the Fourteenth Article. Although the list does not indicate degree of blood, names and historic data show only seventeen full-blood Choctaw men and nine full-blood Choctaw women on the lists.[52]

Ward's registers of claimants were woefully incomplete. The agent appointed by the Secretary of War to identify the lands to be set aside for Choctaws under the Fourteenth Article, George Martin, heard numerous complaints that Ward had actively discouraged claimants—he had told them that he would not register them, or he had not written their names in his book, or he had lost pages from the register. Martin discounted the claims as the work of white lawyers and land speculators who inspired Indians to make claims they could represent in exchange for part of the land to be gained. Nevertheless, confronted with possible clouds on legal titles, Congress established a commission to investigate the validity of the claims.[53]

Two commissions were necessary to deal with the complexity of the claims. One met during 1837–38 and the other from 1842 to 1846. The first investigated 261 cases. Of the 244 records of testimony in the National Archives, fifty-eight of the claimants were female and 186 were male. Of the 401 cases reported in Ralph Graves's journal, there were seventy female claimants (thirty-six of whom were deceased, their claims represented by others), and sixty-four widows representing their husbands' claims.

The rights of Choctaw women dwindled under the increasingly bureaucratic and legalistic operations of the United States government. The Choctaws, because of the matrilineal kinship system, considered that a woman's husband, whether Indian or not, became part of her family. Several white men with Choctaw wives and children had filed claims with the 1837 commission. The treaty provided that Choctaw heads of families were eligible for claims, and the commission interpreted that language to include white men who had married into the Choctaw Nation and had acquired rights therein because of Choctaw custom. By 1842, however, Congress changed its mind, to the disadvantage of Choctaw women. The law establishing the commission in that year explicitly forbade claims made by white men with Indian families. Indian women who had the misfortune to marry white men found themselves and their children deprived of lands that under traditional Choctaw custom would have been theirs. It also indicated the increasingly more apparent desire of the state of Mississippi to see all the Choctaws removed from its borders.[54]

Women's rights and traditional roles in their own societies were subsumed in the legal system that defined land rights under the Treaty. Female headed households constituted a significant proportion of the Choctaw population in Mississippi after 1830. They and their kin suffered significant dislocation because of forcible dispossession, but they managed to maintain traditional patterns of social relationship. Women maintained their households, although in a number of cases their husbands had gone west. The Treaty of Dancing Rabbit Creek was blind to sex in designating heads of families for purposes of claims. Women could claim as heads of families, and they could also claim on the basis of widow's rights. The Treaty implicitly put in place the conventions of English common law with regard to women's rights.[55]

Claims of both men and women, based on the legalities of treaty rights and federal legislation, were finally denied by the American legal system. Of the 1073 claims placed on the docket of the 1842 commission, only 163 claimants were finally awarded land.[56] The female claimants on the lists were mixed-blood women or widows, not full-blood women claiming in their own right.

The status of women in Choctaw society changed as a result of laws and treaties. The control of land and descent that they exercised by virtue of matrilineal clan affiliations passed out of their hands. The social change was reflected in kinship patterns, which were part of the basic fabric of traditional Choctaw culture. Traditional Choctaw matrilineal kinship terminology grouped the father's sisters and their female offspring through all generations together under the term "aunts" ("grandmother" in the Six Towns district in the southern part of the nation). As John Edwards, a Presbyterian missionary put it, they counted "aunts in a row."[57]

Although the laws passed by the Choctaws in the Indian Territory gave men and women equality in rights to property, men came to dominate government and family life. The kinship terminology reported by Cyrus Byington in 1859 revealed a pattern in which the father's male relatives formed a distinctive lineage. The father's sister's son and his descendants through males were classified as fathers. The new system cut across matrilineages and matrilineal clans and emphasized descent through the male line.[58]

The shift to male lineage was a function of new systems of property ownership, elected government, and subsistence introduced by white men, both those who implemented government policy and those who entered Indian nations and married Indian women. These new notions of property were most explicit in the treaty-making process when Indian men bargained away land rights traditionally controlled by women.[59]

The Choctaws who remained in Mississippi after 1830 lost virtually all their property, but through at least the 1840s they maintained customs and communities and a traditional kinship system based on female lineages.[60] Anecdotal evidence appeared in the testimony given by claimants before the two government commissions investigating claims under the Fourteenth Article of the Treaty of Dancing Rabbit Creek. In several instances in testimony before the 1842 commission, witnesses identified female claimants as "aunt," although the commissioner (Ralph Graves) noted that they were only distantly related. Women's sons and sons-in-law still came to live with them.[61]

By the 1930s, the kinship systems in Mississippi and Oklahoma were very similar. They had largely changed in Indian Territory by 1859, when Cyrus Byington made his reports. There is no historical evidence to indicate when they began to change in Mississippi, but they had disappeared by 1933, when Fred Eggan did his fieldwork.[62]

It is obvious that women's roles in Choctaw society were changing as non-Indian men came into and influenced the nation. In Indian Territory, women became subject to the laws of an emerging Choctaw Nation that was fashioning itself along the lines of American society. In central Mississippi, women played an important role in providing stability to the communities who were deprived of land and legal standing in Mississippi after the treaty of Dancing Rabbit Creek in 1830. The persistence of matrilineal kinship systems, matrilocal residence patterns, and female-oriented farming indicates that the Choctaws in Mississippi after 1830 retained an important part of their cultural identity even as they lost the land that had traditionally anchored their communities and as they entered a new economic system. Men picked cotton for wages, but they also went off to hunt. Women made baskets to sell in Mobile and New Orleans, but they also continued to farm when land was available.[63]

Women in Mississippi never entered the system of land ownership which federal Indian policy had tried to impose upon them. They retained their traditional roles as centers of kin groups and providers of an important part of the subsistence base. When they entered the market economy by selling firewood and baskets, they capitalized on female activities. The ultimate decline of matrilineage in Mississippi was probably due to the shifting population patterns caused by often forcible dispossession.

The different adaptations of Choctaws west of the Mississippi River, and those who remained behind in Mississippi are evidence of the roles that women played both in the introduction of new influences into Choctaw life through their marriages with white men and in the persistence of traditional cultural forms of kinship and community.

NOTES

1. Joseph A. Gilfillan, "The Ojibways in Minnesota," *Collections of the Minnesota Historical Society* 9 (1901): 54.

2. Peggy R. Sanday, "Female Status in the Public Domain," in *Woman, Culture, and Society*, ed. Michelle Zimbalist Rosaldo and Louise Lamphere (Stanford: Stanford University Press, 1974), 189–90.

3. Rosaldo asserts a general principle that the more men and women participate equally in the household tasks, and the more equal their contributions to the resource base, the more equal their status. See Michelle Zimbalist Rosaldo, "Woman, Culture, and Society: A Theoretical Overview," in *Woman, Culture and Society*, 17–42.

4. See for example Louise S. Spindler, "Menominee Women and Culture Change," *American Anthropological Association Memoir 91* (Menasha, Wisconsin: American Anthropological Association, 1962), 16–17.

5. By the term proto-Choctaw I mean that the historical entity known to Europeans as the Choctaw tribe emerged in response to changes among Indian people caused by European contact, and that the unity of the Choctaw tribe was recognized and fostered as much by European leaders as it was by the Choctaws themselves. For an overview of Choctaw tribal identity, see Christopher S. Peebles, "Paradise Lost, Strayed, and Stolen: Prehistoric Social Devolution in the Southeast," in *The Burden of Being Civilized: An Anthropological Perspective on the Discontents of Civilization*, ed. Miles Richardson and Malcolm C. Webb. Southern Anthropological Proceedings, No. 18 (Athens: The University of Georgia Press, 1986), 24–40.

6. Edward Gaylord Bourne, ed., *Narratives of the Career of Hernando de Soto in the Conquest of Florida as told by a Knight of Elvas and in a Relation by Luys Hernandez de Biedma, factor of the Expedition*, trans. Buckingham Smith, two vols. (New York: Allerton Book Co., 1922; reprinted New York: AMS Press Inc., 1973); Garcilaso de la Vega, *The Florida of the Inca*, transl. and ed. John Grief Varner and Jeannette Johnson Varner (Austin: University of Texas Press, 1988), 298–99.

7. John R. Swanton, "An Early Account of the Choctaw Indians," *American Anthropological Association Memoir 5* (1918), 22.

8. Bernard Romans, *A Concise Natural History of East and West Florida: Containing an account of the natural produce of all the southern part of British America in the three kingdoms of nature particularly the animal and vegetable. Illustrated with 12 copper plates and 2 whole sheet maps* (New York: Printed for the Author, 1775), vol. 1, 72. By the early nineteenth century, men's names could be recognized by the suffix "tubbee" or a variation thereof, a conventionalized spelling of the Choctaw word "abi" or "ubi"—killer. H.B. Cushman, *History of the Choctaw, Chickasaw and Natchez Indians*, ed. Angie Debo (New York: Russell & Russell, 1962), 51; Cyrus Byington, *A Dictionary of the Choctaw Language*, ed. J.R. Swanton, and H.S. Halbert. The Smithsonian Institution, Bureau of American Ethnography, Bulletin 46 (Washington, D.C.: Government Printing Office, 1915), 73.

9. George Catlin, *Letters and Notes on the Manners, Customs and Condition of the North American Indians* (New York: Dover Press, 1973), vol. 1, 123.

10. H.B. Cushman, *History of the Choctaw, Chickasaw and Natchez Indians* (Greenville, Texas: Headlight Printing House, 1899), 133.

11. John Swanton, *Source Material for the Social and Ceremonial Life of The Choctaw Indians*, Bureau of American Ethnology Bulletin, No. 103 (Washington, D.C.: Government Printing Office, 1931), 140–141.

12. Swanton, "An Early Account," 68.

13. Cushman (1962), 180.

14. Swanton, "An Early Account," 59.

15. Henry S. Halbert, "Nanih Waiya, the Sacred Mound of the Choctaws," *Publications of the Mississippi Historical Society* 2 (1899): 230. The names of the moieties given by the French were *kashapa okla* and *okla in holahta* or *hattak in holahta* (the French versions) or the *inhulahta* and the *imoklasha*.

16. Cushman (1962), 309–310.

17. John Edwards, "The Choctaw Indians in the Middle of the Nineteenth Century," *Chronicles of Oklahoma* 10 (1932): 393.

18. Byington, *A Dictionary of the Choctaw Language*, 180; Halbert, "Nanih Waiya, the Sacred Mound of the Choctaws," 230; Swanton, *Source Material*, 55–56, 76–77. The divisions were identified by French observers as the *okla hannali*, the *okla falaya*, and the *okla tannap*. The Choctaw word for "people" is *Okla*. See various accounts in Dunbar Rowland and A.G. Sanders, *Mississippi Provincial Archives: French Dominion* (Jackson, Miss.: Press of the Mississippi Department of Archives and History, 1927–32), vol. 1, 84, 95, 151–53; Cushman, (1899), 150.

19. Daniel B. Usner, Jr., *Indians, Settlers, & Slaves in a Frontier Exchange Economy: The Lower Mississippi Valley Before 1783* (Chapel Hill: University of North Carolina Press, 1992), 96.

20. Richard White, *The Roots of Dependency: Subsistence, Environment, and Social Change Among the Choctaws, Pawnees and Navajos* (Lincoln: University of Nebraska Press, 1983), 96–146.

21. Charles J. Kappler, *Indian Affairs: Laws and Treaties* (Washington, D.C.: Government Printing Office, 1904–41), vol. 2, 69–70, 87–88, 137.

22. Cyrus Byington to Jeremiah Evarts, Yaknokchaya, 20 July 1829, vol. 3, folder 93, Series 18.2.3, Papers of the American Board of Commissioners for Foreign Missions, Houghton Library, Harvard University (hereafter cited as ABCFM); Cushman (1962), 331; James P. Morrison, *Seven Constitutions (Anumpa Ulhpisa Untuklo). Government of the Choctaw Republic, 1826–1906* (Durant, Oklahoma: Choctaw Bilingual Education Program, Southeastern Oklahoma State University, 1977), 2.

23. Journal of Mayhew Mission, 23 March 1822, vol. 1, folder 79; Cyrus Kingsbury to Jeremiah Evarts, at Mingo Mushulatubbee's, Choctaw Nation, 7 Oct. 1822, vol. 1, folder 109; ABCFM.

24. Kingsbury to Jeremiah Evarts, Elliot, 3 August 1820, vol. 2, folder 66; Kingsbury to James Finley, 12 August 1819, vol. 2, folder 32; Kingsbury to Jeremiah Evarts, Elliot, 26 February 1820, vol. 2, folder 52; ABCFM.

25. John F. Schermerhorn, "Report Respecting the Indians Inhabiting the Western Parts of the United States," *Collections of the Massachusetts Historical Society*, vol. 2, second series (Boston, 1814; reprinted Charles C. Little and James Brown, 1846), 20–21; Journal of Hearings held by Murray and Vroom, Entry 270, Choctaw Removal Records, Record Group 75, National Archives; "Journal of Proceedings," kept by Commissioner Graves, Entry 275, Choctaw Removal

Records, Record Group 75, National Archives (hereafter "Journal of Proceedings"); Jedidiah Morse, D.D., *A Report to the Secretary of War of the United States, on Indian Affairs, Comprising a Narrative of a Tour Performed in the Summer of 1820, Under a Commission from the President of the United States, for the Purpose of Ascertaining, for the Use of the Government, the Actual State of the Indian Tribes in our Country: . . .* (Washington, D.C.: Davis & Force, et al., 1822), 11, 182–83.

26. Morse, 183.

27. Greenwood was Rebecca's son. Florence Rebecca Ray, *Chieftain Greenwood Leflore and the Choctaw Indians of the Mississippi Valley: Last Chief of Choctaws East of Mississippi River*, 2nd edition (Memphis, Tenn.: C.A. Davis Printing Company, Inc., 1936), 33.

28. Ralph Folsom and Alberta Fitzpatrick McBride, "Choctaw Folsoms," delivered at Hibernian Hall, Charleston, South Carolina on August 11, 1979, at the 64th Annual Reunion and 70th Anniversary of the Folsom Family Association of America, Inc.; Cushman (1962), 328.

29. W. David Baird, *Peter Pitchlynn: Chief of the Choctaws* (Norman: University of Oklahoma Press, 1972), xv.

30. Cushman (1962), 290; Dunbar Roland, *Mississippi, Comprising Sketches of Counties, Towns, Events, Institutions, and Persons, Arranged in Cyclopedic Form*; 3 vols. (Atlanta: Southern Historical Publishing Association, 1907), Vol. 2, 72; Baird, 21–22.

31. Journal of Elliot Mission, vol. 1, Folder 1, p. 6, ABCFM.

32. Kingsbury to Choctaw chiefs, 11 August 1819, vol. 2, folder 33, ABCFM.

33. Journal of Elliot Mission, 9 August 1819, vol. 1, folder 1, p. 8, ABCFM. Although there is no list of the men present at the council, the list of signatories to the Treaty of Doaks' Stand in 1820 includes the names of a number of mixed-blood men: Captain Bob Cole, Captain Jerry Carney, Captain William Beams, Captain James Pitchlynn, Captain James Garland, Captain Joel H. Nail, Captain Daniel McCurtain, George Turnbull, Captain Thomas McCurtain, Captain John Cairns, William Hay, Captain Samuel Cobb, Lewis Brashears, Captain Sam. Magee, Joseph Nelson, Greenwood Leflore, Archibald MaGee, Ben Burris, Lewis Perry, Captain Charles Durant, and Pierre Durant. Kappler, vol. 2, 194–95.

34. The first book published in Choctaw was a spelling book, which appeared in 1825. Alfred Wright and Cyrus Byington, *A spelling Book, written in the Chahta Language, with an English Translation; Prepared and Published Under the Direction of the Missionaries in the Chahta Nation, with the Aid of Captain David Folsom, Interpreter* (Cincinnati: Published by Morgan, Lodge and Fisher for the Missionary Society, 1825). See James Constantine Pilling, *Bibliography of the Muskhogean Languages* (Washington: Government Printing Office, 1889) for a list of extant early Choctaw texts.

35. Byington to Evarts, Gibeon, 2 Sept. 1826, vol. 3, folder 78; Byington to Evarts, Aikhuna, 7 July 1826, vol. 3, folder 77; Byington to Evarts (extract), Aikhuna, 1 July 1826, vol. 3, folder 76; ABCFM.

36. Kingsbury to Evarts, Elliot, Sabbath evening, 2 Sept. 1821, vol. 2, folder 85, ABCFM.

37. At Mayhew, the second mission established by the American Board, in 1827, the older boys harvested wheat, oats, and rye, for which they received a wage of $.50 per day. The younger boys chopped wood for $5 a month. The girls had made

thirty-five shirts, sixty-six pairs of pantaloons, four coats, one cloak, fifteen vests, seven hunting frocks, sixty-nine dresses, sixty-three aprons, thirty pair of stockings, sixty dozen candles, and three barrels of soap. *Missionary Herald* 23 (September 1827), 279.

38. *Missionary Herald* 16 (February 1820), 32; Congress, House, Board of Commissioners—Foreign Missions, *Memorial of the Prudential Committee of the American Board of Commissioners for Foreign Missions, Respecting the Property of the Board in the Choctaw Nation*, Document No. 194, 22nd. Cong., 1st sess., 2 April 1832, p. 14.

39. Hannah Bradshaw finally accepted the cake when she was told that her little sister would have something "when the opportunity presented," and the sister, Frutilla Townsley, finally joined the school. *Missionary Herald* 20 (August 1824), 251.

40. *Missionary Herald* 18 (September 1827), 281.

41. American Board of Commissioners for Foreign Missions, *Report of the American Board of Commissioners for Foreign Missions, Compiled from Documents Laid Before the Board, at the Eighteenth Annual Meeting, Which was held in the City of New York, October 10, 11, 12, 13 & 15, 1827* (Boston: Printed for the Board by Crocker and Brewster, 1827), xxvi–xxvii; Ray, 47. Major evidence for land usage patterns and descent come from the Journal of Hearings held by Murray and Vroom and the "Journal of Proceedings."

42. *Missionary Herald* 24 (January 1823), 6.

43. Testimony of Tomalachah in case of Jim Tom, half negro and half Indian, Case 91; testimony of Tomalachah in case of Sally Hoyo, Case 92; Testimony of Tomahlachah, Case 86; Testimony of Tishopiah in case of Hachah, Case 98; "Journal of Proceedings."

44. Ishtahka, Case 96; Hochefo, Case 97; "Journal of Proceedings."

45. Testimony of Tahombee in case of Aoahtonubbee, Case 51, "Journal of Proceedings."

46. Testimony of Ioola, Case 342, "Journal of Proceedings."

47. A. Hutchinson, comp., *Code of Mississippi: Being an analytical compilation of the public and general status of the territory and state with tabular references to the local and private acts from 1798 to 1848. With the national and state constitutions, assigns of the country by the Choctaw and Chickasaw Indians, and acts of Congress for the survey and sale of the lands and granting donations thereof to the state* (Jackson, Miss.: Price & Fall, State Printing, 1848), 136.

48. Theda Perdue, "Cherokee Women and the Trail of Tears," *The Journal of Women's History* 1 (1989): 15.

49. Henry S. Halbert, "The Story of the Treaty of Dancing Rabbit Creek," *Publications of the Mississippi Historical Society* 6 (1902): 382.

50. Grant Foreman, *Choctaw Removal*, new edition (Norman: University of Oklahoma Press, 1953), 44–70.

51. Kappler, vol. 2, 313.

52. Another thirteen men whose names imply that they were white (although they might have been mixed bloods) also appeared on the lists. Congress, Senate, *In Relation to the Location of Reservations Under the Choctaw Treaty of the 27th of September, 1830*, Document No. 1230, 23rd Cong., 1st sess., 11 April 1834, in *American State Papers*, Indian Affairs, vol. 2, p. 133.

53. The documents concerning the Choctaw claims are contained in the National Archives microfilm series M234, Choctaw Emigration and in entries, 262, 268–280, Choctaw Removal Records, Record Group 75, National Archives.

54. T. Hartley Crawford to J. C. Spencer, 7 March 1843, in 28th Cong., 1st Sess., *Message from the President of the United States Transmitting the Correspondence in Relation to the Proceedings and Conduct of the Choctaw Commission, under the Treaty of Dancing Rabbit Creek,* Senate Document 168, 30 January 1844, p. 75, 168.

55. Testimony of Tishopiah in case of Tiacubbee, Case 115; Miya, Case 183, "Journal of Proceedings."

56. Congress, House, *Message from the President of the United States Transmitting a Report of the Secretary of War Relative to the Claims Arising Under the Choctaw Treaty, in Compliance with a Resolution of the House of Representatives of the 31st of December Last,* House Document 189, 29th Cong., 1st sess., 27 April 1846, pp. 2–3.

57. John Edwards, "The Choctaw Indians in the Middle of the Nineteenth Century," *Chronicles of Oklahoma* 10 (1932): 401–402.

58. Angie Debo, *The Rise and Fall of the Choctaw Republic* (Norman: University of Oklahoma Press, 1961), 77; Fred Eggan, "Historical Changes in the Choctaw Kinship System," *American Anthropologist* 39 (1937): 25, 36.

59. See John Phillip Reid, *A Law of Blood: The Primitive Law of the Cherokee Nation* (New York: New York University Press, 1970) for a discussion of the similar change in women's status among the Cherokees.

60. The data on kinship that mark this shift from a matrilineal to a patrilineal system were gathered in Oklahoma from 1859 through 1947 and in Mississippi in 1934. The earliest data were collected by Lewis Henry Morgan, based on schedules filled out by missionaries, and published in *Systems of Consanguinity and Affinity of the Human Family,* Smithsonian Contributions to Knowledge, vol. 17 (Washington, D.C.: Government Printing Office, 1871). Subsequent studies were done by Swanton, who published his kinship data in *Source Material,* 85–89; by Fred Eggan; and by Alexander Spoehr, *Changing Kinship Systems: A Study in the Acculturation of the Creeks, Cherokee, and Choctaw,* Field Museum of Natural History, Anthropological Series 33 (January 1947), 187–196.

61. Lucy, Case 90, "Journal of Proceedings." The witness, Tomalacha, called Lucy's mother, Onahhoka, "grandmother," a regional variant of matrilineal terminology. Ab-be-chunk-tah, Case 110; Hogla, Case 125; Nogue ah, Case 134; Testimony of Oglahtubbee (Jim Belongonah), Case 25; Testimony of Nemahtubbee, Case 134, "Journal of Proceedings."

62. Choctaw kinship terminology followed the anthropologically defined Crow model of matrilineal descent. Fred Eggan, "The Choctaw and their Neighbors in the Southeast: Acculturation Under Pressure," in *The American Indian: Perspectives for the Study of Social Change* (Chicago: Aldine Publishing Company, 1966), 19–20.

63. T.C. Stuart to I. L. Cochrane, Philadelphia, Mississippi, 31 October 1848, Office of Indian Affairs, Letters Received, Microfilm Series 234, roll 186, National Archives.

6

CAROL DOUGLAS SPARKS

THE LAND INCARNATE
NAVAJO WOMEN AND THE DIALOGUE
OF COLONIALISM, 1821–1870

The Navajos are an Athapaskan-speaking people who migrated into the Southwest, probably in the fourteenth or fifteenth century. Within two to three centuries, the Navajos encountered Hispanic and then Anglo expansion, and fought a series of wars to defend their land in what is now northern Arizona and New Mexico. First, the Navajos fought the Spanish, and then after Mexican Independence in 1821, the Navajos fought against the Mexicans. After the Anglo conquest of Mexico in 1848, uneasy Anglo-Navajo relations eventually erupted into full-fledged war in the late 1850s. As part of their campaign to subdue the Navajos, the U.S. Army envisioned a reservation and outpost, Ft. Sumner, at the Bosque Redondo (an arid, unhealthy locale further to the south in New Mexico), as a permanent home for them and for certain Apache tribes. Navajos who wanted peace with the Anglos as well as captured "hostile" Navajos were forced on the "Long Walk" to Ft. Sumner. Many Navajos died on the "Long Walk" and at Bosque Redondo, where disease and shortages of decent water and food created desperate conditions. Recognizing the failure of Bosque Redondo, the U.S. signed a peace treaty with the Navajos in 1868 that allowed them to return to their homeland, now to be recognized by the U.S. as the Navajo Reservation. Carol Douglas Sparks's article deals with Anglo images of Navajo women from the Spanish period to the Bosque Redondo period.

In October 1846, a small detachment of thirty American soldiers under the leadership of Captain John W. Reid forged into northwestern New Mexico, seeking the homeland of the Navajo Indians. Hoping to persuade tribal leaders to treat with American military officials, the Reid expedition carefully wound through looming mountains and precipitous gorges. Springs and meadows unexpectedly dotted stretches of apparent wasteland. Black seas of lava gave mute testimony of a violent geological past, and led soldiers to dream of precious metals and jewels blooming unseen in the earth.

Finally, the expedition stumbled into the heart of Navajoland, where hundreds of mounted warriors with their families surrounded the fragile party. Although surprised by their uninvited guests, the Navajos befriended the travelers, feting the Americans with food, games, races, and dancing. As his men gawked at this lavish display of exotic peoples and produce, Reid consulted with the aged, nearly crippled Narbona, frail headman of an aggressive tribe known to Anglo-Americans and Hispanos as the "Scourge of New Mexico."

All seemed to be going well until Narbona's wife, a woman denigrated by an American eye-witness as "a little squaw about fifty or sixty years of age, apparently, and dried and wrinkled," stood to denounce the intruders. Pointing to a notorious massacre of Apaches by an American-led party, this Cassandra prophesied a similar fate for her people should they accept Reid's invitation. So moving were her words that warriors surrounding the Americans began to murmur threateningly.

Fearing an imminent massacre, the American party desperately prepared for the worst. But Narbona quietly defused the crisis. At his signal, two young men stole up to his "cunning" wife, lifted her by the elbows, and carried her out of the camp. Instantly, an American observer reported, the gathering recovered its earlier equanimity.[1]

Similar images of Navajo harridans dominating a chaotic physical and social landscape grew more frequent in subsequent Anglo narratives, contrasting sharply with their earlier reputation as passively beautiful incarnations of a welcoming land. Pocahontas princess and emasculating harpy—these dichotomous images of nineteenth-century Navajo women served as archetypes of Anglo-American hopes, dreams, and fears of a mysterious land where wealth and glory, or sudden and violent death, lay in wait for the white adventurer. Deconstruction of these signs, or symbols of cultural significance, not only reveals the gender-coded fabric of nineteenth-century American colonialism and its patriarchal environmental ethos, but also peels back layers of Orientalist imagery to uncover the historically "real" women beneath.[2]

Textual analysis provides a useful tool in deconstructing such colonial imagery, but this exegesis must be firmly rooted in a broader historical context which incorporates political, social, economic, and intellectual factors.[3] Many Anglo texts exist which can be examined in this manner: letters, memoirs, poems, newspaper articles, even military and scientific reports. The "factual" content of most of these documents conceals their fictive origins: colonial authors created a reality drawn from their immediate surroundings, but filtered through their experiences and expectations.[4] Often, Anglo-American "fact" dramatically conflicted with the reality of Others.

Admittedly, this method reveals more about the way in which colonizers perceived and shaped those whom they colonized than it does the viewpoint of Others. Unfortunately, almost all early- and mid-nineteenth century accounts about Navajo women were left by colonialist males, and so reflect that orientation. Then how can we uncover this Other reality, especially that of women traditionally overlooked or manipulated by Anglo chroniclers? Anthropology provides important insights into the lives and culture of these women; traditional histories detail the chronology of events which affected them. But too often, individual Indian women are visible only in the documents of white colonizers, who saw rather than heard them. When utilizing these documents, we must decode female characters, both to decipher their utility to white, almost exclusively male, chroniclers, and to see the real women who actually participated in these events.

Vision reflected the relationship of Anglo-Americans to these women and to Nature. While native peoples enjoyed a mimetic relationship with their environment, Anglos perceived Nature—and those they considered its representatives—from outside.[5] This detachment gives extraordinary power to the viewer, who can look or turn away at will.[6] Likewise, the viewer controls the interpretation of vision, as he or she utilizes both past experiences and present agendas to interpret what is seen. Just as the eye cannot see without the brain to translate the retina's signals, neither can the viewer interpret vision without the medium of culture. Both the process of seeing and the resulting vision depend more upon the observer than the observed.

Hearing represents a much different process, as the speaker has more power to impose his or her voice upon a listener than an object has to force vision upon a viewer. As historians who seek native women's voices, we have to listen to what is seen, to hear that which is inaudible. By dissecting colonial constructions of women, we can read their actions as a "sign language" through which they communicate directly with us.

To properly decipher these women's signs, we must first place them within their cultural and historical context. Navajos of the first half of the nineteenth-century were a band people who ranged over the northwestern half of modern New Mexico, as well as northeastern Arizona. Like

Apaches, Navajos belong to the Athapaskan linguistic group, and probably migrated into the Southwest as late as the fourteenth or fifteenth century. Navajos and Apaches quickly became adept at attacking Pueblo and Hispanic settlements. Although the acquisition of the horse made marauders from both tribes far more efficient, Navajo territory was distant enough from Hispanic settlements and trade routes that agriculture and husbandry became as important as raiding to the Navajo economy.[7]

Anthropological research has helped recreate an image of nineteenth-century Navajo women's lives. Navajo society was matrilocal, with small bands revolving around older women, their daughters, and their families. Although men held prominent political positions as war and peace leaders, women also enjoyed economic power through their control of vast herds of sheep, as well as their ability to weave exquisite blankets valued throughout the Southwest.[8]

But Navajo women also played an important role within an elaborate cycle of raid and retaliation in the multicultural Southwest. Navajo men usually raided Hispanic settlements during spring and summer for vast quantities of sheep, horses, and occasionally cattle. Rather than slaughter the animals for immediate use, Navajos drove the stolen herds into their remote, impenetrable canyon homeland, where the flocks grew even larger. During these warm seasons, Navajo women and children planted and nursed crops. By autumn, depredations tapered off as the Navajos attended their harvests; raiding usually ceased during the winter. With spring, the cycle began anew.[9]

Navajo captive-taking remained incidental to stock-napping; although Navajos sometimes carried Hispanic shepherds away with their flocks, desire for livestock motivated most raids. But Hispanic counter-raiders targeted Indian women and children to sell throughout the Southwest and even Mexico. These captive-raids only provoked further Navajo depredations—which in turn justified even more captive-taking. By the time of the Mexican War, an elaborate cycle of raiding and retaliation had become central to the economy of Hispanos and Indians alike.[10] Navajo women were pivotal to this economic system, both as producers of valuable trade goods and as commodities themselves. In addition, Navajo women served as a human conduit facilitating contact between cultures and peoples.

Anglo-American trappers, traders, and travelers of the early nineteenth century stumbled into this cycle, but failed to understand—or deliberately misinterpreted—the roles of its participants. By the time the Santa Fe Trail opened in 1821, Anglo-Americans had already mythologized the Southwest's inhabitants and created their own fantastic Cibolas populated by

Orientalist Others. During the Spanish and most of the Mexican periods, Hispanos provided the most obvious Other for Anglo-American observers, as they represented their primary political and economic rivals.[11] But the Southwest was a multicultural arena, forcing Americans to evaluate not only their relationship with each group but also the interactions between these peoples. Hispanos and various Indian tribes became a set of Others against which Americans defined themselves and their role in the Southwest.[12]

Early nineteenth-century Anglo portrayals of Navajo women reflected colonial myths far more than accurate observation. To some degree, this was inevitable: the Navajo tribe lay to the northwest of most Anglo trade routes within New Mexico.[13] Untroubled by immediate reality, white colonizers used imagination to create a people who legitimized the American presence. Trappers, traders, and travelers portrayed Navajos as de facto allies who threatened Hispanic hegemony. American traders such as Peg-leg Smith even excused Navajo attacks upon themselves as mistaken attempts to fight abusive Hispanos; others, such as the trapper James Ohio Pattie and the trader Thomas James portrayed Navajo attacks as the result of years of Hispanic oppression.[14]

Reflecting American political and economic aspirations in the Southwest, pre-Mexican War observers paid extraordinary attention to the physical appearance and moral behavior of Indian women they encountered. These descriptions provided more than local color or human interest to American tales; instead, they conveyed metaphorical information to contemporary readers. For centuries, native women served Anglo-Americans as an incomparable symbol of *terrae incognitae*. The West has long associated women with Nature's creative forces and with its uncontrolled "irrationality"; nineteenth-century Euro-Americans also perceived Indians as the personifications of untamed nature.[15] Indian women thus presented a doubly powerful symbol of the unknown land, as they were twice removed from white man—the standard of true humanity—by race and by sex.[16] The resulting images of human landscapes usually had little to do with the reality of these women's lives; instead, they reflected the colonizers' relationship with a land they coveted. American descriptions of Navajo women over the fifty-year period from 1821 to 1870 uncannily mirrored the evolving American colonialist relationship with the Southwest.

The Pocahontas trope was especially popular in early nineteenth-century descriptions of Navajo women. Already popular in art and literature, Pocahontas was invariably young and beautiful, yet still untouched. An erotic virgin, Pocahontas invited and welcomed the white male adventurer, rejecting her own culture and heritage as inferior. Symbolically, the land she represented surrendered itself to the redeeming touch of the white male colonizer.[17] This Pocahontas trope riddled factual documents, indicating the extent of myth in shaping perception. Trappers and traders such as James Ohio Pattie, Peg-leg Smith, Thomas James, and William Hamilton described Navajo women as the epitome of the Cult of True Womanhood: not only physically attractive and very white, these paragons of domestic virtue made wonderful wives, mothers, and lovers.[18] Others, including Josiah Gregg and Albert Pike, praised the beautiful, watertight blankets these women produced, which could serve as trade goods both in the States and among other Indian tribes.[19] Industrious, loyal, generous, and welcoming—these desert madonnas recognized the superiority of the American male. Interestingly, almost all of the Navajo women described by the trappers and traders of the 1820s and 1830s were not only beautiful, but also young—an indicator of a virgin land to be explored and (literally) made fertile by the white male explorer.

In a rare twist, the traveler Albert Pike described a very different Navajo woman in his short story, "San Juan of the Del Norte." In this tale, a lazy Spaniard, obsessed with greed, attempts to bribe an ancient Navajo servant to use her sorcerous powers to reveal her tribe's riches to him. The crone—who even has a feline familiar!—rejects his offer and violently drives him away, but San Juan perseveres in his quest. After a mystical dream of Navajo gold, he is captured and enslaved by Indians. Pike ends this lurid tale with a caution: "He was a prisoner to the Spaniard's foe; and his task was, to grind meal upon his knees till his death. *So much for a hankering after WEALTH!!*"[20]

This tale strikingly reveals the multiple Othering Americans projected upon the Southwest. San Juan embodies every "unmanly" stereotype Americans held of Spaniards: he is cowardly, superstitious, illiterate, and greedy. Most damningly, Pike sneers that even the Indians despise San Juan for his laziness. His feminine antipodes, the Navajo woman personifies a death- crone who directs her rage against those who seek to rape her land. Noble though her purpose be, her very essence is terrifying and fatal, and her land is barren except for the minerals which can be ripped from its womb.[21] Pike had no love for the Southwest embodied by this witch-hag; he visited it in 1831 but returned to the South the next year.[22] His vision of an inhospitable and savage feminine landscape serves as a jarring foreshadowing of a later generation's relationship to the Southwest.

Most American writers of the 1820s and 1830s found expansion into New Mexico far more alluring than did Pike. Vistas of new lands and markets titillated traders, who utilized Orientalist fantasy to shape the pre-Mexican War image of Navajo society and life-style. Navajos, announced American observers, lived beyond almost impassable mountains in permanent towns and villages made of stone buildings. Men raised superb crops of corn, peaches, melons, beans, and wheat, while ranging huge herds of cattle—an animal prized more by the Americans than the Navajos—upon the most fertile lands of the Southwest. Rufus Sage effused about this earthly paradise:

> The[ir] valleys . . . are unrivalled in beauty, and possessed of a delightful climate, as well as an exuberant fertility of soil. In these valleys winter is comparatively unknown and vegetation attains an extraordinary size. The mountains abound with game, and are rich in all kinds of minerals. Some of the most valuable gold mines in Mexico are supposed to be held by the Navijos [sic].[23]

Even more startling were American depictions of Navajo polity as an orderly "patriarchy" in which "great men" dominated a society tempered by individual democracy. Men inhabited the public sphere of war, government, and the economy; women restricted themselves to the domestic realms of home and family. Here the women performed Anglo-approved domestic arts such as home-making, weaving, and producing "civilized" foods such as butter and cheese. Navajo women supposedly responded passively to the directions and needs of both Indian and white men in a male-dominated Shangri-la.[24]

The Navajos of the American imagination thus inhabited a "moral" social and physical landscape. Men and women supposedly followed strictly differentiated gender roles that paralleled American sexual spheres of influence—a stark contrast to most American stereotypes of Indians.[25] Even more striking was the gender-coded environmental ethos Anglos imposed upon these Navajos of fantasy. Navajos controlled feminine, irrational Nature through male-dominated agriculture, ranching, and perhaps mining. The result was a land and a society where Reason rather than Passion held sway.[26]

Yet this vision of pastoral bliss carried darker overtones. A few Anglo-Americans represented Navajo women as Pathetic Dusky Heroines, a variation of Pocahontas. Race inexorably doomed the Pathetic Dusky Heroine to a tragic end, which paradoxically affirmed the superiority of Anglo-American civilization.[27] The trapper Peg-leg Smith especially utilized this trope in his description of an encounter with a young Navajo woman wounded in a Ute attack upon her party. Because of her extensive wounds, her group had to travel on without her, though they promised to return shortly. The girl had survived on a small cache of supplies, supplemented by roots she gathered. The Americans gently tended her injuries and offered to take her to their own destination, an Hispanic settlement. She refused and the Americans left, lauding her traits of loyalty, love, and doomed bravery.[28]

The Navajo woman in this tale is little more than a colonial archetype plugged into the Southwest. She could be a character from a novel by James Fenimore Cooper, or a heroine from a penny dreadful. As a nameless literary device, she served as a cultural sign to the colonizer. A noble but savage princess, she was safely admired as the embodiment of a lush wilderness quietly fading before the vitality of white adventurers.

But to only examine this woman as a literary figure is to perpetuate an intellectual colonialism.[29] To rediscover her as an historical actor, we must uncover her drowned voice. Admittedly, she left no records of her thoughts, emotions, or actions. But her actions provide a "sign language" through which we can hear her.

Most importantly, the Navajo woman rejected the Americans' offer to carry her to an Hispanic outpost. It seems unlikely that Peg-leg Smith and his party were as ignorant of the captive trade as they appeared to be; Smith had built a major business by selling mules to Hispanic settlers, collaborating with Indian raiders to steal these animals, and then fencing the "hot" mules in California.[30] Smith certainly understood the intricacies of Indian-Hispanic relations. By refusing to accompany the Americans, the young woman chose to avoid Hispanic captivity—an action which belied the passivity of either Pocahontas or the Pathetic Dusky Heroine. Her strength of will, however, did not conform with Smith's vision of his own presence in the Southwest, and so was reconstructed in his account.

This vignette illustrates an important theme in colonialist texts: the land and its people *needed* the intervention of the would-be colonizer.[31] Most commonly, nineteenth-century Americans expressed this through use of the squaw drudge motif. A debased beast of burden, squaw drudges slaved in fields while their men lazed about hunting and fishing.[32] To some degree, this may have reflected honest misunderstanding of Indian gender roles, but it also served a more sinister purpose: the squaw represented both a land and a people in need of American-style redemption. Significantly, American observers never portrayed Navajo women as complete drudges, a testament to their undeniable social and economic position in their society. Limited use of the squaw motif only began during the Mexican War, when the colonialist dialogue between the United States and the Southwest altered drastically.

Instead, white writers of the 1820s and 1830s used the Pathetic Dusky Heroine to express the need for American intervention in Navajoland. Brave and noble though Navajo men were, they could not adequately protect their domestic circles against the incursions of heinous Mexican oppressors. Americans such as Josiah Gregg—who understood the semi-nomadic, raiding character of the Navajo tribe—excused Navajo depredations as the brave attempt of civilized men to defend their women, children, and land against Hispanic "acts of cruelty and ill-faith well calculated to provoke hostilities."[33] The trader Thomas James reported witnessing a Navajo man begging a cruel and tyrannical Mexican governor: "We are tired of war and we want peace. . . . [Ou]r crops are destroyed, our women and children are starving. Oh! give us peace!"[34] In these pre-Mexican War texts, Navajoland emerged as the citadel of civilization holding against Hispanic barbarians of the south. Despite their strength, Navajos needed the protection of Americans—who also needed to justify their presence in the Southwest.

The Mexican War of 1846 altered this preferential status of the Navajo tribe and their land in the American imagination. The change was not immediate: especially during the war, Americans continued to cast Hispanos in the role of Oppressors of Indians and the Land. Soldiers such as Marcellus Ball Edwards told of the misdeeds of Hispanos who abused Indian women and children, stole Indian lands, and—paradoxically— proved too cowardly to defend themselves against the righteous wrath of natives.[35] In this vein, Private Philip Gooch Ferguson detailed the plight of a sixteen-year-old female Navajo captive liberated by American troops from the Mexicans. Described sympathetically as a "poor girl" who "wept bitterly" while signing her concern for her fellow captives, the girl was kidnaped again by Hispanos and retaken by Americans before finally making her own escape from both sets of captors.[36]

Good and Evil are patently obvious in Fergusson's account: Hispanos "kidnaped" the girl; Americans "rescued" her. Ironically, Fergusson failed to notice that the Navajo girl made no such distinction between her two sets of captors. Indeed, Fergusson's account of this passive young woman echoed that of white heroines in popular contemporaneous American captivity narratives.[37] A quiescent Pathetic Dusky heroine, the girl finally evaporated from Fergusson's account, instead of actively freeing herself. Yet it is in that action that we can "see" the voice of the Navajo women:

content neither to stay in Hispanic nor American captivity, the young girl evaded both sets of would-be colonizers to make her own way home.

Despite Fergusson's pretty tale, the American relationship to the Southwest had irrevocably changed, and with it the colonizers' vision of the colonized. No longer wistful outsiders gazing into a land of mystery and wonder, Americans found that they now possessed a region torn by internecine struggles. The War itself presented a troubling dilemma for American chroniclers: although Hispanos were the formal enemy of American soldiers, marauding Navajos caused more problems for troops charged with protecting the residents of the Southwest. American soldiers were hard pressed to identify enemy or ally in this confusing land.[38]

As Americans began to venture into Navajoland, mirages built by earlier travelers crumbled. Navajo territory seemed a wild and untamed mystery, rather than the pastoral Shangri-La described by Sage. Ridges and labyrinthine canyons twisted insanely across the Navajos' wilderness home, defying American soldiers who sought to apprehend raiders. Danger lurked throughout the Indian territory; the same outcroppings and gorges which daunted soldiers offered safe haven to the natives. Lieutenant James H. Simpson, one of the first visitors to Navajoland, vividly expressed his impression of a land where nothing seemed to meet Anglo expectations:

> The idea I pertinaciously adhered to when in the States, before ever having seen this country, was that . . . it was also, like the country of the States, generally fertile and covered with verdure.
> But never did I have, nor do I believe anybody can have, a full appreciation of the almost universal barrenness which pervades this country, until they come out, as I did, to "search the land," and behold with their own eyes its general nakedness.[39]

Simpson described Canyon de Chelly, the heartland of the Navajo people, in more positive terms, but hastened to assure his readers that all references to fertility or beauty were only in relation to the rest of New Mexico, and not to the eastern United States. Despite these rebuttals, he portrayed the Navajo heartland as an awesome citadel whose sheer cliffs "look as if they had been chiseled by the hand of art," and whose denizens scampered up and down its walls as if in defiance of gravity.[40]

Anglo images of Navajo women uncannily mirrored these changing perceptions of their land. During the Mexican War, romantic observers such as the soldier Jacob S. Robinson continued to see these women in a favorable light, though one quite different from a generation earlier. Instead of the quietly passive nurturers described by visitors of the 1820s, the new Navajo heroines played raucous games and galloped their horses like Valkyries across an equally wild landscape.[41]

But most American men were more charmed by feminine helplessness than Byronic unrestraint, and so found these outspoken, vigorous women disturbing. John T. Hughes first articulated the growing uneasiness with which Anglo men viewed Navajo women. In his account of Captain Reid's encounter with the Navajos, Narbona's wife emerged as a manipulative troublemaker, a hag who contrived to "convince and sway men." Only the prompt and effective action of her male counterpart, who returned the female gadfly to her proper domestic sphere, prevented violence.[42]

The witch-like image of Narbona's wife signaled an arresting shift in Navajo imagery: no longer was the Navajo woman a young virgin who tremulously awaited the touch of the white male savior. Instead, American men of the post-Mexican War period almost invariably portrayed Navajo women as middle-aged or even elderly. More like Pike's sorceress than kindly grandmothers, the oldest hags menaced both white and Indian men. At best, Americans of the 1850s and 1860s portrayed Navajo women as married women of power—a status which carried Victorian connotations of defilement and secret knowledge.[43] Neither was the land innocent: Americans found that the Southwest of reality was far harsher and less forgiving than that of the imagination.

More than any other Navajo woman of this period, Narbona's wife provided a native feminine voice. Her denunciation of the Reid expedition demonstrates that Navajo women were neither ignorant nor indifferent to the events sweeping the Southwest. In warning her people of the dangers of associating with Americans, this anonymous woman referred to the infamous Johnson massacre of 1837, in which an American-led party lured a group of Apaches to a wagon mounted with a hidden gun, then killed several non-combatants. Within twenty years American legend altered the nationalities of the perpetrators—Johnson became British and his followers Hispanos—and exaggerated the number of Apache victims.[44] These changes vilified Hispanic rivals of the Southwest while emphasizing the need for American control there. Narbona's wife obviously understood where responsibility for the massacre lay, and rejected any vision of Americans as guardian angels who would save Indians from Hispanic oppressors.

Despite this woman's clarity of vision, the grumbling which met her denunciation of Americans and her subsequent removal from the meeting illustrated tension within the tribe. Navajos, too, were confused and unsettled by the changes in the Southwest. An elderly peace leader with well-established flocks, Narbona had much to lose from war with the Americans. Younger men, such as Manuelito, would profit from increased raiding. And women such as Narbona's wife could lose flocks, family members, and their own freedom in raids—or they could gain increased wealth and revenge upon long-established enemies. In either case, Narbona's wife's actions display an already-present distrust of American soldiers and their promises.

With the Mexican War, Anglo relationships with Hispanos changed as well. By the 1850's, however, Hispanos no longer represented foreign rivals, but were important social and economic partners in a new American territory. Most importantly, Hispanos—now American citizens —enjoyed the franchise, and so were courted by Anglo would-be politicians eager to please their electorate. Navajo raids upon Hispanic settlements could no longer be considered amusing forays against a mutual enemy, but dangerous and expensive assaults upon American property.[45]

Anglos now realized that previous reports grossly exaggerated Navajo agriculture and sedentariness, but military and government officials began to err in the opposite direction, claiming that these Indians were nomads who ceaselessly roamed a barren land, hunting and raiding. A decade after the Mexican War, Navajoland evoked images of a stony mountain fortress held by bandits ready to swoop down upon the pacific Pueblo and Hispanic peoples of the fertile valleys.[46]

Despite this, Navajo lands never completely lost their allure. The Indians's immense herds of sheep and horses confirmed the presence of excellent grazing lands. Colonialist apologists such as Superintendent of Indian Affairs David Meriwether and Electus Backus, commander of Fort Defiance, claimed that Navajos could develop extensive agricultural resources, *with proper guidance*.[47] Most importantly, rumors that the Navajos possessed vast deposits of garnets, opals, diamonds, and other precious stones crescendoed, and were to be found in everything from Private Josiah M. Rice's doggerel to the official reports of William Watts Hart Davis.[48] Instead of the Jeffersonian agrarian ideal which Navajo territory evoked to colonialist dreamers of the 1820s, Navajoland now appeared an area of potential rather than realized fertility—a land which would have to be forced to surrender its wealth.

As Anglos gained more knowledge of Navajo culture—and as the American relationship to the Southwest changed—apparent inversion of "natural" gender and environmental relationships among Navajos became more noticeable. Rather than the patriarchal system early visitors had envisioned, Navajo women owned vast herds of sheep and other livestock, and so enjoyed economic power. To a limited degree, Anglos approved of these freedoms as preferable to the abuses heaped upon the squaw drudges of other tribes.[49]

But Americans found squaw drudges far more comfortable than these outspoken and powerful women, whose presence defied colonial rationalizations. Not only could the squaw be pitied, but her very existence justified American intrusion into her land and society. The status and power of Navajo women thwarted this argument. "They [the Navajos] treat their women better than any other Indians on the continent," remarked William Watts Hart Davis. "They [the men] eat with them, share their property with them, and do not oblige the weaker sex to do the hardest work of the household and in farming. The women never saddle their horses or hoe their corn."[50] If anything, Anglo men seemed hard pressed to identify what Navajo women *did*, except to intrude into the masculine public sphere. Davis and Doctor P.G.S. Ten Broeck even "humorously" disparaged Navajo women as New Mexican versions of Bloomers and women's rights activists.[51]

Anglos could not approve of this environmental-economic system which women appeared to dominate. Even Commander Electus Backus of Fort Defiance—a man given to far less hyperbole than others in similar positions—assured his superiors that Navajo women's economic power allowed them to invade men's political sphere, where they exerted an inappropriate amount of influence.[52] Women's usurpation of patriarchal privilege supposedly poisoned Navajo families as well. Although husbands paid a bride price for their wives, Navajo women seemed to have an inordinate amount of freedom after their marriages. Divorces were easy and common, and a husband had to maintain "a constant watch upon his wife, lest she stray from the paths of rectitude; . . . [V]enereal diseases are by no means uncommon."[53] Men's relationships with their children fared no better: Navajo women effectively emasculated their husbands. Doctor Jonathon Letterman, stationed at Fort Defiance, reported to the Smithsonian Institution that Navajo men feared for their own lives:

> They [the women] have entire charge of the children, and do not allow the father to correct their own offspring. In fact, an Indian has said that he was afraid to correct his own boy, lest the child should wait for a convenient opportunity, and shoot him with an arrow.[54]

Although most Americans continued to praise Navajo women as producers of useful and artistic blankets, this did not offset their growing reputation as "notorious thieves" whose morals were "extremely loose." Even their hospitality was suspect, as only self-interest prevented them from harming American men who visited them.[55]

In 1858, the association of women and land reached lurid heights with the murder of Jim, the slave of Major Brooks, commander of Fort Defiance. For several weeks, Brooks and Manuelito, a young Navajo war chief, had argued over the ownership of a meadow close to the fort. Manuelito claimed it as a grazing ground; Brooks declared that it belonged to the army post for the same purpose. In May 1858, Manuelito sent a herd of horses to the disputed field, where the Army promptly butchered them. Several deceptively quiet weeks passed while both sides pondered. On July 12, an anonymous Navajo shot Jim with an arrow. He died a few days later, ushering in the final period of violence preceding the Long Walk.[56]

Obviously, the altercation over the meadow and the ensuing slaughter of Manuelito's horses prompted the attack upon Major Brooks's slave. Yet the Navajo agent, S. M. Yost, blamed the assassination upon a woman's lack of proper deference to her husband:

> The Indians say that the murderer had had a difficulty some days before with one of his women. He wished her to go some place with him. She refused and at a dance he tore from her all the clothing that covered her person. She still refused, whereupon, to appease his feelings, he started out (as is the custom of the Navajo Indians) to kill some one outside of his nation. This he succeeded in doing in the person of the negro [sic] boy. The Indian returned to the place where his woman was, and she proceeded with him to the place originally desired by the Indian.[57]

In this bizarre twist, American officials explained Jim's death as a blood offering to an angry goddess, rather than the sordid outcome of bickering between Major Brooks and Manuelito. As symbol, the land-as-woman had turned dangerously capricious.

Newspaper reports and military documents still recognized Hispanic and Pueblo violence against Navajo women; however, Anglos no longer perceived Navajo women as helpless victims who must be protected from their oppressors.[58] Capable of whipping warriors into a blood-frenzy, these forceful women could care for themselves economically and physically. Indian agent John Greiner wearily reported that a group of Navajo boys and women went to Cubero to sell pinons when they were attacked by a larger party of Hispano and Pueblo men, who stole six animals. "[T]he navajoes [sic] ran away for they were scared, but instead of run[n]ing the way from danger, they ran upon the alcalde who had taken their animals[.]" The small Navajo party of "defenseless" women and children ended up robbing the robbers.[59]

Even when Hispanos and Pueblos succeeded in their attacks upon Navajo women, Anglo observers continued to blame the victims. Many intimated that the power and wealth of Navajo women provoked attacks upon them—a variation of "she-had-it-coming." One newspaper article of May 22, 1858, discussed the murder of a Navajo woman by a Zuni man. Unconcerned with her death, the article focused instead upon the incredible value of the jewelry the assailant stole from her corpse.[60]

Similar images of violence, both against and involving Navajo women, escalated in the next seven years as raids and retaliations between these Indians and Americans increased. Navajo women continued to present a troubling dilemma, as they could not be neatly categorized. Producers of beautiful woven blankets, possessors of vast herds of sheep, owners of valuable and exquisite jewelry, Navajo women emphatically were neither alluring virgins nor abject drudges. On the contrary, their freedoms *exceeded* the boundaries of civilization. Neither could their tribe be easily dismissed, as it also seemed to ride the boundary between civilization and savagery. This "middle-ground" made Navajo women especially vulnerable to the image-making of the colonizers.[61] Finally, the land itself posed a dilemma. The Southwest was far more arid and inhospitable than many Americans had previously believed, but reports of agricultural oases and excellent grazing lands in Navajoland persisted. Even more importantly, rumors of incredible mineral wealth in this area expanded.

By 1864, Navajo depredations could no longer be ignored by the federal government, which had been distracted by the Civil War. A scorched-earth policy destroyed the homes, crops, and herds of thousands of Navajos, who were forced to surrender to the Army. Officials believed that only by removing this troublesome people from their beloved homeland, with its inaccessible mountains, canyons, and mesas, could the Southwest have peace. Once captured, seven to ten thousand Navajos were taken to Ft. Sumner at the Bosque Redondo in eastern New Mexico, where the government envisioned a Jeffersonian agrarian utopia, complete with houses, irrigation ditches, corn fields, and rice paddies.[62] Immediately, Anglo officials portrayed Navajo gender roles as falling into a more natural order. Within days of incarceration, the army reported, women began to set up their looms, symbol of domestic produce.[63]

As the experiment at the Bosque Redondo continued, New Mexican newspapers rhapsodized that Navajo men diligently worked the fields, while industrious women and docile children remained within the homes, all busy within their proper spheres.[64] But eventually the problems of the camp became undeniable: in 1868, General Sherman and General Tappen reported inhumane conditions similar to those of Andersonville. In addition, Navajos themselves were now victims of Comanche, Kiowa, and Apache aggression.[65] Worms, drought, and unrealistic methods based upon eastern experiences destroyed the experiment so thoroughly that the commander of the settlement confessed: "To save the crops from complete destruction, they were turned over to the Navajo chiefs."[66] Despite this tacit admission that Navajos already knew and practiced agricultural methods appropriate for this arid region, the report included Charles McClure's ringing endorsement of the experiment:

> After all the labor and care expended on the farm this last season, it must be confessed that the result is rather discouraging; but when we reflect that it has been the means of teaching agriculture to a large number of a very formidable and warlike tribe, and has been the nursery in which they have received their first lessons in civilization, much consolation may be derived.
>
> It was my fortune to be at Fort Sumner in April, when the planting was going on, and it was not without emotion that I saw the whole tribe working earnestly and cheerfully on their farm, and on their own gardens; these very same Indians with hoes in their hands, who, but a little more than two years before, had been the terror of every family from Albuquerque to the borders of Old Mexico.[67]

Indeed, Secretary of War Edward Stanton's 1868 Report painted a picture of agriculturally-based domestic harmony: Navajo men valiantly irrigated their doomed fields, while "squaws" dug holes and "papooses" planted seed.[68] Although Anglos admitted the difficulties suffered at the Bosque Redondo, the image of renewed harmony, subjugated passion, and societal order triumphed. The Navajo tribe—now emasculated by Anglos—had become objects of pity and redemption.

The army released the Navajos, who returned to their homeland to become one of the more prosperous and popular tribes of the late nineteenth century. Anglos continued to admire the personal wealth and talent of Navajo women. By the 1870s and 1880s, however, most visitors to the Southwest believed these women to be little more than the chattel property of their husbands. Indeed, Navajo women had come full circle by 1868, once more perceived as frequent victims of Hispanic peonage and slavery who needed American help.[69] In short, Navajo women had become glorified squaw drudges, a comfortable and safe image for a colonial iconography.

◆　　◆　　◆

Images of nineteenth-century Navajo women provide an extraordinary barometer of American colonialism in a land shaped by the imagination. Beautiful princesses transmogrified into harpies, only to be tamed and made squaws. Likewise, Navajo land mirrored these changes. Described as an agrarian utopia by early trappers and traders, by the 1850s Navajo territory mutated into a stony mountain fortress held by marauding savages. Transfigured by the Long Walk, the same lands became a subjugated internal colony by the 1870s.

A gender-coded polarization of mind and Nature, man and woman, structured these American perceptions of their relationship to the Southwest and its inhabitants. In 1864—the same year the Long Walk began—George Perkins Marsh wrote in *Man and Nature*: "[T]hough living in physical nature, he [man] is not of her, . . . he is of more exalted parentage, and belongs to a higher order of existences than those born of her womb and submissive to her dictates."[70] To nineteenth-century Americans, the correct relationship of man to nature correlated with that of man to woman: patriarchal control and guidance of the land-as-woman.

Yet there was another voice in this dialogue: that of the Navajo women themselves. Throughout this troubled period, anonymous women such as Narbona's wife, the wounded woman described by Peg-leg Smith, and the captive girl encountered by Ferguson, sought to maintain their traditional roles while vigorously reacting to the American intrusion in their world. Despite the attempts of early American colonizers to force them into passive categories such as the Pathetic Dusky Heroine or Pocahontas, Navajo women emerged as actors rather than victims.

Later, during the Mexican War and the territorial period, Navajo women continued to defy the common stereotype of the squaw drudge. Instead, their wealth, power, and strength of character stymied American officials who saw in them a strength that threatened colonial hegemony. Women such as Narbona's wife demonstrated the political awareness and clout Navajo women exercised. Producers of their own reality, Navajo women protected their traditional roles while actively responding to developments in a multinational drama.

Disparate though the realities of Americans and Navajo women were, they did overlap in key areas. Anglo representatives were forced to rewrite their Land-as-Woman metaphor, as neither Navajo women nor their territory corresponded to American expectations. Events thus entered a dialogue with culture, as Navajo women served both as actors and as signs in this colonialist arena.

Because of lack of documentation, it is more difficult to discover nineteenth-century Navajo women's revisions in their own perceptions of Americans. But by decoding their silent voices in colonialist documents, we can examine these women's participation in volatile events. Most importantly, we can see them as conscious actors rather than as reactors and symbols.

NOTES

1. Two sources are valuable in detailing Reid's expedition: John T. Hughes, *Doniphan's Expedition: Containing an Account of the Conquest of New Mexico and California*, ed. William Elsey Connelly (Topeka, Kansas: 1907), 166–85; and Jacob S. Robinson, *A Journal of the Santa Fe Expedition under Colonel Doniphan* (Princeton: Princeton University Press, 1932; repr. New York: Da Capo Press, 1972), 42–51. Hughes' account is more "official" than is Robinson's; after all, Hughes was the appointed chronicler of the expedition. Robinson, a young man from Rhode Island who enlisted in the Army of the West on a lark, displayed far more romanticism and spontaneity.

2. Several sources have inspired this textual analysis and symbolic study, including: Robert Darnton, *The Great Cat Massacre and Other Episodes in French Cultural History* (New York: Basic Books, 1984); Clifford Geertz, *The Interpretation of Cultures* (New York: Basic Books, 1973); Peter Hulme, *Colonial Encounters: Europe and the Native Caribbean, 1492–1797* (New York: Metheun, 1986); Marshall Sahlins, *Islands of History* (Chicago: University of Chicago Press, 1985); and Edward W. Said, *Orientalism* (New York: Pantheon Books, 1978).

3. William Roseberry especially makes this critique in *Anthropologies and Histories: Essays in Culture, History, and Political Economy* (New Brunswick: Rutgers University Press, 1989).

4. Hayden White, *Tropics of Discourse: Essays in Cultural Criticism* (Baltimore: John Hopkins University Press, 1978), 144.

5. Carolyn Merchant, *Ecological Revolutions: Nature, Gender, and Science in New England* (Chapel Hill: University of North Carolina Press, 1989), 47–48.

6. Margaret R. Miles, *Image as Insight: Visual Understanding In Western Christian and Secular Culture* (Boston: Beacon Press, 1985), 45.

7. David M. Brugge, "Navajo Prehistory and History to 1850," in *The Handbook of North American Indians*, general ed. William C. Sturtevant, vol. 10, *Southwest*,

volume ed. Alfonso Ortiz (Washington, D.C.: Smithsonian Institution, 1983), 489–501.

8. Carolyn Niethammer, *Daughters of the Earth: The Lives and Legends of American Indian Women* (New York: Macmillan Publishing, 1977), 23; Gary Witherspoon, "Navajo Social Organization," in *Handbook of North American Indians, Southwest*, 524–535. Navajo men, as well as women, own extensive flocks of sheep. Because of the matrilocal nature of Navajo society, however, most of the men's sheep are eventually merged with those of their wives. See Witherspoon, 528.

9. Some historians, such as Jack Forbes in *Apache, Navaho, and Spaniard* (Norman: University of Oklahoma Press, 1960), believe Spanish slave-raiding triggered the vicious cycle of raid and retaliation in the Hispanic Southwest. Others maintain that Navajo raiding was countered by Spanish captive-taking as a defensive measure. By the time of the American entrada, this cycle was so entrenched that assigning blame is pointless.

10. For the extent of Navajo captive-taking during the Spanish and Mexican periods, see David M. Brugge, *Navajos in the Catholic Church Records of New Mexico, 1694–1875* (Tsaile, Arizona: Navajo Community College Press, 1985). See also Thomas D. Hall, *Social Change in the Southwest, 1350–1880* (Lawrence: University Press of Kansas, 1989), for a discussion of the Southwest within a multinational economy.

11. There were other reasons for American anti-Hispanicism, including Anglo-Saxon racism and anti-Catholicism. See Ray Allen Billington, *The Protestant Crusade, 1800–1860: A Study of the Origins of American Nativism* (New York: Rinehard & Company, 1938); and Reginald Horsman, *Race and Manifest Destiny: The Origins of American Racial Anglo-Saxonism* (Cambridge: Harvard University Press, 1981). David J. Weber provides an extraordinary discussion of anti-Hispanic prejudices in the Southwest in "'Scarce More than Apes,' Historical Roots of Anglo American Stereotypes of Mexicans in the border Region," in *New Spain's Far Northern Frontier: Essays on Spain in the American West, 1540–1821*, ed. David J. Weber (Albuquerque: University of New Mexico Press, 1979).

12. A major problem with using the Other as a model for colonial relationships is that its binary nature can be too simplistic. For example, the relationship of a wealthy white female to a poor man of color can be seen in binary sexual terms: woman/man. On the other hand, their relationship can be seen as one of economic power, which would make the woman more "masculine"—yet the basic polarization remains. Said (p. 7) suggested the use of "flexible positional superiority" as a model of the colonizer/Other which adjusts to individual situations. For a discussion of the gender-coded nature of relationships, see Joan Wallach Scott, *Gender and the Politics of History* (New York: Columbia University Press, 1988), 28–50.

13. Susan Reyner Kenneson, "Through the Looking-Glass: A History of Anglo-American Attitudes toward the Spanish-Americans and Indians of New Mexico" (Ph.D. diss., Yale University, 1978), 119.

14. See Thomas James, *Three Years among the Mexicans and the Indians* (Waterloo, Ill.: Office of the "War Eagle," 1846; repr., Chicago: Rio Grande Press, 1962), 148–49; James Ohio Pattie, *The Personal Narrative of James O. Pattie of Kentucky*, ed. Timothy Flint, introduction and notes by Milo Milton Quaife (Chicago:

Lakeside Press, 1930), 188; "Sketches from the Life of Peg-Leg Smith," published serially in *Hutching's Illustrated California Magazine* 5 (October–March, November 1860), 205–6.

15. See Rayna Green, "The Pocahontas Perplex: the Image of Indian Women in American Culture," *Massachusetts Review* 16 (Autumn 1975): 701–2; Hugh Honour, *The European Vision of America* (Cleveland: Cleveland Museum of Art, 1975); Hulme, xii; Nancy Jay, "Gender and Dichotomy," in *A Reader in Feminist Knowledge*, ed. Sneja Gunew (London: Routledge, 1991), 88–92.

16. John McBratney, "Images of Indian Women in Rudyard Kipling: A Case of Doubling Discourse," *Inscriptions* (1988): 47–57.

17. Green, 701–2. For a more general study of land-as-woman, see Annette Kolodny, *The Lay of the Land: Metaphor as Experience and History in American Life and Letters* (Chapel Hill: University of North Carolina Press, 1975), 4–11.

18. See William T. Hamilton, *My Sixty Years on the Plains: Trapping, Trading, and Indian Fighting*, ed. E.T. Sieber (Norman: University of Oklahoma Press, 1960), 71; James, 148–49; Pattie, 187–88; and "Sketches from . . . Smith," 205.

19. Josiah Gregg, *Commerce of the Prairies*, 2 vols., (New York: Henry G. Langley's Astor House, 1844; repr., Ann Arbor: University Microfilm, 1966), 1: 286; Albert Pike, "The Inroad of the Nabajo" and "San Juan of the Del Norte," in *Prose Sketches and Poems Written in the Western Country* (With Additional Stories), ed. David J. Weber (Albuquerque: Calvin Horn Publisher, 1967), 149–50, 255.

20. Pike, "San Juan of the Del Norte," 249–56.

21. The juxtaposition of aged women, violence, and threatening nature is an ancient trope in Western culture: see Bernadette Bucher, *Icon and Conquest: A Structural Analysis of the Illustrations of de Bry's Great Voyages*, trans. Basia Miller Gulati (Chicago: University of Chicago Press), 43–118, passim; and Carolyn Merchant, 104–7.

22. David J. Weber, "Introduction" to *Prose Sketches and Poems*, xi–xix.

23. Rufus B. Sage, *Rufus B. Sage, His Letters and Papers, 1836–1847*, eds. LeRoy R. and Ann W. Hafen, vols. 4 and 5 in the Far West and the Rockies Historical Series (Glendale, Cal.: Arthur H. Clark, 1956), 5: 94.

24. Albert Pike, "Inroad of the Nabajo" in *Prose Sketches and Poems*, 149–50. Despite his antipathy to the Southwest, Pike's anti-Hispanicism allowed him to build the heroic reputation of Navajo warriors.

25. David D. Smits, "The 'Squaw Drudge': A Prime Index of Savagism," *Ethnohistory* 29 (1982): 281–85.

26. Merchant, 127.

27. Priscilla Sears, *A Pillar of Fire to Follow; American Indian Dramas: 1808–1859* (Bowling Green: Bowling Green University Popular Press, 1982), 36.

28. "Sketches from . . . Smith," 205–6.

29. Chandra Talpade Mohanty, "Under Western Eyes: Feminist Scholarship and Colonial Discourses," *Boundary* 2 (Spring/Fall 1984): 333–358.

30. Floyd F. Ewing, "The Mule as a Factor in the Development of the Southwest," *Arizona and the West* 5 (Winter 1963): 310.

31. Said, 31–110, passim.

32. Smits, 281–85.

33. Gregg, 1: 287.

34. James, 148–49.

35. Marcellus Ball Edwards, "Journal of Marcellus Ball Edwards, 1846–1847," in *Marching With the Army of the West, 1846–1848*, ed. Ralph P. Bieber, Southwest History Series (Philadelphia: Porcupine Press, 1974), 215.

36. Philip Gooch Ferguson, "Diary of Philip Gooch Ferguson, 1847– 1848," in *Marching with the Army of the West, 1846–1848*, ed. Ralph P. Bieber, Southwest Historical Series (Philadelphia: Porcupine Press, 1974), 328–33.

37. Glenda Riley, *Women and Indians on the Frontier, 1825–1915* (Albuquerque: University of New Mexico Press), 17–19.

38. Edwards, 215.

39. James H. Simpson, *Navaho Expedition: Journal of the Military Reconnaisance from Santa Fe, New Mexico to the Navaho Country made in 1849*, ed. Frank McNitt (Norman: University of Oklahoma Press, 1964), 159. See also Hughes, 166.

40. Simpson, 90–92.

41. Robinson, 46–48.

42. Hughes, 294–95.

43. In the Western binary construction of gender, man is associated with transcendent mind and spirit, women with somaticism and death. Virgins represented idealized women untouched by original sin, yet ripe for masculine direction. See Miles, 84.

44. An article by Rex Strickland neatly charts the evolution of the Johnson myth; however, he does not consider any reason for the changes other than normal exaggeration. Rex W. Strickland, "The Birth and Death of a Legend: The Johnson 'Massacre' of 1837," *Arizona and the West* 18 (Autumn 1976): 257–86.

45. Hall, 24, 147–63.

46. Major Electus Backus to McFerran, 7 May 1852, copy from National Archives, found in RAC 52, Frank McNitt Collection, New Mexico State Records Center and Archives (NMSRCA), Santa Fe, New Mexico; Dodge to Meriwether, 17 April 1855, transcription from New Mexico State Indian Affairs (NMSIA), Record Group (RG) 75, roll 2, in McNitt Collection; Dodge to Meriwether, 16 May 1856, transcription from NMSIA, RG 75, roll 2, in McNitt Collection; Captain J. H. Eaton to 1st Lieutenant A. Pleasanton, 7 August 1852, RAC 1852, McNitt Collection; Kendrick to Meriwether, RAC 1855, McNitt Collection; *Santa Fe Gazette*, 19 February 1853.

47. E[lectus] Backus, "An Account of the Navajoes [sic] of New Mexico," in *Historical and Statistical Information Respecting the History, Condition and Prospects of the Indian Tribes of the United States* [hereafter cited as Schoolcraft], ed. Henry R. Schoolcraft, (Philadelphia: Lippincott, Brambo & Co., 1854), 4: 212; Dodge to Meriwether, 13 June 1856, transcription from NMSIA, RG 75, roll 1, in McNitt Collection; Meriwether's Annual Report to the CO, 1 Sept. 1854, transcription from NMSIA, RG 75, roll 2, in McNitt Collection; Meriwether to Manypenny, transcription from RG 75, rolls 1 and 2, in McNitt Collection.

48. William Watts Hart Davis, *El Gringo: Or, New Mexico and Her People* (repr., Chicago: Rio Grande Press, 1962), 247; Davis to Thompson, 10 September 1857, Governors' Papers: David Meriwether, Folio #4, NMSRCA. See also Josiah M. Rice's fanciful poem, "The Valley of the Diamonds," reprinted in *A Cannoneer in Navajo Country: The Journal of Private Josiah M. Rice, 1851*, ed. Richard H. Dillon (Denver: Denver Public Library, Old West Publishing Company, 1970). Although tongue in cheek, the poem exemplifies the type of tall tales which surrounded the little-known country.

49. Davis, 235.

50. Davis, 235.

51. Davis, 235; P.G.S. Ten Broeck, "Manners and Customs of the Moqui and Navajo Tribes of New Mexico," in Schoolcraft, 86.

52. Backus, 214; Jonathon Letterman, "Sketch of the Navajo Tribe of Indians, Territory of New Mexico, by Jona. Letherman [sic], Assistant Surgeon U. S. Army," in *Extracts from the Correspondence of the Smithsonian Institution, 10th Annual Report, 1856* (Washington: Smithsonian Institution, 1856), 294.

53. Letterman, 294.

54. Letterman, 290.

55. J. H. Eaton, "Description of the True State and Character of the New Mexican Tribes," in Schoolcraft, 4: 217; Letterman, 294; and George Archibald McCall, *New Mexico in 1850: A Military View, ed. Robert W. Frazer* (Norman: University of Oklahoma Press, 1968), 100.

56. Frank McNitt, *Navajo Wars: Military Campaigns, Slave Raids, and Reprisals* (Albuquerque: University of New Mexico Press, 1972), 317–32.

57. Agent S. M. Yost, Ft. Defiance, to Collins, 31 August 1858, NMSIA, RG 75, in Frank McNitt Collection.

58. Col. B.L.E. Bonneville to Maj. Nichols, 8 February 1858, from National Archives, RG 98, in McNitt Collection; Gen. Garland to Lt. Col. Thomas, 1 March 1858, from National Archives, RG 98, McNitt Collection. Although attacks upon Navajo women annoyed Army officials who worried about native reprisals, most civilians did not share this concern.

59. Annie Heloise Abel, "Journal of John Greiner," *Old Santa Fe* 3 (July 1916): 197.

60. *Santa Fe Weekly Gazette*, 22 May 1858.

61. American officials found it particularly disturbing that a tribe as wealthy as the Navajos should continue to raid, and speculated this behavior was due to a basic moral weakness. See Calhoun to Medill, 1 October 1849, in Annie Heloise Abel, ed., *The Official Correspondence of James S. Calhoun: While Indian Agent at Santa Fe and Superintendent of Indian Affairs in New Mexico* (Washington, D.C.: Government Printing Office, 1915), 32–33.

62. There are numerous studies of Ft. Sumner, ranging from the dispassionate to the highly charged. For a brief, well-balanced account, see John L. Kessell, "General Sherman and the Navajo Treaty of 1868: A Basic and Expedient Misunderstanding," *Western Historical Quarterly* 12 (July 1981): 251–72.

63. *Santa Fe Weekly Gazette*, 21 February 1861.

64. *Santa Fe Weekly Gazette*, 11 June 1864.

65. Kessell, 258–59; *Santa Fe Weekly Gazette*, 2 October 1864; *Ibid.*, 3 December 1864.

66. Lieutenant R. McDonald, in "Letter from the Secretary of War," Ex. Doc. No. 248, 40th Congress, 2d Session, 1867–68, 15: 5

67. Brevet Major Charles McClure, in "Letter from the Secretary of War," 2.

68. McDonald, 7.

69. *Congressional Globe*, 40th Congress, 2d Session (Washington, D.C.: 1868), 4462, 4501.

70. George Perkins Marsh, *Man and Nature*, ed. David Lowenthal (Cambridge: Harvard University Press, 1965), 37.

7

KATHERINE M.B. OSBURN

"DEAR FRIEND AND EX-HUSBAND"

MARRIAGE, DIVORCE, AND WOMEN'S PROPERTY RIGHTS ON THE SOUTHERN UTE RESERVATION, 1887–1930

As part of a larger package of policies aimed at the assimilation of Indians into the general populace, Congress passed the Dawes Act in 1887. The Dawes Act provided for the allotment of reservations into small, individually owned plots of land. The Southern Ute Reservation in Colorado, like the majority of Indian reservations in the U.S., was broken up into small tracts of about 160 acres per family. The U.S. sold the surplus lands, usually to white settlers, and then even more reservation land fell into non-Indian hands as individual Indians lost their allotted land through tax forfeiture, sale, and fraud. Osburn's essay assesses the impact of the Dawes Act on divorced Indian women, who were especially hard-hit by changes resulting from cultural assumptions about women and the family guiding the allotment process.

In 1905, a recently divorced Ute woman wrote to her ex-husband: "Red Dog: Dear friend and ex-husband. I drew your annuity money here and enclose you $8.00. Your friend and ex-wife, Ma ma chi roo." Beneath her message the reservation trader, who had apparently written the note for her, remarked, "as the pro-rata was $17.00 and Mr. Red Dog owed me nothing, I do not know what she did with the other $9.00."[1] At the time the note was written, Ma ma chi roo's husband had left her for another woman, and she was living with her son—who could "ill afford to support her."[2] She does not explain why she felt entitled to a portion of her ex-husband's annuities, but her behavior reflects the willingness of several Ute women to insist on sharing resources belonging to their former spouses. In fact, in 1920, Ma ma chi roo received money from Red Dog's estate after he died.[3]

What processes were at work in this and other examples of Ute women demanding assets from their ex-husbands? Had Ute women abandoned their former economic independence and internalized the Euro-American idea of the dependent wife? On what grounds did they base their claims to resources? An examination of ten divorce cases involving allotment property addresses these questions and provides insights into Ute women's adjustment to the late-nineteenth- and early-twentieth-century Indian reservation.

The Office of Indian Affairs (OIA), also known by its later designation as the Bureau of Indian Affairs (BIA), was the federal agency within the Department of the Interior responsible for administering Indian reservations throughout the country. Once relocated to reservations, in the late nineteenth century, Ute families underwent the OIA program of directed culture change which shifted power within the family toward the husband. Government-assigned property, granted according to Euro-American perceptions of women's roles within the family, complicated marriage and divorce for Native American men and women. Government ideology concerning property, divorce, and gender roles represented a departure from the pre-reservation pattern of the Southern Utes and was characterized by attempted coercion and women's resistance.

In pre-reservation, post-contact Southern Ute culture, a woman's position in her family and in society was equal to a man's. Living in bilateral extended families which formed hunting and gathering groups, women's contribution to the survival of the group was so valued that matrilocality was the preferred post-marital residence pattern.[4]

Women frequently took the initiative in courtship, and the Bear Dance courtship ritual was ladies' choice. Although pre-marital sex was not encouraged, no double standard applied if the couple were caught. No male relative could force a woman to marry and any woman unhappy in her marriage could either ask her husband to leave or join herself to another family. Women's economic equality with their husbands contributed to this easy divorce. An abandoned or widowed woman was never left destitute for she was part of a larger group with whom she exchanged labor. Finally, authority within the family was based on age rather than gender.[5]

Ute lifecycle rituals reinforced the idea that women were, by virtue of their labor and their ability to bear children, powerful members of their communities.[6] Although the division of labor followed gender lines, women's labor was not considered secondary, relegating them to a private domestic "sphere." Women participated in trade with outside groups and frequently followed men into battle to scalp and gather loot.[7] While military and communal economic activities were generally directed by men, women could still have input into public decisions for the men ruled only as long as they were supported by public opinion. Further, individual families were free to leave the band at any time and in all individual disputes within the band the family acted as the primary agency of social control.[8] In short, Southern Ute culture was egalitarian with respect to gender roles in the pre-reservation period.[9] Once they were confined to the reservation, however, all of this began to change.

In 1868, under the terms of the Great Ute Treaty, the U.S. government created the original Ute reservation, which covered about one quarter of the Colorado Territory. After the San Juan Cession of 1873, and the removal of the White River and Uncompahgre bands to the Uintah-Ouray reservation in Utah in 1880–81, the three remaining bands of Utes—the Mouache, the Capota, and the Weminuche—were settled on a narrow rectangle of land in southwestern Colorado which became the Southern Ute reservation. There the Mouache and Capota bands agreed to take allotments and a program of directed culture change began.[10]

Inspired by the stories in popular weekly magazines of Indian mistreatment, a group of reformers including federal officials, churchmen and women, and professional educators gathered at Lake Mohonk, New York to plan the "uplifting" of Native Americans. The resulting legislation, known as the Dawes Act, was designed to bring peace and social justice to the Indians through assimilation to a Euro-American model of civilization. Through the Dawes Act, the OIA attempted to make Indians into yeoman farmers and farm wives by assigning to them individual land holdings known as allotments. The Act was signed into law in 1887 but was implemented on a tribe by tribe basis over the next several decades.[11]

Throughout the years in which the Dawes Act was the blueprint for Indian affairs, the federal government tried to create a new family structure for Native Americans. In the Euro-American paradigm, the family was viewed as a male-headed nuclear household in which economically dependent women were under the control of their husbands—who owned the family property and "supported" their families through wage work.[12] In placing families on male-owned allotments, and in limiting women's property rights with respect to marriage and divorce, OIA agents sought to impose this concept on Ute women. Further, by making married women vulnerable to the loss of allotment property if they married and divorced according to tribal custom rather than Euro-American law, reservation personnel attempted to force women to comply with state sanctioned marriages. The Euro-American ideal of female economic dependency within marriage was vastly different than the marital economy of traditional Ute society in which women controlled their own property within marriage and divorced their mates without significant economic loss. On the Southern Ute reservation, several Native American women attempted to assert their traditional rights to divorce and property despite OIA sanctions.

The OIA imposed a Euro-American family structure on the Utes during the allotment process. In 1895 Congress passed the Hunter Act, providing for the allotment of the Ute reservation according to the provisions of the Dawes Act. That same year, the Commissioner of Indian Affairs (CIA) Daniel M. Browning defined the reservation family for the Southern Ute Allotting Commission. He noted that allotments were to be granted to the head of the family, ideally the "husband and father." Yet Browning also recognized that his preferred pattern might not fit reservation realities: "the term is rather a relative one and means, in general, any person who has charge of and provides for a family; and to constitute a family there must be at least two persons related by ties of blood, marriage, or guardianship residing under the same roof."[13] Browning acknowledged that widows, single men or women, or older children caring for siblings may all be heads of households and thus entitled to land.[14] OIA policy at Southern Ute, then, did not exclude women from land ownership; it did, however, with two exceptions, exclude wives.

The Dawes Act contained a clause providing allotments "to each orphan child under eighteen."[15] Browning initially argued that this did not apply to married women under eighteen but later reversed his position, grudgingly instructing the allotting agents to give these women their own land. "This is a manifest absurdity," he wrote, "but it is the law nevertheless and it cannot be disregarded."[16] Further, women who married outside of the Southern Ute bands were supposed to be given allotments and counted on the census roll as heads of the house.[17] Thus the presence of a husband did not automatically disqualify a woman from receiving an allotment. Nevertheless, the regulations stipulated that if a woman married within her tribe and was over eighteen years of age her husband, as the head of the house, received the family land.[18]

Although the majority of wives had no land of their own they were considered co-owners with their husbands. The agents were told to record the wife's name next to her husband's in order to indicate that, although she was not "counted or numbered on the schedule as an allottee," the land allotted to her husband was also hers. This provision was supposed to hold for couples married by tribal custom; a legal marriage license was not required if the two were man and wife before allotment.[19]

Laws concerning Indian marriages, however, were not always clear. Native Americans residing on reservations during the Dawes Era were subject to two legal jurisdictions—federal and state. (The OIA ran token Indian Courts of Offenses staffed with OIA-appointed judges but these had no real legal power. They ruled on violations of OIA regulations pertaining to reservation conduct of Indians.) Because there was no federal law circumscribing marriage and divorce, noncitizen Indians were, ostensibly, allowed to follow tribal practices.[20] Nevertheless, women without legal documents were left without property if their marriages broke up because the granting of an allotment impacted the legal status of their marriages.

Cato Sells, the Commissioner of Indian Affairs in 1917, ruled that once Indians accepted allotments, they became citizens, and should marry according to state law. He wrote: "While Indians maintain tribal relations they may marry and divorce themselves but not after they become citizens."[21] Although the question of Indian citizenship (and thus their specific legal rights with respect to their tribes) was interpreted differently within different OIA administrations, commissioner Sells was rather conservative on the question of wives' marital property rights: without a legal marriage, divorced women had no legal land claim. In this manner, Indian women could only take advantage of state laws concerning married women's property if they had legal marriages.

For Southern Ute women with state-sanctioned marriages, their right to certain kinds of property was clearly protected by statute law. The Colorado civil code stated:

> The property, real and personal, which any woman in this state may own
> at the time of her marriage, and the rents, issues, profits, and proceeds
> thereof, and any real, personal, or mixed property which shall come to
> her by descent, devise, or bequest, or the gift of any person except her
> husband shall remain her sole and separate property, notwithstanding

her marriage, and shall not be subject to the disposal of her husband, or liable for his debts.[22]

Allotments undoubtedly fell under these provisions, provided they were initially assigned to the women. Legally, then, single, widowed, and "exception wives" with a state marriage license had legal title to their property. Legally wed, co-allotted wives had no legal rights to the family property because it was their husbands's property. They could probably claim something under the divorce and alimony statutes which provided support for divorced women; Ute women with tribal marriages could not.

Commissioner Sells admitted that the OIA's position sometimes hurt Indian women who literally lost their property by virtue of receiving it— unless they were immediately legally wed. Sells imagined this problem could be solved if ex-husbands would share their property at the request of the reservation superintendents.[23] In the reservation family, then, dependent wives were subject to their husbands's authority in vitally important matters.

Many Southern Ute women lived out their lives as wives or widows and were untouched by the limitations which the OIA placed on their property rights as tribally married women, but other women were profoundly affected by this policy. A total of sixty-one wives were listed as co-allottees in the Bureau of Land Management (BLM) allotment book.[24] Of these women, forty-six remained married until one of the partners died. Twenty-eight were widowed, nine were divorced, and six are untraceable in the records. All of the twenty-eight widows inherited their husbands's allotment, but in the divorce cases the co-allotted wives found they had no legal claims to the land they supposedly shared with their husbands.[25]

There were ten divorce cases among the original allottees at Southern Ute from 1905 to 1917. These cases include one woman who was a second wife and not listed on the allotment roles as co-allottee. No data is available for two of these women concerning whether or not they attempted to get land from their former spouses. In eight of the ten divorces, however, the women appealed to the agent to help them retain a portion of the land they viewed as theirs; they actively resisted their newly assigned position of economic subservience.

The reasoning behind the women's attempts to get a portion of this land are not exactly clear. In pre-reservation Ute culture a woman wishing a divorce simply asked her husband to leave or she herself left, usually going to live with another family member.[26] A lack of real property (in the

Euro-American sense) and the semi-nomadic economy of pre-reservation Ute culture meant that women probably did not ask their husbands for anything when they ended their marriages. Why, then, did post-reservation women expect part of the allotment when they left their husbands? While pre-reservation women never owned land, they did have property rights over anything they made, including tipis.[27] Perhaps they extended this concept of ownership to their new homes. Or perhaps something else was at work.

Examination of the eight divorce cases gives some insight into the divorced women's property claims. In 1906, Southern Ute agent William D. Leonard wrote to the Commissioner of Indian Affairs on behalf of four women who had been co-allotted when the original lands had been assigned. The women had been married by tribal custom and were now divorced, also according to tribal custom, and their husbands had remarried. Leonard asked that Sarah Buck, Peggy Washington, Ada Russell, and Daisy Baker be given a portion of their husbands's allotments. According to Leonard, the first wives were not legally married, but their listing as wives on the allotment rolls legitimated their claims to some of these lands.[28] The outcome for these four women was either negative or uncertain. Sarah Buck and Daisy Baker never got any land; what happened to Ada Russell and Peggy Washington is unknown.[29]

In four other cases ex-wives received land. A notation in Benjamin North's petition to sell some of his allotment disclosed that he had previously deeded 160 acres of land to his former wife Elmira.[30] In 1916, agent Walter West reported that John Tyler had deeded some acres to his ex-spouse Anne; the next year West noted with some satisfaction that when Alfonso Kuebler sold his land he paid his "discarded" wife $500.00 even though she was legally entitled to nothing.[31] In 1917, West forwarded Topsy Plato's divorce papers to Washington, explaining that her former mate had ceded forty acres of his land to his minor children "as a settlement of any claim which [Topsy] might have on his property."[32] Topsy was not a co-allottee, having married John Tyler after his divorce from Anne, who, as mentioned earlier, received a portion of the original lands. Although Topsy's settlement gave the land to her children by John Tyler, the property was in effect hers because she lived on it until her death.[33]

The reasons for these women's success are not clear from the existing records nor do the agents record anything about the women's view of their property rights. The women's good fortune may have been a result of agent West's forceful or persuasive personality or of their husbands's generosity. There is no evidence that the agent brought sanctions or employed force against any of these husbands. In all of these cases, the only issue mentioned in the granting of land is children. Since Topsy was not Tyler's wife at the time of allotment, her children would not have been assigned land with their father; apparently all the parties involved agreed that they should receive a portion of their father's holdings. Thus Topsy gained her property only indirectly—by virtue of being the children's mother rather than by having been John's wife.

The records do not indicate whether Topsy appealed for land on this basis, but it would not have been inconsistent with pre-reservation culture for her to feel her former husband owed his children support even after the marriage broke up. While there are no ethnographic accounts of "child support" payments in pre-reservation Ute culture, there was considerable emphasis on family responsibilities to off-spring. A father's role was underscored during the rites of passage surrounding birth when his family gave him ritual meat and blessed his hunting prowess because the baby's survival depended on his ability to provide meat.[34]

Further, in the Ute conception of family, children belonged to all consanguineal lines—each of which shared in the tasks of feeding, clothing and enculturating the child. Utes believed that a child might have more than one father, for they thought that conception occurred when, over time, semen—*wana'tcpi*—filled up an amniotic sac—*no'gup*.[35] Thus the obligations to a child were not necessarily restricted by residence in the immediate family unit and men may very well have felt a duty to provide for their children after divorce.

Another Ute wife attempted to get a property settlement on these grounds, but where Topsy Plato succeeded, Daisy Spencer Baker failed. Her case is especially illuminating because she is the only woman who left letters about her divorce. Daisy's struggle against her ex-husband, James Baker, began in 1905 when agent Burton B. Custer posted a notice that: "Daisy Spencer—former wife of James Baker—has no control whatever of the land allotted to them jointly . . . [and that] those who trespass do so at their own risk and will be handled according to law."[36] The true injustice of the message, of course, lay in the phrase "no control whatever of the land *allotted to them jointly.*" There is no record of Daisy's response to this message, but since the "law and order" section of the agents' annual reports did not record any trouble with trespassing over the next decade, she probably respected the warning.

She did not, however, accept the idea that she had no share of the family property. In 1916, agent Walter West replied to a letter she had sent him (apparently dictated to her daughter Mary) asking about the inheritance settlement of her two dead children's allotments. West explained that the Secretary of the Interior had ruled that James Baker was sole heir to the allotments. He regretted that he could not help Daisy in this case.[37] In June of 1917 Daisy wrote again—this time to the Commissioner of Indian Affairs—demanding half of James's 340 acres because "we were allotted together and now we are not living together [sic] he has said that he did not take me as his wife [sic] as i think he should give me 1/2 of the 320 acres he has." She told the Commissioner that she had asked the Southern Ute agent to write but that she doubted he had. She concluded, "Do with me what you think the best."[38]

Agent Edward E. McKean took up Daisy's cause in a letter to the OIA in 1917. He described how she and James Baker were married by Indian custom and, although she had no legal right to the land, she "is still a woman in vigorous health and I believe if it were possible for her to secure any part of the allotment given to her former husband James S. Baker, that she would be greatly assisted in supporting herself."[39] The Commissioner responded by explaining that since Indian marriages and divorces were not valid after "they become citizens by allotment or otherwise," James Baker owed his wife nothing; he suggested McKean try to convince him to deed "the Indian" some land.[40] James refused, however, and in the process said some very unkind things about Daisy.

Daisy responded to these remarks in a letter to McKean in January of 1918. She accused the Commissioner and McKean of siding with her former husband "just so we will be quarrelling about it."[41] Apparently James reiterated that Daisy had never been his wife and that he was not the father of her children. She expressed wounded outrage at these charges writing:

> Jim Baker says with his own tongue I was not his wife, he says he just lived with me like any lose [sic] animal. What more worse name can he give me than to call me an animal. If I was an lose animal what does he want my land for he makes fun of me . . . I had my children and this man who says he was not my husband gets all the money out of them and I don't get any one penny. it is because you say he is heir. he want to be the heir but he don't want to take children as his children.[42]

Three times Daisy demanded her land and she ended her letter by claiming, "I am going to get my land some way if you can't do."[43]

Some time after Daisy's angry letter, James capitulated and offered her 160 acres—one of her deceased children's allotments—if she would sign a statement relinquishing any future demands on the rest of "his" land.[44] Daisy, obviously still smarting from his earlier accusations of promiscuity, refused to sign the waiver, writing, "I don't want to give my childs [sic] land to Jim Baker. he says they are not his children. Before I sign anything like this I will go to court with him." She demanded more land because of the large number of children she had.[45] The Commissioner wrote and asked if McKean could "have a talk with the Indian and with James Baker and see if some satisfactory settlement cannot be made."[46] No further letters are available, but evidently Daisy never got her land.

On August 13, 1927 James Baker died at the age of 77. His heirship papers list four wives, including Daisy's sister Eliza, who died in 1907 and may have been co-wife with her sister. Daisy is listed as deceased in 1920 and as having no land. Baker had eleven children by his four wives. Five were Daisy's and all of them were dead by 1926.[47] For all her efforts on behalf of herself and her children, Daisy Spencer Baker died with nothing—an example of the vulnerability of married women, particularly tribally married women, under the Euro-American imposed definition of the reservation family.

The stories of Daisy Baker and Topsy Plato provide a glimpse of women's perceptions of their rights within the family—Daisy's by direct statement and Topsy's by implication. Both women's claims rested primarily on their role as mother rather than on their role as wife. Perhaps the women felt that the former claim would carry more weight with the agent than the latter or perhaps the argument reflected the women's own view of what their husbands owed them. Were they asking for "support" in the Euro-American sense? Was this a middleground where OIA agents and Ute women agreed that women and children should be sustained by men? While reservation personnel seemed to hold the latter position, an examination of Ute ideology of gender and familial obligations suggests that Ute women viewed the situation differently.

In traditional Ute culture, a woman's identity was closely tied to her reproductive functions. Women's power to give life was celebrated in birthing rituals and emphasized during menstruation—when she was isolated in a wickiup and told to refrain from eating meat or fish because her spiritual power was intense while her menstrual blood flowed and she might injure the ability of her male relatives to hunt or fish.[48]

The idea that a woman's value was tied to her role as mother also appears in myth. Except where the Ghost Dance or Peyotism were found, Great Basin mythology generally did not include the concept of "mother earth."[49] The Ute pantheon, however, did include a key life-giving figure and female archetype, Water Grandmother. In some Ute versions of the creation myth, the earth began as a vast sea, and Water Grandmother floated upon the waters in her basket and created land from her body.[50] Her importance to the Utes is demonstrated in their Woman's Dance, or Round Dance, which she mandated at the beginning of time.[51]

In some Ute myths, women also take part in the initial creation of human life. Several tales speak of how Wolf or Coyote had sex with women and human beings were created. Coyote was then given a sack containing the children that he and the women have created, and he spilled its contents, scattering the tribes across the earth.[52] A related myth tells of how the Ute Culture hero—the younger Shin-au-vi brother—swallowed a baby and then had great difficulty in delivering it. After his ordeal he concluded, "these birth pains are more than men can endure; hereafter the women must bear children."[53] While this story could be interpreted as a male deity palming off an unpleasant task on women, it may also be regarded as an indication of admiration and respect for women's strength and fortitude as mothers.

Specific tales depicting women as mothers are also very complimentary of this role. While the mythic portrayal of Ute women as wives or sexual partners is not always flattering, Ute mothers are brave, selfless, and resourceful—at least with regard to their own children. The wife of principle culture hero Sunawavi flees to the heavens with her children (where they become stars) to protect them from his incestuous advances.[54] Crane's wife is captured by Stone Shirt, who orders her to kill her baby, but she saves the baby at great risk to herself.[55] Turtledove braves a witch (or a ghost, depending on the version) to rescue her son, and Dove, Bear, and a nameless woman all work hard to provide for their children.[56]

In short, the role of mother gave a woman dignity and identity. Her entrance into the adult female role occurred when she became capable of bearing children—at her first menstruation. Further, the Ute practiced a type of fertility dance called the Bear Dance. According to mythology, a bear once told a Ute hunter that he would improve his sexual and hunting abilities if he would perform a dance to propitiate bears. The dance functioned originally as a courtship ritual and was organized so that women chose their dancing partners. It was performed in the spring when bears ended their hibernation and the earth was once again fertile. In precontact times, it could also mark the end of a girl's puberty ritual.[57] The Utes, therefore, sought supernatural aid and blessing in areas crucial to their survival—hunting and reproduction. Both roles were equally valued and celebrated in Ute culture.

Thus, for a woman to point to her children was to point to a highly valued accomplishment. To be a mother was, for Ute women, to be a fully participating member of Ute society. When Daisy Baker wrote "I had my children" she most probably meant "I have fulfilled my role in this society—I count." Her demand for land was most likely not a demand that her husband support her because she, being a wife and mother, was economically dependent on him, but that she, as a productive adult, be allowed equal access to the new subsistence base—land. While she may have felt her husband had an obligation to her children, she probably did not assume he had an obligation to provide for her once her marriage was over. Her request was probably an attempt to secure resources in order to provide for herself.

Southern Ute agents agreed that the women should have a share of the reservation resources, but they viewed this right from a different perspective. Their behavior must be understood by reference to Euro-American concepts of wives' economic dependency as reflected in the OIA rulebook and in Colorado divorce laws. A husband's duty to support his wife and children was clearly spelled out in the OIA rulebook, first published in 1883. An offender in this regard lost his rations until he proved to the agent that he "will provide for his family to the best of his ability."[58]

Further, the rulebook mentioned the dilemma of ex-husbands refusing to provide for their former families. The book blamed this problem on tribal marriage and divorce customs, but rather than establish sanctions for Indian husbands who failed to care for families abandoned under tribal divorces, the rulebook instructed agents to try and force Indian couples to stay together and to allow divorce only through legal channels.[59] The OIA, then, provided sanctions to coerce men to support wives as long as the family remained intact, but placed the question of ex-wives' access to family assets under the jurisdiction of state courts.

Since Southern Ute agents insisted that marriages and divorces conform to Colorado state law, they may have viewed Ute women's land claims as the equivalent of asking for alimony, which Colorado law provided for divorcing wives.[60] The 1881 and 1891 statute laws of Colorado allowed women to sue for divorce on the grounds of impotency, adultery, cruelty, drunkenness, desertion, or failure to provide, and made provision for them to receive alimony and child support (although they did not always get custody of the children) not in excess of two thousand dollars or half the husband's income.[61] A woman's right to alimony was contingent on certain conditions. Payments were determined by her need for support and her husband's ability to pay; if she had "the necessary means" to support herself, her petition was denied. If a woman's behavior brought about the divorce, she was still allowed alimony unless she was currently living in adultery or "her conduct has been very gross." Finally, the idea that women needed financial support from husbands was so deeply imbedded in the law that a divorced and remarried woman could still receive alimony payments from her first husband if she could prove that her second spouse could not properly sustain her.[62]

Thus while agent McKean hoped to secure land for Daisy so that she "would be greatly assisted in supporting herself," he considered her petition for land in the context of her husband's obligation to provide for her and their children. Additionally, McKean did not mean that Daisy and James should share the family property, but that he should grant her a portion of the resources properly belonging to him. "Since the [land] patent has been granted to James Baker," he wrote, "I do not know whether Daisy S. Baker could claim any of the land."[63] In McKean's thinking, since James was the rightful property owner, Daisy's claim to the allotment was not that of an equal but of a dependant.

McKean does not say whether or not he intended that Daisy work the land herself, but it would be highly unlikely that he would expect such behavior. Most women who owned property but had no husbands either leased it, sold it, or hired someone to work it for them, often paying them by giving them part of their holdings. While these women may have actually run their farms, they were usually not independent of a man's labor.[64]

Had any of the original co-allottees chosen to legalize their marriages, their rights to the family property would have been more secure. Southern Ute agent William D. Leonard promised as much in 1906 when he told a gathering of Ute women that they could expect no guarantee of property, either in alimony or inheritance, if they persisted in their "illegal cohabitations."[65] Although Leonard despaired that the Utes were "opposed to giving up their custom of tribal marriage which carries divorce with it any time the parties see fit," reservation marriage license records recorded ten marriages at the agency and four at the local Catholic Church in 1906: this represented more licenses than in any other year in agency records.[66]

The number of legal unions rose steadily in the first two and a half decades of the twentieth century, but all of these licenses were issued to couples married after allotment. There are no records of any of the original allottees "legitimizing" their marriages with state licenses.[67] Agents aimed their arguments for state-sanctioned marriages at women who were vulnerable to the loss of allotment property, but land ownership did not prompt any of these couples to adopt Euro-American marital customs.

The impact of these arguments on the later couples who sought marriage licenses is not clear.

SUMMARY AND CONCLUSIONS

In the process of allotting lands to Native Americans, wives were relegated to a dependent position with regard to property. The allotting commission assigned land to husbands. Wives's rights to that land in cases of divorce were contingent upon the legality of their marriages. This was a significant change from the pre-reservation pattern in which women's rights to divorce and property were not restricted by men. The majority of co-allotted wives, however, were not hurt by this policy. Most marriages in this age cohort survived—forty-six out of the fifty-five for which data is available—although, to the agents's frustration, they survived as tribal unions.[68]

Government dictates concerning marital property, however, created a new male-dominated social and economic system, and Ute women who chose to divorce suddenly found themselves subjected to men's control in ways unfamiliar to them. Without legal marriages, they had no titles to their homes and were dependent on the generosity of their former husbands. Agents attempted to help women attain a portion of their "co-allotted" lands, but they could only try to persuade the men to aid their former spouses; they had no means of bringing sanctions against men who refused, for OIA regulations requiring men to support their wives and children applied only to intact families. Divorced Ute women could appeal to state marriage laws, but tribally married women had no legal recourse should their husbands decline to share the family allotment.

Ute culture founded woman's power and identity in her productive tasks and her maternal role, both crucial to the survival of the group. Thus Ute women's demands for property were most likely grounded in their conception of themselves as equal participants in the subsistence quest. In contrast, Euro-American law codified both a husband's duty and a wife's right (should she be unable to care for herself) to financial support. It was in this legal and economic context that agents attempted to help divorced Ute women attain property. The agents's ideological framework for this undertaking—based on a notion of dependency—therefore differed greatly from that of the Ute women—founded on a belief that they were entitled to equal access to the means of subsistence.

Nevertheless, while Anglo agents and Ute women envisioned women's property rights from very different perspectives, they seemed to agree that the women had legitimate claims. Further, although the concept of "mother" meant divergent things to either side, both the agents and the women stated the women's requests by reference to the maternal role. Thus, the idea of motherhood functioned as a middle ground in the process of land negotiations.[69]

Reservation life affected men and women differently. In order to comprehend fully the early reservation years, historians must account for women's experiences as well as men's. Ute men lost a critical part of their identity when they could no longer make war and hunt buffalo; Ute women, in addition to losing their former productive role as food collectors and processors, also found themselves subservient to men in the new reservation economy. Yet far from acquiescing to OIA dictates, several Ute women sought to preserve their autonomy by demanding a share of the reservation resources. They were not always successful, but Ute women were always active participants in the reservation community.

NOTES

1. Ma ma chi roo, Uintah Ouray Reservation (UO), Fort Duchesne, Utah, to Red Dog, Southern Ute Reservation (SU), Ignacio, Colorado, 28 February 1905, Records of the Consolidated Ute Agency (RCUA), 44012: General and Statistical: Outgoing Correspondence, 005, Bound Letterbooks, National Archives and Records Administration (NARA), Rocky Mountain Region, Denver, Colorado.

2. William B. Fry, Southern Ute agent (SUA) to Jewell D. Martin, Uintah-Ouray agent (UOA), 10 February 1913, RCUA, 44015: General and Statistical: "Alphabetical Status Files of Indians, 1879–1939," Box 5, "Red Dog File," NARA, Denver.

3. Albert H. Kneale, UOA, to Edward E. McKean, SAU, 10 March 1920, "Red Dog File," 44015, RCUA.

4. Marvin K. Opler, "The Southern Ute of Colorado," in *Acculturation in Seven American Indian Tribes*, ed. Ralph Linton (New York: Harper & Sons, 1940), 128–129. According to Opler, matrilocality was the preferred post-marital residence pattern but the couple sometimes lived with the family which needed their labor the most. Also see Donald Callaway, Joel Janetski, and Omer C. Stewart, "Ute," in *Handbook of North American Indians*, general ed. William C. Sturtevant, *Great Basin*, vol. 11, vol. ed. Warren L. D'Azevedo (Washington, D.C.: Smithsonian Institution, 1986), 340–52.

5. Opler, 124, 146–53; Jan Pettit, *Utes, The Mountain People*, revised edition (Boulder, Colorado: Johnson Books, 1990), 91–94.

6. Ute lifecycle rituals reinforced this concept. See Opler, 137–40; Callaway et. al., 350–52.

7. Opler, 132–35, 158–69, 166; Callaway et. al., 340–43.

8. Opler, 163–65; Callaway et. al., 353–54.

9. The data from Southern Ute supports Peggy R. Sanday's hypothesis that societies in which women make a significant contribution to the economic survival of the

group are generally more egalitarian with respect to women's social and political roles. See Sanday, "Female Status in the Public Domain," in *Woman, Culture and Society*, ed. Michelle Zimbalist Rosaldo and Louise Lamphere (Stanford, California: Stanford University Press, 1974), 189–205. Martha Knack has developed this concept for Great Basin women. See, Knack, "A Comparative Analysis of Women's Status in Great Basin Cultures," 1989. Typescript in author's possession.

10. J. Donald Hughes, *American Indians in Colorado*, second edition (Boulder, Colorado: Pruett Publishing Company, 1987), 62–72; Pettit, 40–46; Callaway et. al., 354–58.

11. In related policies, the Office also hoped to acculturate Native Americans by instructing them in Anglo patterns of thought and behavior in Indian service schools, and replacing native religion through missionary work. Frederick E. Hoxie, "The Curious Story of Reformers and the American Indian," in *Indians in American History*, ed. Frederick E. Hoxie (Arlington Heights, Illinois: Harlan Davidson, Inc., 1988), 205–28. For an in-depth study of this topic see Hoxie's book, *A Final Promise: The Campaign to Assimilate the Indians, 1880–1920* (Lincoln: University of Nebraska Press, 1984).

12. This model of the Euro-American family is summarized in the introduction to *Women and Colonization: An Anthropological Perspective*, eds. Mona Etienne and Eleanor Leacock (New York: Praeger, 1979), 25–41.

13. D. M. Browning, Commissioner of Indian Affairs (CIA), to the Southern Ute Allotting Commission (SUAC), 15 August 1895, RCUA, 44017: Tribal and Administrative, Box 11, Folder: "Land: Regulations and Circulars, 1887–1942," NARA, Denver.

14. Browning to SUAC, 15 August 1895.

15. Browning to SUAC, 15 August 1895.

16. Browning to SUAC, 15 August 1895.

17. Browning to Henry Page, SUA, 8 July 1881, RCUA, 44017, Box 11, "Land," NARA, Denver.

18. Browning to Page, 8 July 1881. Edith Day Spencer, fourteen-year-old wife of Joseph Spencer, received an allotment under the first "exception" provision. The two Ute women who were married to non-Ute men at the time of allotment, however, were not given land. Melissa Nelson Cooper saw her allotment go to her husband Job, a Taos Indian, and Bella Clay Douglas's allotment went to her Northern Ute husband Fred. The allotting agents did not offer any explanation for their failure to comply with the "exception" provisions. See RCUA, 44001, III, 300, Tract Book: Allotments Approved, 1896–97, NARA, Denver.

19. Browning to Page, 8 July 1881, RCUA, 44017, Box 11, "Land," NARA, Denver.

20. Laurence F. Schmeckebier, *The Office of Indian Affairs*, (Baltimore, MD: The Johns Hopkins Press, 1927), 257–8. Schmeckebier quotes the Board of Indian Commissioners's 1919 ruling on the subject of marriage and divorce laws.

21. Cato Sells, CIA, to McKean, 28 December 1917, Records of the Southern Ute Agency (RSUA), Central Classified Files (CCF), 104064, NARA, Washington, D.C. The Dawes Act originally provided for citizenship in twenty-five years when the trust period for the land patents expired and Indians were issued fee patents for their lands. (See Public no. 43 in RCUA, 44017, Box 11, "Land," NARA, Denver.) In 1905, however, the U.S. Supreme Court ruled, in *Matter of Heff*, that Indians became citizens at the beginning of the trust period when they accepted

allotments. See Janet McDonnell, *The Dispossession of the American Indian, 1887–1934.* (Bloomington: Indiana University Press, 1991), 88–89. In 1906, Representative Charles H. Burke of South Dakota introduced an amendment to the Dawes Act which once again postponed the granting of citizenship for twenty-five years but which also allowed the Secretary of the Interior to grant patents to competent Indians. The purpose of this legislation was to protect unacculturated Indians from being tricked out of their lands by allowing them a special trust status reserved for non-citizens. Indians who were deemed sufficiently acculturated to buy and sell their property without supervision, however, were allowed to do so by becoming citizens. See Michael T. Smith, "The History of Indian Citizenship," in *The American Indian Past and Present*, ed. Roger L. Nichols, third edition (New York: Alfred A. Knopf, 1986), 232–41. Despite this amendment, Commissioner Sells was notorious for granting patents to Indians and declaring them citizens before they were really ready and against their wills. The result of his actions was a terrible alienation of Indian lands. See McDonnell, chapter eight.

22. General Statutes, State of Colorado, 1883, (Denver, CO: Colorado Times Stream and Publishing House, 1884), 694–5.

23. Sells to McKean, 13 June 1918, RSUA, CCF-104064, NARA, Washington D.C.

24. Allotment Tract Book Bureau of Land Management (BLM) at the BLM office, Denver.

25. BLM Tract book; Southern Ute Census Records, The Omer Stewart Collection (OSC), Series II, Box 4, Western Historical Collections, Norlin Library, University of Colorado, Boulder, Colorado; Southern Ute Death Records, Tri-ethnic files, Omer Stewart's personal collection, University of Colorado, Boulder, Colorado; Walter Runke, SUA, to Mr. Guy Tucker, Slater Hotel, Durango, 6 January 1914, RCUA, 44012: General and Statistical, Outgoing Correspondence, Bound Letterbooks, NARA, Denver.

26. Opler, 151.

27. Opler, 128–29.

28. William D. Leonard, SUA, to CIA, 6 November 1906, RCUA, 44012, NARA, Denver.

29. Walter Runke, SUA, to CIA, 21 March 1914, RCUA, 44011: General and Statistical, Outgoing Correspondence, Bound Letterbooks, NARA, Denver; RCUA, 44015, "Alphabetical Status Files of Indians 1879–1939," Box 4, Baker File, NARA, Denver.

30. "Petition for the Sale of Land by the Original Allottee, Benjamin North," RSUA, CCF–310–136344, NARA, Washington, D.C.

31. Walter West, SUA, to CIA, 29 September 1916 and 9 March 1917, RCUA, 44013: General and Statistical, Outgoing Correspondence, Bound Letterbooks, NARA, Denver.

32. West to CIA, 9 March 1917, 44013, NARA, Denver.

33. West to CIA, 9 March 1917.

34. Opler, 137–38; Pettit, 60–5.

35. Opler, 133–34.

36. Burton B. Custer, SUA, TO ALL IT MAY CONCERN, 6 June 1905, RCUA, 44013, NARA, Denver.

37. West to Daisy Spencer Baker, Pagosa Junction CO, 6 June 1916, RCUA, 44013, NARA, Denver.
38. Daisy Spencer Baker to CIA, 26 November 1917, RSUA, CCF, 310–104064, NARA, Washington, D.C.
39. McKean to CIA, 26 November 1917, RSUA, CCF, 310–104064, NARA, Washington, D.C.
40. CIA to McKean, 28 December 1917, RCUA, 44015, Baker File, NARA, Denver.
41. Daisy Spencer Baker to McKean, 21 January 1918, RCUA, Baker File.
42. Daisy S. Baker to McKean, 21 January 1918, Baker File.
43. Daisy S. Baker to McKean, 21 January 1918, Baker File.
44. McKean to Daisy S. Baker, 22 January, 15 February, 11 March 1918, Baker File.
45. Daisy S. Baker to McKean, 15 March 1918, Baker File.
46. CIA to McKean, 15 June 1918, Baker File.
47. "Heirship Report of James Baker, 1927," Baker File.
48. Opler, 137–40; Pettit, 62–3; Callaway et. al., 350–52.
49. Ake Hultkrantz, "Mythology and Religious Concepts," in *Handbook, Great Basin*, 630–639.
50. James Goss, "Ute Myth as a Cultural Charter," Paper presented at the Great Basin Anthropological Conference, Reno, Nevada, 1990, 2. In author's possession.
51. Goss, 16.
52. Hultkrantz, 638–39.
53. John Wesley Powell, *Anthropology of the Numa*, Smithsonian Contributions to Anthropology Number 14, eds. Don Fowler and Catherine Fowler (Washington, D.C.: Smithsonian Institution Press, 1971), 88–89.
54. Robert H. Lowie, "Shoshonean Tales," *The Journal of American Folklore* 37 (1924): 28–30.
55. Anne Smith, "Ute Tales." Manuscript from her 1940 dissertation from Yale, in my possession. Dr. Smith's work, "An Analysis of Great Basin Mythology," 2 vols., was unavailable to me in its bound form.
56. Powell, 45–47; Smith, 4, 20–22, and 44–47.
57. Joseph G. Jorgensen, "Ghost Dance, Bear Dance, and Sun Dance," in *Handbook, Great Basin*, 662–63. In post-contact times the primary focus of the dance shifted from sexual and hunting success to healing and well-being. This was obviously a response to the stress of contact.
58. "Rulebook for the Court of Indian Offenses," RCUA, 44016: General and Statistical: Reports and Enrollment, Box 7, NARA, Denver.
59. "Rulebook for the Court of Indian Offenses," RCUA, 44016.
60. The agent's annual reports to the CIA included a "Law and Order" section in which virtually every agent from 1906 to 1929 told how they stressed the need for legal marriages.
61. *General Statutes of the State of Colorado, 1883* (Denver, CO: Times Stream Printing and Publishing House, 1883), 397–98, 244. The 1891 statute book elaborated on these provisions but did not alter them in any way. See *General Statutes of the State of Colorado, 1891*, 1035–1050.
62. *General Statutes*, 1891, 1044–46.
63. McKean to CIA, 26 November 1917, RSUA, CCF, 104064–310, NARA, Washington, D.C.

64. 44011–44013, *passim*, RCUA, NARA, Denver.

65. Leonard to CIA, 3 November 1906, RCUA, 44011, NARA, Denver.

66. Annual Report to the Commissioner of Indian Affairs (ARCIA), 1907, 44011, RCUA, NARA, Denver, CO; "Southern Ute Marriage Records, 1901–1911," Stewart Collection, Series II, Box 3, Norlin , Boulder, CO; Agent's Annual Statistical Reports, 1912–1925, RCUA, 44016: General and Statistical, Reports and Enrollments, Box 8, NARA, Denver.

67. Annual Report to the Commissioner of Indian Affairs (ARCIA), 1907, 44011, RCUA, NARA, Denver, CO; "Southern Ute Marriage Records, 1901–1911," Stewart Collection, Series II, Box 3, Norlin , Boulder, CO; Agent's Annual Statistical Reports, 1912–1925, RCUA, 44016: General and Statistical, Reports and Enrollments, Box 8, NARA, Denver. Also see "Southern Ute Census Records, 1880, 1900, 1912, 1923, 1932," Stewart Collection, Series II, Box 4; "Southern Ute Death Records," Tri-ethnic Files.

68. "Southern Ute Census Records, 1880, 1900, 1912, 1923, 1932," Stewart Collection, Series II, Box 4; "Southern Ute Death Records," Tri-ethnic Files. I was able to trace fifty-five of the couples through death and census records, individual Indian files, and agent's correspondence.

69. I am grateful to Richard White for helping me to clarify this concept. While he uses the term middle ground with respect to contact relations based on the political autonomy of Native Americans, the broader sense of the term refers to an idea or cultural convention which may form a common basis for understanding between the cultures. To say that two sides on the contact continuum found a middle ground is not to argue that they viewed a given idea or convention in exactly the same way. Indeed, one or the other side usually distorted the other's meaning according to their own cultural premises. Nevertheless, a cultural congruence in which both sides pursued the same goals often resulted from the middle ground. See Richard White, *The Middle Ground: Indians, Empires, and Republics in the Great Lakes Region, 1650–1815* (NY: Cambridge University Press, 1991).

8

CLIFFORD E. TRAFZER

HORSES AND CATTLE, BUGGIES AND HACKS

PURCHASES BY YAKIMA INDIAN WOMEN, 1909–1912

An 1855 treaty between the United States and several different tribal groups living on the Columbia Plateau marked the boundaries for the Yakima Reservation in what is now south-central Washington State. Although the Indian signers of the treaty tried to preserve rights to traditional root-gathering and fishing spots, they also incorporated farming and ranching activities into their economy. Under the Dawes Act, the Yakima Reservation was allotted into individually owned plots of land in 1892, thereby encouraging the Yakimas to invest more heavily in farming and ranching. Despite the provisions for Indian citizenship and individual self-sufficiency explicit in the philosophy behind allotment, the Bureau of Indian Affairs (BIA) continued to maintain a paternalistic surveillance over reservation Indians. BIA purchasing records, which Clifford Trafzer has used to study women's participation in the reservation economy, are one by-product of BIA supervision over the ordinary, daily life of individual Indians.

Women played powerful roles within the various bands of Indians of the Pacific Northwest Plateau. Traditionally, Yakima and other Plateau Indians were patrilineal but women served as religious leaders and Indian doctors, helping their people in many ways. They advised male leaders about important decisions, and they fought alongside men in battle. Women often led the family and served as primary providers by gathering nutritious roots, berries, onions, mosses, and other foods. Yakima women fished and hunted, and they preserved a variety of nutritious foods upon which their families survived from year to year.[1] For generations the Yakima and their neighbors lived by following a "seasonal round," moving from their permanent villages on the Yakima River in the spring to gather roots, only to return in the summer to fish salmon. In the fall they left again as women dug late roots and gathered berries while men hunted, gambled, and traded horses. Women also dressed, smoked, and dried meat and fish for their families and for trade during this season. In the late autumn, "the time when the tamaracks turn yellow," the men, women, and children returned to their homes along the Yakima River and its tributaries, completing the seasonal rounds through which the people lived.[2]

Before the arrival of whites in the Pacific Northwest, women were influential in the economic life of the Yakima people. They continued to play a significant role in the tribe's economy after the arrival of whites and the establishment of territorial government by the United States. Life changed dramatically for women and men in 1855, after the United States negotiated a treaty with the Indians in the Walla Walla Valley.[3] A few of the male leaders of the tribe signed the Yakima Treaty of 1855, which established the Yakima Reservation in central Washington Territory. Governor Isaac Ingalls Stevens placed the names of several different tribes in the preamble of the treaty, including the Yakima, Palouse, Wenatchee, Wanapum, and Wishram. Other tribes and bands were made party to the treaty, including people from three distinct language families. The agency considered all of these Indians to be "Yakima," and in the documents all of the people are categorized by whites as such. In reality some of them were from other tribes or of mixed tribal ancestry, but all of them living on the Yakima Reservation were subject to the policies of the United States government. All of the Indians residing on the Yakima Reservation had to cope with a new system which was imposed on them by the Bureau of Indian Affairs. The federal government established its dominance over Indian people through the Yakima Treaty and a military conquest conducted between 1855 and 1858.[4] Agents of the United States forced men, women, and children to accept life under a system designed to destroy elements of Yakima culture.[5] The government was successful to some extent, but the Yakima survived the invasion of their lands and the policies of the Bureau of Indian Affairs. The Yakima adapted to their new situation, preserving portions of their culture and acculturating elements of new ways.

By the early years of the twentieth century, the Yakima ranched and farmed in order to supplement their traditional economy of gathering, hunting, and fishing.[6] They turned to ranching and farming partly in response to the Dawes Act, by which part of the reservation was divided into parcels of 160, 80, or 40 acres. By 1909, Indian Agent Samuel Young wrote the Commissioner of Indian Affairs that "if judged by ideal standards," the Yakima "are backwards." But in comparison "with other tribes," the Indians under his charge were "doing well." He made these comments in relation to the Indian economy, the first measure of concern discussed in his annual report.[7]

According to Agent Young, the men and women of the Yakima Nation had made a "commendable" start "in the way of farming and stock raising." The Indians had planted fields of varying sizes "ranging . . . from small patches to areas of respectable size." They grew gardens of "fruits and berries, and small grains." The agent felt that farming methods used by the Indians were "not satisfactory, but it is encouraging to note that genuine efforts are being made."[8] In order to improve agriculture, the agency urged Indians to purchase farm equipment in the hope that technological devices would improve production. By 1912 Agent Donald M. Carr reported that "During the past three or four years a considerable amount of individual Indian money has been spent in the purchase of good serviceable teams, wagons, harness and implements." The Yakima men and women had made "progress" in the construction "of small homes and stables." The agent went on to say that the purchase "of implements for the Indians will not assist them materially in their farming operations."[9]

Regardless of Carr's opinion, the Indians believed that they had something to gain from the purchase of farm equipment, harnesses, hacks, and a host of other items. The Yakima people earned their own money through land-leasing, farm labor, ranch work, freighting, government employment, and domestic labor.[10] The federal government did not give the people cash for merely being Indian, as is often believed, but men, women, and children worked and leased their lands. Since the Yakima made their own money, they decided for themselves how they would spend it. Indians chose to buy a number of goods with their earnings, and a detailed record of their buying has survived, focusing on purchases made by Yakima women and men for a limited amount of time in the early twentieth century. According to the Yakima Agency Census of 1910, 2679 men, women, and children lived on the Yakima Reservation. According to one scholar, about 225 people farmed, but the author provides no indication of the farmers' gender. Documents kept by the Bureau of Indian Affairs provide a closer view of purchases made by females and males on the reservation, and these shed some light on the reservation economy, particularly with regard to gender.[11]

Significantly, the Bills of Sale For Personal Property reveal that Yakima women were the major buyers on the reservation, which suggests that in spite of the reservation system, women continued to play an important role in the tribe's economy during the first two decades of the twentieth century.

Between 1909 and 1912, the agents working on the Yakima Indian Reservation recorded Bills of Sale For Personal Property as part of an effort to legally record every business transaction made by Indians under their jurisdiction.[12] In addition to recording the purchases, the agents also described—often in some detail—the items purchased by an Indian. The national policy of recording and describing every purchase made by Native Americans on an Indian reservation was an outgrowth of the Progressive Era. Convinced that non-Indian traders were taking advantage of them, Progressives in the Bureau of Indian Affairs decided to track every purchase made by an Indian. Of course, this was paternalism on a massive scale, but the Progressives determined that it was justified and the only way to prevent whites, particularly licensed Indian traders doing business on the reservation, from taking advantage of Indians.

The national policy of recording and describing the Bills of Sale began in 1909. According to Secretary of the Interior R. A. Ballinger and to Commissioner of Indian Affairs R. G. Valentine, they ordered the Bills of Sale to be executed on every Indian Reservation in order to place all business "dealings with the Indians . . . on a strictly cash basis" and to allow the agent to review each purchase made by an Indian. In this way the agent conceivably could prevent whites from cheating. It was also a way in which an Indian agent could monitor the purchases of Indians and advise them of "wasteful" expenditures.[13] The agents kept copies of the Bills of Sale until 1912, when the Bureau of Indian Affairs ended the procedure. Officials working at the Yakima Agency kept all of these documents and ultimately deposited a total of 572 Bills of Sale in the National Archives, Pacific Northwest, in Seattle, Washington. Of the 572 purchases, women made 315 and men made 250, with seven individuals unidentified in terms of their gender.

The data described in the Bills of Sale include many variables that were coded for the present study of the Yakima economy. The documents provided descriptions of the items bought, including detailed discussions of the type, quality, and quantity. All of the items fell into six broad categories: horses, cattle, wagons-buggies-hacks, harnesses-collars, farm equipment, and household goods. The household goods included flour, salt, coffee, eating utensils, and the like. It also included lumber, fencing, tools, roofing, etc. All of the items purchased were coded into one of the six categories mentioned above. The agents provided discussions of all of the items, including graphic descriptions of horses and cattle—their breeds, brands, weights, colors, and ages. These descriptive variables were not coded, but some samples of them have been provided in the narrative. The agents also noted the year, amount, and geographical location of the purchases. They recorded the individual or company from which the items were purchased as well as the buyer's gender. These two variables were coded as well as the literacy of the buyers. All of the Bills of Sale were signed by the parties involved. If the buyer could write her or his name, the document had the person's signature. However, if the individual could not write their name, the agent typed the person's name and had them place a thumbprint on the document. If the person could write their name, they were coded as literate, and if they provided a thumbprint, they were coded as non-literate.[14] Because the amounts spent ranged from $1 to $350, it was determined to arrange them in the following categories: $1 to $50, $51 to $100, $101 to $200, $201 to $300, and $301 to $500. All of the geographical places of purchase coded are found in Washington state, and they include such major sites as Fort Simcoe, Toppenish, Wapato, North Yakima, and White Swan. If the purchases were made by the Indians outside of these areas, they were coded as "other."

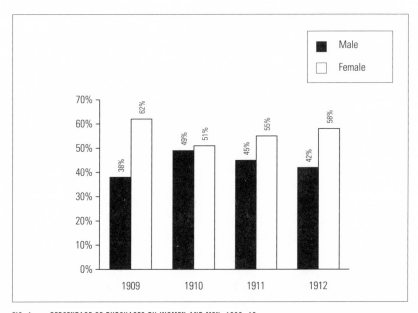

FIG. 1.   PERCENTAGE OF PURCHASES BY WOMEN AND MEN, 1909–12.

Overall, between 1909 and 1912, women made 315 (66%) of the purchases, while men made 250 (44%) of them. During the four-year period, women made more purchases than men, and they spent more money in each of the four years. In 1909 women made 39 (62%) purchases while men made 24 (38%) of them. The next year, purchases by women and men were fairly even, with women buying goods 76 (51%) times and men doing so 74 (49%) times. In 1911 women made 113 purchases (55%), while men made 92 (45%). This ratio increased slightly the next year with women making 77 (58%) of the purchases and men making 55 (42%). Although the difference in percentages of purchases made by females and males was generally not great, it is clear that women made more purchases than men each year, which indicates a high degree of activity in purchasing goods on the reservation (Figure 1).

The item purchased most often by women and men was horses. Women made 111 (53%) of the horse purchases during this time, while men made 99 (47%) of them (Figure 2). Horses first arrived on the Columbia Plateau around 1750, and the Indians of the region—particularly the Yakima— quickly adopted the horse culture.[15] Men and women bought, traded, and owned horses, and the animals served as a means of exchange for many

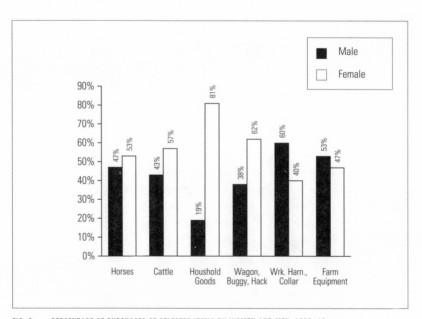

FIG. 2. PERCENTAGE OF PURCHASES OF SELECTED ITEMS BY WOMEN AND MEN, 1909–12.

years. Horses were an important element of Yakima Indian culture through-out the nineteenth century, and they continued to be an important component of Yakima culture into the twentieth century. Indeed, horses remain an integral part of Yakima culture at the end of the twentieth cen-tury, although their usefulness has diminished markedly. During the era studied, Yakima people relied heavily on horses for work, transportation, and trade. According to the Bills of Sale, the Yakima bought a variety of horses, described in the documents in many colorful ways. One Yakima woman bought a buckskin mare in foal with a star on her forehead, "the season [breeding] being paid," while another woman bought a cream-colored gelding of sixteen hands with a wire cut and a "fleabitten grey." On April 22, 1911, Yehamloot bought two horses for $250, including "one sor-rel mare nine yrs. old branded **N** on left shoulder stip in face both hind feet white weight 1150" and "one black mare nine years old star in face right hind foot white branded **T** on Right stifle 1150 lbs." On August 2, 1911 Stauce Talpocken bought two horses for $350, including "one bay horse 9 yrs. old branded **HP** on right shoulder weight 1200 lbs.," and "one bay mare seven yrs old light branded left side of neck **8** wire cut left shoulder weight 1200 lbs." Jennie Tainwasher bought a "sound and true" team of horses on April 25, 1911, described by Charles Whitaker of the Yakima Agency as "one white horse brown spots on him brown ears branded **A** on left shoulder six yrs old weight 1300 lbs.," and "one bay mare four yrs star in face snip on nose left hind foot white weight 1250 lbs." On May 3, 1911 Wanitha Sharnute paid $400 for "one roan horse branded **G** on left shoul-der five yrs. old blaze face left hind foot white wight 1300 lbs." and "one sorrel mare unbranded nine yrs. old weight 1400 lbs."[16]

Women not only purchased more horses than men, they also bought more cattle. From 1909 through 1912, women made 20 purchases of cat-tle (57% of total), while men made 15 (43%) (Figure 2). As was the case with horses, often a person bought more than one item in a single pur-chase. The Bills of Sale offer informative descriptions of the cattle bought by Yakima people, including the color, sex, and brands used to mark the animals. On October 28, 1911 Jennie Tainwasher paid $60 for "one white cow three years old branded **C** on right hip natural muley." On March 21 of the same year, Maggie Cree spent $100 for "one red cow with white face and white joints Branded thus an H right shoulder" and "one red cow." On January 20, 1911, Lillian Cleparty spent $395 on "one dark red muley heifer Branded **0** in right hip two years old, One red heifer white line down back both ears notched two years-old, One light red heifer white belly 2 years old, One light red heifer branded **Ln** left side three years old." And Susan B. Brown bought "one red cow six years old branded **A.Y.** on right hip" for $50. According to the Bills of Sale, women bought more horses and cattle than men between 1909 and 1912.[17]

Women also bought more household goods. During the era under discussion, women made 30 purchases of household items (81% of total), while men made 7 (19%). This is a significant finding, since household goods included much more than foodstuffs and items normally considered in this category. For the purpose of this study, household items included a wide range of goods needed for the maintenance of a home, farm, and ranch. Such items as beds, mattresses, and dining chairs were coded as household items. Home improvement items such as paint, rugs, and linoleum were also coded in this category. Larger appliances such as cook stoves, heating stoves, washing machines, and sewing machines were coded as household goods. In addition, lumber, barbed wire, nails, staples, troughs, chains, and shingles were placed in this category. Tools such as hammers, screwdrivers, cornseeders, planes, bits, braces, pliers, and the like were also coded in this general category. On December 24, 1910, Heneset Sitwell of Toppenish bought "one cook stove and utensils" for $75. In February of the same year, Anna Riddle bought "Six (6) Dining Chairs" for $14, "40 yards of Linoleum" for $30, and "1 Rug (9'x12')" for $6. Julia Abram bought "One Ideal Brown Range, # 816" for $50 on October 20, 1910. Many other items were included in this category, and women purchased a vast majority of them.[18]

Women also bought wagons, buggies, and hacks more often than men. During the period from 1909 through 1912, women bought 96 (62%) of these vehicles, while men bought 53 (38%) of them (Figure 2). Some of the best descriptions written by the officials of the Yakima Agency were those discussing these vehicles. On August 11, 1910, for example, Heimstulle Whitefoot spent $163 for a "No. 212 Michigan mountain spring wagon" and a "set double work harness with collars." Sally Ann Tainewasher spent $175 on "One top buggy with pole" and "One set of double driving harness." Minnie Boone spent the same amount on a "Birdsell Wagon Complelet, with box and seat" and "One set Heavy double work harness, Red Special 1 1/2" tug with Boston Team Collar." Agatha Abkahter Emowtenesshet spent $125 on a "Winona Wagon complete with box seat and whipple trees." According to the Bills of Sale, Yakima women bought Molino Wagons, Studebacker Hacks, and Moon Brothers Top Buggies with red gears and rubber tires.[19]

Like horses, cattle, and tools, vehicles are often perceived as being items of material culture associated with males. This was certainly not the case among the Yakima, where men and women purchased, owned, traded, and sold such items. Once they were introduced into Plateau Indian culture, women and men dealt in horses and cattle. Yakima women made, purchased, and owned their own household tools, such as knives, awls, needles, scrapers, and hatchets. Women were also responsible for taking care of the camp, dismantling and reestablishing tipis and mat lodges, and moving from root grounds to fishing areas. Thus, in one form or another, Yakima women had long been involved in acquiring and maintaining material culture that was used to enhance the well-being of their families, and they continued to do this once the United States confined them to the reservation.

In the other two categories coded from the Bills of Sale, men bought more goods than did women. Men made 33 purchases of work harnesses and collars (60% of total), while women made 22 (40%). Men also made more purchases of farm equipment than did women, with men making 41 (53%) of all purchases and women making 37 (47%) of them (Figure 2). In terms of farm equipment, Yakima women were involved in a good many purchases, in part because agriculture was closely tied to the well-being of the family. Yakima women had always played major roles in gathering, preserving, and preparing roots, berries, and other natural foods for their families. Once the United States forced them onto the reservation and white farmers and ranchers destroyed ancient Indian food sources, Yakima women and men were forced to concentrate more of their attention on agriculture and ranching.[20]

Since food-getting had traditionally been a function of women as well as men, females became involved in the efficient production of foods that whites had introduced to them after the establishment of the reservation. In sum, women purchased work harnesses-collars and farm equipment, but not as often as men (Figure 2). According to the documents the Yakima paid for hay derricks, mowers, binders, and plows. The Bills of Sale Reveal that on June 30, 1911, Susan Smattie bought "One 3-1/4" Mitchell Farm Wagon, with 13 foot California Stake rack bed" for $130. Anna Barlow bought "One New Four, 5 Ft. Cut McCormick Mower" for $60. In June of 1910, Anna Boone bought a "ten foot McCormick rake" for $37.50, and in July, Jennie Charles spent $175 on "One 6' cut McCormick Binding with truck." Ruth Supie Sohappy spent $100 on a "McCormick Mower, 5-Ft." and "One McCormick Rake."[21]

Women spent more money than men in every category of size of purchase. In that category of expenditure from $1 to $50, women made 43 purchases (55% of total), while men made 35 (45%). In that category of cash from $51 to $100, women made 80 purchases (58%), and men made 59

(42%). In that category of money from $101 to $200, women made 109 transactions (55%), while men made 90 (45%). Women also made more purchases in that category between $201 and $300. Women made 38 purchases (53%) while men made 34 (47%). Finally, in that category from $301 to $500, women made 46 purchases (55%), while men made 37 (45%). It is clear from these statistics that women made more purchases than men in general, and women made more purchases of every size (Figure 3).

When Yakima women and men bought items, they preferred to buy them from other Indians rather than non-Indians or from trading posts. The Yakima made 147 purchases among themselves (26% of all purchases) and 101 (17%) between Yakima and non-native people who were not associated with trading posts. Of all purchases made by Yakima, 248 (43%) of the transactions were between Native Americans and non-Indians who were not traders (Figure 4). Of those purchases made by Yakima with other Indians, 84 (57%) were made by women and 63 (43%) were made by men. Women preferred to purchase goods from other Indians, and they did so more often than did men. However, of those purchases made by Yakima with non-Indians who were not traders, 53 (52%) were made by men and 48 (48%) were made by women. This represents a

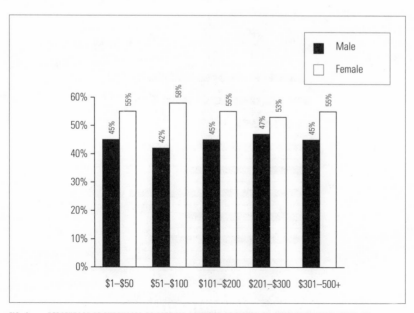

FIG. 3.   PERCENTAGE OF PURCHASES OF SPECIFIC AMOUNTS OF MONEY BY WOMEN AND MEN, 1909–12.

fairly even split, and gender does not appear to be a major factor in terms of purchases made between Indians and those made between the Yakima and non-Indians (Figure 4).

However, gender seems to have played a role in purchases made by Yakima women and men at three trading posts. Most important were the purchases made by women at the Toppenish Trading Company. This trading post was located in Toppenish, Washington, which became the agency headquarters in 1922.[22] The trading post was situated in an area with a large Indian population, and during the period, Yakima women and men made 79 (8%) of all purchases at it. This company had more commerce with the Yakima than any other trading post on the reservation during the four-year period. Of those purchases made there, women made 45 (76%) while men made 34 (24%) (Figure 4). A similar, but less dramatic, situation is found at the Wyman Sheldon Company which had trading posts in Fort Simcoe and North Yakima. Of the total number of purchases made at these stores, women made 17 (61%), while men made 11 (39%). Men, however, made more purchases at Otto Lubbes Trading Post in Toppenish, Washington. Of all the purchases made at this trading post, men made 16 (59%) and women made 11 (41%). Men also made more purchases at the Coburn

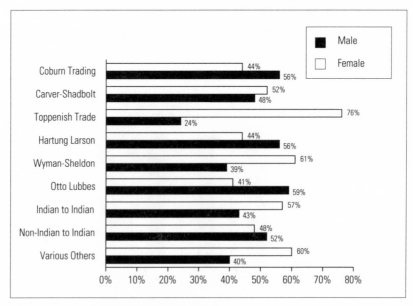

FIG. 4.   PERCENTAGE OF PURCHASES BY WOMEN AND MEN
WITH INDIVIDUALS AND TRADING COMPANIES, 1909–12.

Trading Company of White Swan and the Hartung Larson Trading Post of Wapato, but not by great margins (Figure 4). Since there was roughly an equal number of men and women in the population, perhaps it was the operation of particular trading posts that appealed to Yakima women and men. The companies that attracted women may have catered to them, employing women, including native women, who spoke Yakima and understood the culture. Since Yakima women were less literate than Yakima men (Figure 6), they may have felt more comfortable dealing at a company that hired Yakima speakers, male or female.

In any case, gender was a factor at some trading posts, but the location of the trading post also influenced purchases made by women. Women were generally more assertive in their buying at Toppenish and Wapato, places that had long been used by the Yakima as village sites. This may have been the result of the fact that women ran the family ranches while men picked crops, did day labor, and freighted goods for a living.[23] Before the arrival of the railroad to Toppenish in 1883, this Indian community prided itself on its traditionalism, and long into the twentieth century it maintained a *ka'dnam* or longhouse where *Washat* ceremonies were conducted regularly.[24] Toppenish was a *traditional* Indian town where women, not men, were more intimately involved in the economy as in a traditional setting— women were the economic power in a traditional Indian setting. Toppenish was also located some distance from Fort Simcoe, where the United States maintained the Yakima Agency headquarters until 1922. At Toppenish, women conducted 154 business transactions between individuals and all trading companies (60% of total), while men made 66 (40%). A similar situation emerged in Wapato, where women made 39 transactions (68%) and men conducted 24 (32%). Men were more economically minded in towns closer to whites where they were influenced by white males. Thus, men did more business at Fort Simcoe, White Swan, and North Yakima. At Fort Simcoe, men made 89 transactions (58%), while women made 64 (42%). At White Swan men made 14 purchases (56%), while women made 11 (44%) of them. At North Yakima, an area influenced by the influx and power of non-Indians, Yakima men made 49 (64%) of the purchases, while women made 27 (36%) of the deals (Figure 5). Thus, geographical areas influenced purchases, with women making more purchases in regions farther from the influences of the Bureau of Indian Affairs—an agency that hired more men than women. Overall, women made more transactions and spent more money than men between 1909 and 1912.[25]

The Bills of Sale offer a glimpse into the question of literacy among women and men, since they indicate the purchaser's gender and were signed either with a signature or a thumbprint. It is conceivable that a person signing a Bill of Sale with their signature knew nothing more of written English than their name. It is also conceivable that a person using their thumbprint knew how to read and write. Nevertheless, for the purposes of this study, those who wrote their name were considered literate. Only 67 (21%) of the women who purchased goods between 1909 and 1912 were able to write their names, while 248 (79%) of them signed the documents with their thumbprint. A total of 128 Yakima men (51%) wrote their names, while 122 (49%) made their mark. (Figure 6). The differences in literacy among Yakima men and women was likely the result of a gender bias inherent among agents and school superintendents of the Bureau of Indian Affairs who focused more of their educational endeavors on Indian males. This mirrors an educational bias found in the larger society of the time. Significantly, however, literacy did not influence the purchasing of goods, since non-literate and literate people purchased items, and, in fact, non-literate individuals bought goods more often than literate people (Figure 7).

The documents suggest that literate Indians were more likely to purchase goods from non-Indians, but not by any great margin. The evidence shows that of the Indians who dealt with non-Indians, 52 (53%) were

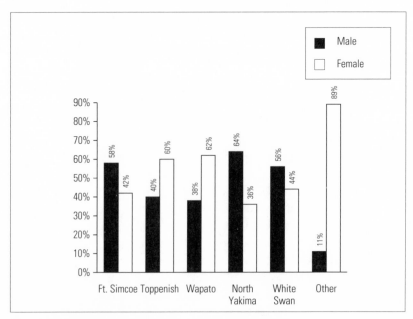

FIG. 5. PERCENTAGE OF PURCHASES BY WOMEN AND MEN AT SELECTED PLACES
ON OR NEAR THE YAKIMA RESERVATION.

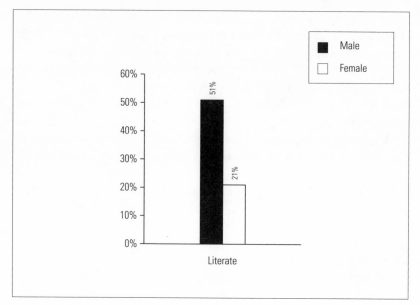

FIG. 6.   PERCENTAGE OF LITERACY AMONG WOMEN AND MEN, 1909–12.

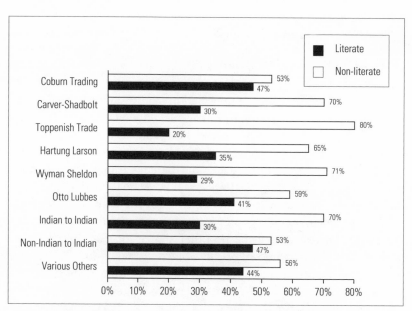

FIG. 7.   PERCENTAGE OF PURCHASES WITH INDIVIDUALS AND TRADING COMPANIES BY LITERATE AND
          NON-LITERATE WOMEN AND MEN, 1909–12.

literate and 46 (47%) were non-literate. The Bills of Sale also illustrate that of the women and men who bought goods from other Indians, 101 (70%) were not literate and 44 (30%) were literate. Most of the purchases made between Indians were made by women who were not literate (Figure 7). Between 1909 and 1912, the non-literate Indians made 370 (66%) of all purchases, and literate Indians made 195 (34%) of them. Again, literacy played no role in deterring men or women from making purchases. This is particularly apparent since women were not literate more often than men, and yet women made most of the purchases and spent more money on the reservation (Figures 1, 2 and 3).

Historically, some white observers viewed Yakima women as subservient to men who forced the women to do the hard labor. While it is true that Indian women engaged in hard work, it is not true that they were subordinate to Yakima men. Traditionally, Yakima women were powerful actors within their communities, particularly in the area of the economy. They provided the bulk of the food by digging roots, harvesting berries, fishing for salmon, and preserving all of the natural bounty. The invasion of whites into the Yakima Valley and the dominance of the Bureau of Indian Affairs radically changed the nature of Yakima life. After 1860 the Yakima were no longer able to live as a free and independent nation, moving in bands across the Columbia Plateau, over the Cascades to the Pacific Coast, or across the Bitterroot Mountains to the buffalo country. Some of the traditional roles of men and women changed as a result of the white invasion, but Yakima traditionalism remained, exhibiting itself in a variety of ways.

The Bills of Sale from 1909 through 1912 provide a limited but illuminating glimpse of Indian life during the early twentieth century. The documents provide a source of information that was not recorded in the agency letterbooks kept by the Indian agents of the time. The documents offer a brief look at the actions of individual Indians through their purchases over a four-year period, and they reveal that women made the majority of purchases and that they out-purchased men when buying horses, cattle, wagons-buggies-hacks, and household goods. The documents do not indicate where the women got the cash to make each purchase or whether their spouses instructed them to make certain purchases, and there seems to be no other source for such information. However, given the traditional role of women in Yakima society in terms of the economy, it seems reasonable to argue that women continued to play an important role in the Yakima economy in spite of the reservation system and the presence of white males who ran the Yakima Agency. The documents show that women made a majority of the purchases on the

Yakima Reservation from 1909 through 1912, and they spent more money than men. Thus, Yakima women, who had always been a powerful part in the tribal economy, continued to do so on the reservation during the first years of the twentieth century.

NOTES

1. Funding for this research was made possible by the American Council of Learned Societies. The author wishes to thank Neal Hickman, Helen Schuster, and Colleen Plante who assisted in producing this essay. Scholarly works about the Yakima recognize the significance of women to the economy of the people. This is seen in the numerous documents assembled for the Indian Claims Commission cases, Record Group 279, National Archives, Washington, D.C. See Helen H. Schuster, "Yakima Indian Traditionalism: A Study in Continuity and Change," Ph.D. Dissertation, University of Washington, 1975, 72–81; Verne Ray, Cultural Relations in the Plateau of Northwestern America (Los Angeles: Southwest Museum, 1939), 14–24.

2. Schuster, "Yakima Indian Traditionalism," 81–87.

3. "Documents Relating to Negotiations of Ratified and Unratified Treaties," Microfilm T494, Reel 5, Record Group 75, National Archives. For an analysis of the Walla Walla Council and the Yakima position regarding the Yakima Treaty of 1855, see Clifford E. Trafzer and Richard D. Scheuerman, Renegade Tribe: The Palouse Indians and the Invasion of the Inland Pacific Northwest (Pullman: Washington State University Press, 1986), 46–59.

4. Accounts of the Plateau Indian War, 1855–1858, involving the Yakima are found in Trafzer and Scheuerman, Renegade Tribe, 60–92, and Alvin M. Josephy, Jr., The Nez Perce Indians and the Opening of the Northwest (New Haven: Yale University Press, 1965), 333–385. The war caused severe factionalism among the Yakima during the early reservation period, 1855–1880, and this is described in Trafzer and Scheuerman, Renegade Tribe, 93–102 and Schuster, "Yakima Indian Traditionalism," 234–248.

5. Schuster, "Yakima Indian Traditionalism," 234–257.

6. Schuster, 260–262; Donald W. Meinig, The Great Columbia Plain: A Historical Geography, 1805–1910 (Seattle: University of Washington Press, 1968), 448–450. Meinig (p. 450) states that "Of the approximately 3,000 Indians on the Yakima Reservation, about 225 were doing 'more or less farming,' a few had herds of cattle or sheep, a good many owned range horses, but an increasing number were found in and about Toppenish . . . doing day labor, freighting or some sort of team work."

7. Agent Young to Commissioner Valentine, 22 July 1909, Yakima Agency, Box 17, Letters Sent, Record Group (RG) 75, National Archives, Pacific Northwest Region, (NAPNW), Seattle, Washington. The author wishes to thank Joyce Justice of the National Archives, Seattle, for her generous assistance.

8. Young to Valentine, 22 July 1909, Yakima Agency.

9. Agent Carr to Commissioner, 19 August 1912, Yakima Agency, Box 20, Letters Sent, RG 75, NAPNW, Seattle. In this letter the newly appointed Yakima agent wrote: "In a great majority of cases, however, I feel that the best results have not been obtained because of lack of the required assistance at the psychological time."

10. Meinig, *The Columbia Plain*, 450; Schuster, "Yakima Indian Traditionalism," 260.
11. Yakima Agency Census, RG 75, NAPNW, Seattle; Meinig, *The Columbia Plain*, 450. According to the Yakima Agency Census, the number of Yakima reported living on the reservation for 1911 and 1912 respectively was 2622 and 3046. The Agency did not record a census for the Yakima in 1909.
12. "Bills Of Sale For Personal Property," Yakima Agency, Box 766, RG 75, NAPNW, Seattle. Robert Grosvenor Valentine served as Commissioner of Indian Affairs from 1909 to 1912, and he ordered the use of Bills of Sale in a sincere attempt "to protect the interests of the Indians." Valentine was a Progressive who wanted to curb the abuses of unscrupulous traders and merchants dealing with Indians. The Bills of Sale emerged with his administration, and they disappeared in 1913 with the appointment of Cato Sells as Commissioner. See Robert M. Kvasnicka and Herman J. Viola, eds., *The Commissioners of Indian Affairs, 1824–1977* (Lincoln: University of Nebraska Press, 1979), 238.
13. Secretary of Interior R. A. Ballinger and Commissioner of Indian Affairs R. G. Valentine, "Trading With Indians," Circular, December 17, 1909, Yakima Agency, Box 70, RG 75, NAPNW, Seattle. According to the census data kept by the Bureau of Indian Affairs, the officials did not take a census of the Yakima Reservation in 1909. However, the census of 1910 reveals that there were 2679 Indians living on the reservation, and the census of 1911 indicated that there were 2622 of them. In 1912 the census indicated that there were 3046 Yakima. See Yakima Census.
14. "Bills Of Sale For Personal Property."
15. Francis Haines, "The Northward Spread of Horses Among the Plains Indians," *American Anthropologist* 40 (1938): 429–437; "The Western Limits of the Buffalo Range," *Pacific Northwest Quarterly* 31 (1940): 389–398; and "Where Did the Plains Indians Get Their Horses?" *American Anthropologist* 40 (1938): 112–117. For a general discussion of horses, see Frank G. Roe, *The Indian and the Horse* (Norman: University of Oklahoma Press, 1968).
16. Case 150, 106, 107, 189, 268, 37, "Bills Of Sale For Personal Property," Yakima Agency, RG 75, NAPNWTC, Seattle. The cases are arranged in the notes in the order they appear in the text.
17. Cases 342, 357, 380, 261, *Ibid.*
18. Cases 324, 332, 326, *Ibid.*
19. Cases 307, 283, 256, *Ibid.*
20. Trafzer and Scheuerman, *Renegade Tribe*, 122–135; Schuster, "Yakima Indian Traditionalism," 246, 250, 252, 254, 260–261.
21. Cases 223, 352, 347, 353, 298, "Bills of Sale for Personal Property."
22. Helen H. Schuster, *The Yakima* (New York: Chelsea House Publishers, 1990), 89–90.
23. Schuster, "Yakima Indian Traditionalism," 260.
24. Schuster, 388.
25. The Bureau of Indian Affairs was the domain of white males who generally hired Indian males and not females. In matters of hiring and education, Indian agents focused their attention on Indian males. This was the case at Fort Simcoe, agency headquarters of the Yakima Agency. See Letterbooks, Yakima Indian Agency, RG 75, NAPNW, Seattle.

9

HARRY A. KERSEY, JR.
AND HELEN M. BANNAN

PATCHWORK AND POLITICS
THE EVOLVING ROLES OF FLORIDA
SEMINOLE WOMEN IN THE 20TH CENTURY

The Seminoles are descended from Creek Indians who migrated from Georgia to Spanish Florida in the eighteenth century. The Creeks who migrated usually spoke either the Muskogee or Mikasuki language. In an 1819 treaty, the U.S. acquired Florida and immediately began putting pressure on the Seminoles to cede land claims and accept a reservation. The Seminoles resisted and fought the U.S. in several wars in the 1830s through 1850s. Captured Seminoles were forcibly removed to Indian Territory (now Oklahoma). A small minority managed to escape capture by retreating into the Everglades. In the twentieth century, these surviving Florida Seminoles worked to solidify claims to reservation land and to organize as tribes. Some of the Mikasuki-speaking Seminoles formed the Miccosukee Tribe and have a reservation along the Tamiami Trail. Five other reservations—Hollywood (formerly Dania), Brighton, Big Cypress, one at Immokalee, and one in Tampa—belong to the Seminole Tribe of Florida. Kersey and Bannan show how Seminole women's entry into politics is a recent, twentieth-century development related to the Seminoles' changing economy.

It seems fitting to use the metaphor of patchwork to discuss the process of evolution that has occurred in Florida Seminole women's roles throughout this century. Patchwork, a "traditional" craft that relies upon the technology of the sewing machine, and expresses individual taste and talent in culturally consistent patterns, authentically reflects the synthesis of heritage and adaptation achieved by Seminole women. Building upon cultural traditions of matrilineal clans and a gender-based division of labor and "spheres," whereby women controlled the home and men the town and relationships with outsiders, Seminole women have expanded their activities and have gained greater recognition of their influence.

Historically, women played an extremely important role as cultural conservators among the Seminoles, a people whose complicated history requires some explanation to understand in terms of both change and continuity in recent times. Today's Seminoles are the descendants of an amalgam of Southeastern Indian peoples who began migrating to Florida in the 18th century. Most were Muskogees from Georgia and Alabama, called Creeks by the English because they were first contacted at Ochese Creek and their towns generally were situated on streams. Internally, the Muskogees were divided into the politically dominant Upper Creeks, who spoke Muskogee, and the Lower Creeks, who spoke the language now called Mikasuki.

In 1704, the English from Charleston, South Carolina, as part of the imperial wars of that period, invaded Spanish Florida and destroyed the Franciscan missions which harbored the surviving Timucuan and Apalachee Indians. Virtually the entire aboriginal population was either killed or carried back to slavery in Carolina. The Spaniards, anxious to fill this void and thwart English expansion, invited the Lower Creeks to move into Florida, where they could occupy the vacated lands, free of both Upper Creek control and encroachment by English settlers from the new colony of Georgia, founded in 1732. The Spaniards promised ample trade and no missionary efforts among the towns.

Several Lower Creek groups accepted this invitation and established towns across northern Florida. A few Upper Creek towns also relocated to Florida in the 1760s. When the English gained control of Florida in 1763, they began calling all Indians in the colony Seminoles, a Muskogee corruption of the Spanish word *cimarrón*, meaning "wild" or "runaway," which had been applied to the migrating Lower Creeks. Following the destructive intervention of Andrew Jackson's forces in the Creek Civil War of 1813–14, a contingent of several thousand of the most virulently anti-American Upper Creeks migrated to Florida. They refused to live under American domination and came to join the Seminoles, since Florida was then under Spanish control, prior to its annexation by the U.S. in 1821.

All of these groups of Seminoles shared a common Southeastern woodlands culture based on town social and political organizations, matrilineal clans and kinship systems, as well as religious beliefs centering on the annual Green Corn Dance. Traditionally, Seminoles were both matrilineal and matrilocal. Following a typically Southeastern, but most particularly Creek, pattern of matrilineal clan and kinship, each Seminole individual inherited a clan identity through the mother. Clan membership determined residence and marriage partners, as well as political and social roles and responsibilities. All knowledge pertaining to clan origins, functions, and ritual roles was transmitted to a child through the mother and her relatives, primarily the matrilineal uncles.

This process was reinforced by the matrilocal living arrangements, according to which a married woman and her husband went to live in the camp of her mother, surrounded by females of her clan and their families. The basic unit of residence and social interaction in Creek society was the nuclear family. Related women and their families maintained households close together, forming matrilineal communities called *Huti*.[1] Each *Huti* was affiliated with a squareground town or ceremonial center known as the *Talwa*, where the chief or *Mico* resided. Early in the nineteenth century there were over 100 *Talwas* in the Creek nation, spread from northern Alabama to Spanish Florida. These were self-contained communities in which the domestic tasks were shared by all female members.

Thus the center of women's power in Creek society was focused on the home, and women's work consisted of child rearing and the cultivation, preparation, and distribution of food. Men's sphere was distinctly different, focusing on the town and hunting, and on relationships with outsiders in their roles as warriors and traders. While women might occasionally accompany the men in these activities, they were always at the periphery.

The old Creek town organization, formally, was a political patriarchy. The clans were separated into two divisions or moieties, with the town political chief (*Mico*) chosen from the White or Peace clans, and the war chief (*Tastanagi*) selected from the Red or War clans. All town officials were males, and women were excluded from daily meetings in the town square and played no significant political role whatsoever. Nevertheless, Creek women appeared to have influenced policy through private means. In a consensual society, the women had a voice in calling for war, determining when revenge had been achieved and peace should prevail, as well as in choosing whether to adopt or torture and execute prisoners. Unlike the Cherokee "War Women" or the Iroquois "Clan Matrons" who wielded obvious political power within their tribes, Kathryn Braund has found that the exact role of Creek "Beloved Women" in political life ". . . remains a mystery."[2]

The pattern of excluding women from public politics persisted among the Seminoles long after they abandoned towns at the time of the Seminole

Wars in 1835–42 and 1855–58. These wars, waged by the U.S. Army attempting to remove the Seminoles to Indian Territory, decimated the population, with only a remnant of a few hundred remaining in Florida. These Seminoles lived in isolated camps that came together as busk groups to celebrate the annual Green Corn Dance with its associated social and judicial functions. Each group was headed by Medicine Men and a council of elders. Even with this attenuated form of political interaction among a small population, Seminole women were allowed no formalized input.

Brent Weisman has made the case that the matrilineal *Huti* were the cultural antecedents of the Seminole camps which developed in Florida following the break up of town life.[3] Large multi-family settlements such as those at Catfish Lake, Fisheating Creek, Miami River, Big Cypress, and the Pine Island complex were prevalent among the Florida Seminoles from the 1850s through the 1890s. These extended family camps, headed by a "Grandmother" (*Posi*), provided a stable setting for child rearing and a nexus of psychological support, social interaction, and physical protection. This stability was especially important because Seminole marriages were fragile, due to the risk of death or captivity men faced in warfare or hunting, and the non-binding nature of the marital bond itself, which could be dissolved at the next Green Corn Dance with the man returning to his lineage.

Moreover, women came to outnumber men in the remnant Seminole population of Florida. In his 1880 study of Seminole settlements, which may have missed some isolated camps, ethnologist Clay MacCauley found but 208 Seminoles. He reported that in the marriageable group, ages twenty to sixty, there were fifty-six Seminole women and thirty-eight men in some form of polygamous or duogamous relationship. Yet among the pre-marriage age group, boys outnumbered girls by a margin of fifty-four to thirty-one, and this disparity foreshadowed a future change in the family structure.[4] Although monogamy became the norm among the Seminoles, there were a few old men who had more than one wife as late as the turn of the century.

In their camps the Seminoles maintained gender-specific economic roles. Women continued to be responsible for the home and for child rearing, and maintained their focus on providing food: planting and tending the family gardens, caring for the animals, harvesting and preparing the wild zamia root for the starch *Coontie*, as well as gathering edible plants and berries. The Seminole home and garden, household goods, animals, and certainly the children were considered possessions

of the mother. Men were responsible for building the thatched roof structures known as *Chikis* and clearing ground for gardens; they contributed
to the family's subsistence by hunting and fishing, cutting the huge
cypress trees and fashioning dugout canoes, and increasingly participated
in trapping and trading.

Starting around 1870, Seminole men began an intensive trade in otter
pelts, bird plumes, and alligator hides. These native commodities were
extremely valuable for resale to the international fashion industry, where
they were converted into alligator shoes, belts and luggage, fur collars for
coats, and feathered millinery. Seminole men used the income produced
by these sales to purchase manufactured goods sold by white storekeepers who set up shops on the edges of the Everglades. By the turn of the
century, Seminole material culture showed an increasing dependence
upon store-bought goods, such as the iron tools used by both the men
and women of the tribe. Seminole women grew accustomed to cloth and
hand-powered sewing machines; their cooking changed as they added
canned foods, and even substituted milled grits for the native *Coontie* flour
in making the food staple *Sofkee*. The men used improved guns and
ammunition to increase the effectiveness of their hunting.

As Seminole men changed their economic goals from subsistence to
commerce in this period, the reciprocity of gender roles within the group
shifted as well. As the exchange with white traders became more profitable, and Seminole men spent more time away from home hunting and
trapping for the commercial market, women assumed more responsibility
for daily decision-making. At the same time, nuclear family units began to
leave the large extended family camps, becoming widely dispersed across
the south Florida. In a reconfiguration of clan support mechanisms,
women continued to rear the family, but they enjoyed less constant interaction with, and support from, their relatives.

Apparently, the trade-off was that by focusing on hunting and trapping, men could provide the cash income needed to purchase more of
the high-quality trade goods that all believed improved the quality of
camp life. By most accounts, Seminole women were not actively involved
in the economic transactions at the trading posts. In the early years of
intensive Indian trade in south Florida, Seminole hunters brought their
pelts and hides to sell at stores around the periphery of the Everglades,
bought goods from the storekeepers, and returned home to their camps.
Infrequently, entire family groups came to the trading posts, usually staying there for several days. Even when the women did accompany the
men, they took a limited part in the transactions because they lacked the

necessary language skills. Very few Seminoles were fluent in English in the late nineteenth century, but over time the men had developed a functional patois for use at the trading posts. Most women had not participated in this language development, and thus were generally limited to using very few English words.

A recently published letter dating from 1925 speaks to this point. Mamie House Smallwood, wife of the trader at Chokoloskee Island in southwest Florida, reported that the Seminoles "are very peculiar people. They never allow their women to speak English and it is almost impossible to teach them our methods of caring for their babies."[5] This comment, from a woman socialized in an American culture in which men had the power to refuse to permit the education of their wives or daughters, may be interpreted in another way. Seminole women may not have been interested in learning to speak English or adopting Anglo ways of child-rearing, preferring their own cultural traditions. This inability, or refusal, to communicate in English had some positive effects on cultural conservation. Anthropologist Alexander Spoehr contended that the Seminole women's "interests are more circumscribed, they have little familiarity with English, and a greater desire to live in their traditional form of family group."[6] Ethnologist Ethel Cutler Freeman also found that "By matrilineal inheritance, the woman is the recipient and preserver of folklore. . . . She is alert to resist the intrusion of white influences and guard against the violation of old usages."[7]

The Florida East Coast Railway arrived at Miami in 1896. As settlements grew and Seminoles lived closer to them, intercultural contacts increased. During the last decade of the nineteenth century, Seminole women began to take a more active role in the trading process. They had traditionally made buckskin leggings, moccasins and braided belts and crafts such as baskets and alligator teeth necklaces for their own use, and prepared foodstuffs such as fresh eggs, vegetables, berries and *Coontie* flour. At this point, they began to spend more of their time producing a small surplus of these items for possible sale in the local frontier communities, although they were not yet making goods specifically for the tourist market. Even though a Seminole woman was free to use the funds derived from these sales, she depended upon her husband to purchase the goods she desired. Author Kirk Munroe, who wintered in the Miami area, reported that "when they visit the trader's store together, he stands up at the counter examining and selecting goods, while she, sitting on the floor in a remote corner . . . indicates her choice by gestures or in low tones to him."[8]

The Seminole couple described were following the traditional pattern of gender division of labor, with the man retaining responsibility for dealing with outsiders in trade. Such transactions were not generally interpreted in this way by the traders. The ultimate sign of the indignity which Seminole women were accorded by traders was the fact that, with a few notable exceptions such as Polly Parker or Annie Tommie, they were not generally recognized by their given names like the men. More typical was the ledger kept by the trader Frank Stranahan in his store in Fort Lauderdale, which listed an account for "Old Charlie's Old Squaw," and elsewhere one for "Old Charlie's Young Squaw."[9]

Early in the twentieth century, a number of causes led to the collapse of the Seminoles' hunting-trapping-trading economy. After the arrival of the railway, white settlement of the lower peninsula rapidly increased, with farms and citrus groves extending into the interior. This forced many Indians from their traditional campsites and hunting grounds. After 1906, the State of Florida authorized a program to systematically drain the Everglades for agricultural development, and that led to a drastic decline in the wildlife population. The final blow was the outbreak of World War I, which cut off European markets for the commodities the Indians had provided.

The status of Seminole women actually strengthened during that difficult period of transition to a new economy. They always remained secure in the knowledge of their position within the tribe, which was seen as complementary to the men, with no overt competition between the sexes. The men retained primary responsibility for dealing with outsiders, and the women continued to focus on domestic subsistence. With trade in pelts, plumes and hides suddenly curtailed as an economically profitable pursuit, the male sphere was somewhat diminished, while women's familial responsibilities continued unabated, in a pattern parallel to that experienced by Plains and Midwestern tribes a generation earlier.[10]

Different groups of Seminoles chose alternative responses to these developments. The traditionalists, mostly Mikasuki-speaking Seminoles, maintained their camps in the Everglades south of the Tamiami Trail and returned to subsistence agriculture supplemented by hunting and fishing. Many other Seminole families who were landless and virtually destitute either became "squatters" near the white communities, or became migrant laborers moving to land owned by white farmers. When three federal reservations were opened in Florida during the 1920s and 1930s, they offered a refuge for many Indian families. Still another group of Seminoles spent part of the year at commercial tourist attractions in Miami and other cities. In each of these settings, the women played an important role in developing patterns for economic survival, one of which was participating in a new kind of commerce focusing on arts and crafts.

The traditionalists attempted to continue their old lifestyle and economic activities in more remote portions of the Everglades that permitted continued reliance on agriculture supplemented by hunting and trapping. In a landmark report to the U.S. Senate in 1930, Roy Nash described life at a Seminole camp in the Big Cypress region, including an ethnocentric, ethnographic sketch of a Seminole woman:

> Sally Cypress, the squaw, is a woman of 38, a tall woman, 5 feet 9 or 10. Although she has given birth nine times, she still carries herself erect; generously fleshed, she yet moves with vigor and alertness. Her costume consists of a skirt, a chemise with sleeves, and a cape. Neither shoes nor stockings nor hat are worn. The skirt sweeps the ground. The chemise slips over the head and hangs down just enough to cover the breasts. A costume dictated by a modesty veritably mid-Victorian. Its structure marks the Seminole as a human being altogether original and unique.[11]

Nash was impressed by more than Sally Cypress's appearance; he also noted with respect her capacity for work and independence, and that she, in addition to household chores and raising the children, found ways to produce cash income.

> Now a skirt that sweeps the ground and 25 pounds of decoration about the neck would seem but poor preparation for a hard day's work. Yet I have seen this Sally Cypress leave camp at 9 in the morning with an umbrella in one hand and 2 feet of quarter-inch rope in the other and be gone until 9 at night, long after dark. On inquiring where she had been, I learned that she had been catching her young pigs, marking and castrating. For the Seminole woman is absolute mistress of her own property, and is frequently wealthier in the matter of hogs than her husband.[12]

Families not so well-off sought other ways to procure their livelihood. Rather than see their families in privation, Seminole women accepted the necessity of picking crops for wages, since such employment was usually the only source of cash income available. Agricultural pursuits had traditionally been part of Seminole women's domestic duties, so they were accustomed to the demands of this work, while the men were not. By working in the fields of others, Seminole women used their old skills to ensure their families' subsistence in new ways. By 1930, some Indian families, many of them headed by women, were already moving about south Florida in search of agricultural employment.[13] In the process of accepting wage labor, Seminole women also modified their clothing and invented a new hair style, combing their hair over a piece of cardboard to produce a practical eyeshade that others perceived as part of their "native" costume.

As the Great Depression worsened, even those Seminoles who had moved to federal reservations often found it necessary for some family members to seek employment in surrounding areas. Federal relief programs such as the CCC-Indian Division and WPA, which were available on the reservations, offered jobs primarily to Seminole males. Women, particularly single mothers, had to look elsewhere for work, and, as the U.S. Indian Agent in Florida, James L. Glenn, reported, they found it "on a nearby farm and have fitted into the industry about them. They are picking peppers, and I am told that they were more careful in handling the vines than either white or Negro labor. Like so much farm work, they were employed only a few weeks of the year, but it does help them provide for their homes."[14]

A third Seminole economic strategy was to spend part of the year in commercial tourist attractions such as Musa Isle Grove and Coppingers Tropical Gardens in Miami. The Indian families who lived there were on constant display to visitors. As part of the show, they made handicrafts for sale, wrestled alligators, and participated in mock ceremonials such as "Indian weddings." BIA agents, missionaries and reformers felt that this existence was totally demeaning to the Indians and constantly urged closing the tourist villages. As advocates of assimilation, they felt that the Indians should live on federal reservations, where they could participate in government employment, education and health programs, and learn the lessons in acculturation such pursuits entailed.

However, Patsy West's interviews with Seminoles who had lived in these attractions has provided an alternative point of view.[15] The Indians went to these villages freely, and the lifestyle was compatible with that they knew in the Everglades, except they were getting paid to let tourists watch them perform their everyday tasks. Most important, according to West, these villages provided a transitional environment, in which some Seminoles could earn a living while preserving many elements of their traditional culture. These culturally familiar enclaves in an urban setting gave the Indians control over the extent of their contact with the outside world, and offered one of a very few viable economic alternatives during the Depression years.

Although the headmen at these attractions became popular figures whose activities were often reported in the press, it was the Seminole women who took a leading role in maintaining cultural continuity there. West found that "The Mikasuki Seminoles adhered to traditional customs while in residence at the tourist attractions. The continuance of such behavior illustrates that the tourist attraction camps were as vital a setting as any Everglades Indian camp, regarding courtships, births, deaths, and council decisions."[16] Moreover, life in the tourist villages allowed the Seminoles to develop a new source of family income; "economic incentives and the generous quantities of leisure time allowed the women, and to a lesser but significant extent, the men, to create craft items for sale."[17]

Wherever they lived, Seminoles continued to adapt tradition to enhance their ability to support themselves, as demonstrated by the development of a craft economy, a strategy used by other tribes living on reservations across the country in this same period.[18] Through centuries of change, the Seminoles had become adept at altering a foreign concept or material trait so that it could be absorbed into their life without greatly impinging on old cultural patterns.[19] Over time, Seminole women mastered the sewing machine, and began to produce patchwork clothing and dolls for sale as a means of supporting their families. By the 1920s, some women took the initiative of selling these items directly to visitors, where formerly such negotiations had been handled by men. Conversely, men increased their involvement in the production of crafts, notably wood carvings. Thus, the boundaries of gender roles bent as necessary to meet the challenges of subsistence. In the 1940s, both men and women served on the governing board of a Seminole arts and crafts cooperative organized at the Brighton Reservation to regulate the production and wholesale marketing of these goods.

Such a sharing of power was also visible in other areas of Seminole life during this transitional period. Men retained their leadership of the Seminole "fires," but as Ethel Cutler Freeman noted in the 1940s, the oldest woman of her camp "is consulted by the men of her clan, and has great influence as the power behind the throne."[20] Occasionally, though, women also had to exert social control in a physical sense over Indian men who had indulged in the use of spiritous liquors which were readily available at most trading posts, and more frequently imbibed by men than women. A storekeeper reported that after one such drinking bout, the Seminole women tied the men up and took away their weapons until their senses returned.[21]

Although Seminole women were always consulted on important matters, they had never participated directly in the selection of leaders. This changed during the 1930s, when the Seminoles were authorized to choose three tribal cattle trustees as supervisors for a beef cattle enterprise begun at the Brighton Reservation with a communal herd provided by the federal government. Women were equally enfranchised in this first Seminole experience with a formalized elective process, in which individual balloting and majority rule replaced their traditional method of building consensus. The agent reported irritably that the Seminole women voted for everyone nominated—he thought possibly to avoid offending anyone—and as a result one of the men elected to the board knew nothing about cattle.[22] Later, when the herd was dispersed into individual ownership, Seminole women had an equal opportunity to apply for loans to purchase cattle individually, and many of them did so.

While the cattle enterprise offered some Seminole women a variety of new economic and political roles, the Christian church presented them with other possibilities. During this period Seminole women became the earliest converts to Christianity and were the staunchest supporters of the reservation churches.[23] Missionary efforts among Florida Indians started in 1907, when Seminole and Creek Baptists from Oklahoma began to work in the camps for a few months each year. In the 1920s the Rev. Willie King, a Creek from Oklahoma, arrived as a permanent missionary. He erected a small mission church on the Dania Reservation, where he preached to a few Indians, most of whom were women and children. When the First Seminole Indian Baptist Church was organized as a full-time church in 1936, its membership of eleven converts was predominantly female. Although the church had two male Deacons, they may not have been baptized, since another official account of the church claims that the first male was not baptized until 1944.[24]

As Christianity spread to the other reservations, the women took a leading role in establishing churches. During the 1930s the Indian Agent at Dania was also a minister, and as one of the women recalled, "We used to go out and sometimes he preached at night. We used to go sing for him. I remember that—Indian songs, Christian songs."[25] Seminole women frequently made singing appearances at local churches and were well accepted; in turn, white Christians visited the reservation church, increasing the occasions of intercultural contact.

However, there were still a number of Indians who resisted Christianity, rejected changing their lifestyle, and refused to relocate to the reservations. In 1962, about fifty of these Indian families living in the vicinity of the Tamiami Trail—a federal highway crossing the Everglades between Miami and Naples—received federal recognition as the Miccosukee Tribe. Although they had a formalized tribal government, the Miccosukees continued to dress and live in a traditional manner and celebrated the busk ritual of the Green Corn Dance. Today, the two tribes co-exist in relative harmony and cooperate on a number of projects of benefit to all Indians in Florida.

Those Seminole families who moved to the reservations took advantage of opportunities for employment, medical care, and education. At Dania, they could send their children to a federal day school. Sometimes there was intense resistance to this from the elderly Seminoles who did not want their grandchildren to have any association with the government. However, a few youngsters, mostly girls, persevered in their pursuit of further study.

The experience of Betty Mae Tiger, born in 1922, illustrates the difficulties faced by the first generation to be educated. Her mother, Ada Tiger, had moved the family to the Dania Reservation about 1928, and she and her brother attended the day school until it closed in 1936 as a Depression-era economy measure. The Bureau of Indian Affairs said it would be preferable for Seminoles to attend public schools, but at that time Indians were not accepted in the public schools of Florida. The Seminole Agent then arranged for a few of the most promising Seminole students to attend the federal School for Indians at Cherokee, North Carolina. Tiger wanted to go to school there, and did, for eight years, against the objections of her grandmother, but with the support of her mother. In 1945, Tiger and her cousin, Agnes Parker, became the first Seminoles to receive a high school diploma. Following graduation Betty Mae trained as a public health nurse at the Kiowa hospital in Oklahoma, and then returned to Florida to work with her people. She married Moses Jumper, a Navy veteran and classmate from the Cherokee School, and tried to settle down to raise a family, but she heard the call of her people and continued to work on their behalf in various roles for forty-two years.[26]

The story of Laura Mae Osceola is somewhat similar, in terms of commitment to education, family, and tribe. Born in 1932, she, too, was raised on the Dania reservation and attended school in Cherokee, North Carolina. Her uncles were prominent leaders of the Seminole community and gave her a legacy of commitment to working for the good of her people. At age 17 she became the first Seminole woman to apply for a marriage license and have a church wedding, after which she settled down to a quiet life. However, in 1954 when a delegation of Seminole elders went to

Washington to testify before a Congressional committee considering the termination of federal services to the tribe, they selected Osceola as their interpreter; she was the only woman to make the trip. Osceola's fiery defense of the tribal position, urging the government to continue its support for another quarter-century while the Seminoles prepared to run their own affairs, was most impressive. When challenged on how far she thought her people could be expected to progress, she retorted, "In twenty-five more years they won't need your help. We will be giving you help!"[27]

Thus, by the 1950s, a group of Seminole women was ready to assume leadership roles that were being created as the tribal government became more highly structured. These young women, all educated Christians, received strong support from the local religious and civic leaders, as well as from BIA officials. More importantly, these women were respected and popular among their own people.

When the Seminole Tribe incorporated in 1957 under the provisions of the Indian Reorganization Act, the most conspicuous group to achieve institutionalized power was Seminole women. From the outset there was no overt discrimination against women holding tribal offices, and they were well represented in tribal government during the first decade. In the first election Betty Mae Jumper won a seat on the Tribal Council and became its Vice Chairman. Laura Mae Osceola was appointed as the Secretary-Treasurer of the Seminole Tribe and served in that capacity for ten years. Charlotte Osceola from the Dania Reservation was elected to both the Tribal Council and as a member of the Board of Directors which managed business affairs for the people, serving from 1957–60. Dorothy Osceola also served on the Board from 1957–60, while Mary Bowers and Alice Snow were Board members from 1964–67. Betty Mae Jumper left the Tribal Council in 1959 and became a member of the Board until 1963, giving her experience in both branches of Seminole government. Then in 1967 she was elected Chairman of the Seminole Tribe, and served a four-year term.

Since 1957, women have usually been appointed to the position of tribal Secretary-Treasurer, which is regarded as the third most influential position in tribal government, although not an elective one. Initially there were two positions, both held by women—Laura Mae Osceola as Secretary and Peggy Alonis, the non-Indian wife of a BIA employee, as Treasurer. The office was combined by 1959, and held by Laura Mae Osceola. She was succeeded in 1967 by a non-Indian woman appointee; after a few years, Dorothy Osceola became Secretary-Treasurer, followed by Fred Smith, the only male to serve in that capacity. In 1979, Priscilla Sayen assumed the office, which she still holds.

After an initial period of active female participation in elective tribal government in the 1950s and 1960s, few women were elected to either of its branches during the ensuing decades. Joann Micco was elected to the Board of Directors in 1971, but served only a few months before resigning. In the Tribal Council, Rosie Buck (later Rosie Billie) from the Brighton Reservation served two terms, from 1967–69 and 1977–79, as the only woman on the Council, and also from 1983–87. She is now considering running again, and, though she is "tired of traveling, she'll do it for her people."[28]

This raises an interesting question of a possible backlash against a woman having achieved the highest elected position in the tribe. As further evidence, when Seminole social and economic programs expanded greatly during the 1970s and 80s, women did not occupy a proportional number of elective or appointive positions within tribal government. Is it possible that a "glass ceiling" has limited upward mobility for Seminole women as it has for American women in general in politics and business? At a recent symposium organized by the co-authors, a panel of Seminole women addressed this point. Carol Cypress, currently tribal housing manager, stated that "men in government look out for each other," and resent women taking more prominent roles. "We women were behind the men, pushing them. Now women are doing things they want to do and this frightens the men." Rather than retreating, however, she predicted that women would continue to take an active role, and "the men will have to deal with it."[29] Laura Mae Osceola concurred: "Men can talk and talk and talk, but it takes a woman to do the things."[30]

Seminole women's strong commitment to serving their people is a consistent theme in their life stories, which also reveal their flexibility, as they respond to changing needs by redirecting their careers. A Seminole woman interviewed by Merwyn Garbarino earned a business college degree and was working at a job she enjoyed in a Miami bank in 1966 when she was asked by her father and the tribal chairman to return to Big Cypress to run a tribal store. She agreed to do so, partially out of concern for her mother, but also stating that "all my life I had wanted to do something to help my people, and I could do that only by leaving my bank job in Miami. . . . I would have felt guilty if I had a chance to help and I didn't."[31] Carol Cypress got involved in education when her children were in school. She became a curriculum development specialist, and then, aware of other tribal needs, she took the personal risk necessary to change her focus and accept positions in tribal health and housing programs.[32] Betty Mae Jumper also changed careers, first from public health to public policy and leadership in tribal government, and later to the editorship of the tribal newspaper.[33] Rosie Billie said she "didn't know what she was doing" when she went into politics, but saw community needs for, among other things, a gymnasium, and did what she could. "In the old days, men used to provide; now, women need to provide for their children," in a variety of different ways.[34]

The example of female leadership was crucial to many of these activists. Betty Mae Jumper credited her initial involvement in public health to her lineage, since she descended from a line of Indian doctors, including her mother, who was a midwife. Carol Cypress credits the tradition of women she considered "my leaders" for giving her the impetus to take an active role in tribal affairs.[35] Rosie Billie mentioned the encouragement of her politically active aunt in convincing her to prepare for involvement in tribal politics by going back to night school to get her diploma. "You need some education to represent your community."[36]

In the early years following tribal organization, most Seminoles still lacked the requisite education and work skills to compete successfully in the world outside the reservations. The Superintendent of the Seminole Agency reported that 67% of youths who entered the first grade in 1956 did not remain to graduate in 1968.[37] One exception was Garbarino's informant, who explained why she and other girls were motivated to attend school in the 1960s: "I think the reason almost all the educated Indians are girls is because a woman's life here on the reservation is harder than the man's. The women have to take all the responsibility for everything. To go to school and get a job is really easier for a woman than staying on the reservation," where women were "sewing all the time or working in the fields."[38] At the urging of tribal leaders, the children soon began to attend public schools, as well as the BIA-run Ahfachkee ("Happy" in Mikasuki) Day School on the Big Cypress Reservation.[39]

Thirty years later, there are nearly two hundred high school and GED graduates, while among the Seminoles who have received postsecondary education women enjoy an educational parity with men. Of the thirty-two tribal members holding Associates or Bachelors degrees, fourteen are men and eighteen women. Two men and one woman hold Masters degrees, while two Seminole men have received the Juris Doctor degree and are practicing attorneys. Forty nine Seminoles are now enrolled in college.[40]

In addition to their more active participation in education and tribal governance, Seminole women's traditional prominence in the domestic sphere has also continued, but some of their husbands share this responsibility in ways previously uncommon. Carol Cypress reported that she and her husband, administrator of the tribal museum, have worked out more of a "50-50" marriage now; he washes dishes and takes the kids to the dentist, rather than having her do it all.[41] However, most Seminole women retain the primary responsibility for childrearing, a task that today's Seminoles see as increasingly complicated.

Teaching children traditional languages has become more problematic as more parents speak English in the home. Most children born after World War II went away to intertribal boarding schools, where they were punished for speaking native languages, and many fell in love with people from other tribes, leading to an increase in intermarriages. While today's grandmothers often learned to speak both Mikasuki and Creek from their grandparents, their children are not fluent in either. Their grandchildren are taught these Seminole languages in bilingual programs at school, but never become fluent if the languages are not spoken at home.[42]

In addition, due to the boarding school experience, few of today's parents have memories of their own parents raising them as adolescents. Some believe that the lack of such guidance by example has increased their difficulty in knowing how to help their own children cope with the drug and alcohol problems prevalent today throughout south Florida and the nation.[43] However, the extended family, particularly the grandmother, continues to provide assistance in childrearing and connection to the Seminole linguistic heritage. Rosie Billie's grandparents taught her that childcare was a grandmother's responsibility, and she follows their example. She speaks to her grandchildren in both Indian languages and brought her year-old granddaughter to the symposium.

The teaching of traditional values remains crucially important to Seminole women. Laura Mae Osceola emphasized her commitment to teaching her own and her adopted children, including current tribal chairman, James Billie, that education was crucial for tribal leadership. Her advice to him provided a clear Seminole definition of what social scientists call acculturation: "You need to take the good out of white man's ways and take the good out of Indian ways, and rule your people." She stated that bitterness was not helpful. "Everybody knows you took our land, why keep harping on it?" She emphasized several traditional Seminole rules of life: "Don't steal. Don't lie. Appreciate trees. . . . 'Respect your elders. Be kind. Respect your culture. If anybody needs help, always be ready to help.'"[44]

In summary, the evolving roles of Seminole women have in great measure reflected the changing fortunes of their people over the last century.

They were always the primary force within the domestic sphere, but at the time of increased contacts with Anglo traders in the late 19th century, they were perceived by outsiders as fitting the then-current derogatory stereotype of "squaw": passive, submissive, and totally dominated by Indian males.[45] As the status of the men as hunters and traders grew, so, too, did the appearance of disparity. However, following the collapse of that economy, women began to assert themselves in response to economic crisis. They led the way in accepting agricultural wage labor, moved their families to reservations or tourist attractions, and perfected the art of fashioning crafts for sale to visitors. Many of them adopted Christianity, accepted medical care and schooling for their children, and began to move into modern housing. After World War II, when the federal government's termination policy threatened the Seminoles' status as a tribe, young, educated Indian women were at the forefront of effective opposition. When the Seminole Tribe of Florida was officially organized, women actively participated in getting the tribal government through its rough early years. When relative tranquility and prosperity returned to Indian life in Florida, the women once again played a less prominent role in tribal government, yet they remain a source of strength and stability.

Today, following various court decisions, settlement of a federal land claims case, and the introduction of bingo and other profitable ventures, the Seminole Tribe is in control of its economic and political destiny. The Seminole Tribe of Florida now has 2010 enrolled members and provides them with over one hundred tribally-funded programs. Most Seminoles live on one of the five reservations, where many men and women are employed by the BIA or tribal government, or by various tribal economic enterprises.[46] The old tourist attractions no longer exist; some Seminoles still demonstrate their traditional crafts and skills for tourists, but most do so within a tribally controlled context. The Seminole Tribe operates a craft cooperative at the Immokalee Reservation, and individual artists display their wares at the annual Tribal Fair and other events throughout the country. Although there is still a market demand for patchwork, it has become less important as a source of income for Seminole women. However, it remains a source of cultural pride and artistic achievement for the women in those families where the skill has been passed from generation to generation. Over time, new designs have been added and new techniques have evolved, yet the essential integrity of the craft is timeless. So, patchwork, like the women who continue to create it, represents both the cultural stability and evolving dynamism of Seminole life.

NOTES

1. John R. Swanton, "Social Organization and Social Usages of the Indians of the Creek Confederacy," *Forty-Second Annual Report of the Bureau of American Ethnology* (Washington, D.C.: Government Printing Office, 1928), 171.

2. Kathryn E. Holland Braund, "Guardians of Tradition and Handmaidens to Change: Women's Roles in Creek Economic and Social Life During the Eighteenth Century," *American Indian Quarterly* 14 (Summer 1990): 242.

3. Brent Richards Weisman, *Like Beads on a String: A Culture History of the Seminole Indians in North Peninsular Florida* (Tuscaloosa: University of Alabama Press, 1989), 30.

4. Clay MacCauley, "The Seminole Indians of Florida," *Fifth Annual Report of the Bureau of American Ethnology, 1883–1884* (Washington, D.C.: Government Printing Office, 1887), 447.

5. Emily Dieterich, "Citizen Progress," *South Florida History Magazine* 4 (Fall 1990): 15.

6. Alexander Spoehr, "The Florida Seminole Camp," *Anthropological Series, Field Museum of Natural History* 33 (25 December 1944), 146.

7. Ethel Cutler Freeman, "The Seminole Woman of the Big Cypress and Her Influence in Modern Life," *American Indigena* 4 (April 1944): 124.

8. Kirk Munroe, "A Forgotten Remnant," *Scribner's Magazine* 7:3 (1893): 309.

9. Harry A. Kersey, Jr., *Pelts Plumes and Hides: White Traders Among the Seminole Indians, 1870–1930* (Gainesville: University Presses of Florida, 1975), 55.

10. George and Louise Spindler, "Male and Female Adaptations in Culture Change," *American Anthropologist* 60 (April 1958): 217–233. Gender-specific patterns of acculturation continue to the present day; see Janet Mancini Billson, "Standing Tradition on Its Head: Role Reversal Among Blood Indian Couples," *Great Plains Quarterly* 11 (Winter 1991): 3–21.

11. Congress, Senate, *Survey of the Seminole Indians of Florida*, report by Roy Nash, 71st Cong., 3d sess., 1931, S. Doc. 314, p. 6.

12. Congress, Senate, *Survey*, report by Nash, 7.

13. Congress, Senate, *Survey*, report by Nash, 21–22.

14. James Lafayette Glenn, *My Work Among the Florida Seminoles* (Gainesville: University Presses of Florida, 1982), 20.

15. Patsy West, "The Miami Indian Tourist Attractions: A History and Analysis of a Transitional Mikasuki Seminole Environment," *Florida Anthropologist* 34 (December 1981): 220–25.

16. West, 210.

17. West, 208.

18. See Terry R. Reynolds, "Women, Pottery, and Economics at Acoma Pueblo," *New Mexico Women: Intercultural Perspectives*, ed. Joan M. Jensen and Darlis A. Miller (Albuquerque: University of New Mexico Press, 1986), 279–300.

19. Freeman, "Seminole Woman," 124–125.

20. Freeman, 125.

21. Charlton W. Tebeau, *The Story of the Chokoloskee Bay Country* (Miami: University of Miami Press, 1955), 55.

22. Interview with Fred Montsdeoca, 4 December 1972 (SEM 76a), University of

Florida Oral History Archives, Gainesville.

23. Harry A. Kersey, Jr., *The Florida Seminoles and the New Deal, 1933–1942* (Gainesville: University Press of Florida, 1989), 31–33. Missionary effort by the Episcopal Church, begun in 1893, had ended by 1914; see Harry A. Kersey, Jr., and Donald E. Pullease, "Bishop William Crane Gray's Mission to the Seminole Indians in Florida, 1893–1914," *Historical Magazine of the Protestant Episcopal Church* 42 (September 1973): 257–73.

24. Betty Mae Jumper, . . . *and with the Wagon came God's Word* (Hollywood, FL: Seminole Tribe, 1980); First Seminole Indian Baptist Church, "Souvenir Brochure, Dedicatory Service, First Seminole Indian Baptist Church (Four Miles West of Dania) Dania, Florida, May 29, 1949," 6.

25. Interview with Betty Mae Jumper, 2 January 1985, SEM 186A, University of Florida Oral History Archives.

26. Betty Mae Jumper, remarks at "From Patchwork to Politics: Evolving Roles of Seminole Women in the 20th Century," a symposium sponsored by Florida Humanities Council, Florida Atlantic University, Boca Raton, 6 March 1993; Harry A. Kersey, Jr., "Betty Mae Jumper," in *Native American Women: A Biographical Dictionary*, ed. Gretchen M. Bataille (NY: Garland Publishing, 1993), 131–132.

27. U.S. Congress, Joint Hearings Before the Subcommittees of the Committees on Interior and Insular Affairs, *Termination of Federal Supervision Over Certain Tribes of Indians*, 83rd Cong., 2nd sess. on S. 2747 and H.R. 7321, Part 8, Seminole Indians, Florida, 1 and 2 March 1954 (Washington, D.C. 1954), p. 1119; Harry A, Kersey, Jr., "Laura Mae Osceola," in Bataille, *Native American Women*, 191–92.

28. Rosie Billie, "Patchwork to Politics."

29. Carol Cypress, "Patchwork to Politics."

30. Laura Mae Osceola, "Patchwork to Politics."

31. Merwyn Garbarino, "Seminole Girl," in *Awakening Minorities: American Indians, Mexican Americans, Puerto Ricans*, ed. John R. Howard (n.p.: Transaction, 1970), 78, 84.

32. Carol Cypress, "Patchwork to Politics."

33. Betty Mae Jumper, "Patchwork to Politics."

34. Rosie Billie, "Patchwork to Politics."

35. Carol Cypress, "Patchwork to Politics."

36. Rosie Billie, "Patchwork to Politics."

37. E.W. Barrett to Senate Subcommittee on Indian Education, 21 January 1969. Quoted in Harry A. Kersey, Jr., "Economic Prospects of Florida's Seminole Indians," *Florida Planning and Development* 20 (December 1969): 2.

38. Garbarino, "Seminole Girl," 84.

39. Harry A. Kersey, Jr., "Educating the Seminole Indians of Florida, 1879–1970," *Florida Historical Quarterly* 49 (July 1970): 16–35; "The Ahfachkee Day School," *Teachers College Record* 72 (July 1970): 93–103.

40. Jill Young Miller, "Speaker of the Tribe," *Sun-Sentinel* (Fort Lauderdale), 21 March 1993, 5 (E).

41. Carol Cypress, "Patchwork to Politics."

42. Betty Mae Jumper and Carol Cypress, "Patchwork to Politics."

43. Carol Cypress, "Patchwork to Politics"; similar point made by Carolyn

212

Attneave, "The Wasted Strength of Indian Families," in *The Destruction of American Indian Families*, ed. Steven Unger (NY: Association on American Indian Affairs, 1977), 30.

44. Laura Mae Osceola, "Patchwork to Politics"; Miller, "Speaker of the Tribe," 1 (E).

45. See David D. Smits, "The 'Squaw Drudge': A Prime Index of Savagism," *Ethnohistory* 29 (1982): 281–306.

46. Priscilla Sayen, "Patchwork to Politics."

10

PÄIVI H. HOIKKALA

MOTHERS AND COMMUNITY BUILDERS
SALT RIVER PIMA AND MARICOPA WOMEN IN COMMUNITY ACTION

In 1879, the Pimas and Maricopas in the Salt River region of central Arizona obtained a reservation by executive order, and later, under the provisions of the 1934 Indian Reorganization Act, they organized a constitutional govern- ment, which is still in place today. Although there exists much anecdotal evidence showing that tribal governments experienced a renaissance in the late 1960s and 1970s, there has as yet been little solid research into the rea- sons why. As Hoikkala shows, one reason is that Lyndon B. Johnson's War on Poverty made new sources of federal grant funding available; this assisted in tribal self-determination largely because the funds were not funneled through the Bureau of Indian Affairs. Instead, federal money went directly to tribes and tribal programs. Hoikkala's article discusses how, in this political revival, women became more involved in tribal government, as elected offi- cials and as appointed employees.

I have gained self-esteem, a sense of accomplishment and satisfaction—a degree of power through involvement. I say to my kids, too, that nothing is impossible; you can do it if you want to.

—Angela Brown

Angela Brown's evaluation of her life[1] summarizes the experience of many Native American women who participated in the programs cre- ated under the Economic Opportunity Act (EOA). President Lyndon B. Johnson signed the act on August 20, 1964 after he had declared an "unconditional war on poverty" as part of his legislative program to create a Great Society. The act proposed "to eliminate the paradox of poverty in

214 the midst of plenty in this Nation by opening to everyone the opportunity for education and training, the opportunity to work, and the opportunity to live in decency and dignity."[2] In essence, it provided a series of programs designed to supplement social security and child welfare with emphasis on helping the young to break "the cycle of poverty." Community action programs (CAP) formed an essential part of these efforts, and by attempting to give the target communities an opportunity to participate in the design and implementation of the programs, the EOA aimed at a restructuring of political decision-making.[3]

While the Economic Opportunity Act made no special provision for Native Americans, reservation Indians clearly comprised a rural group with a strong claim to the resources of antipoverty legislation. In 1964, an estimated seventy-four percent of reservation families earned less than $3,000, the amount that the federal government considered the poverty threshold. The median income of a reservation family was $1,800, or thirty percent of the national average. High unemployment, low educational levels, inadequate housing, and high rates of illness and infant mortality compounded the problem of material poverty in Indian communities.[4]

In light of the history of federal paternalism and control, the encouragement of Indian participation and local leadership development proved especially significant. Although the programs failed to eradicate material poverty, conditions on many reservations improved and new jobs became available, providing viable employment alternatives to young, educated Indians. With grants from the Office of Economic Opportunity (OEO), reservation communities developed programs that brought attention to their particular problems. This access to resources not tied to the Bureau of Indian Affairs (BIA) was pivotal in the emergence of a new generation of tribal leadership, intent on fulfilling the promise of self-determination.

Despite the significance of community action to self-determination, few scholars have explored its implications and impact on reservations.[5] Especially blatant is the exclusion of Native American women from studies of reservation politics and economies. Although their economic, political and ceremonial influence often diminished after the imposition of Western institutions, Indian women held on to their social roles as mothers, wives and educators. The Indian Reorganization Act of 1934 enfranchised women, but community action provided the opportunity to participate in the formal functions of politics and economic and social planning. As a result, women achieved greater visibility in tribal affairs. They participated in OEO-funded training and education programs and developed skills, experience and self-confidence, which propelled them into tribal politics and continued involvement in community development. In short, community action programs broadened the range of activities open to Native American women and empowered them to assume new responsibilities in the arena of public affairs.

This essay explores women's participation and roles in community action in the Salt River Pima-Maricopa Indian Community, located immediately east of the Phoenix metropolitan area in central Arizona. The Pimas and Maricopas successfully employed the concept of community action to reorganize their tribal governmental structure, create social services in the community and improve the economic viability of the reservation. Women participated actively in these developments, extending their powers in the home to involve the arena of public affairs, and they continue to be a dynamic force in the community today.

The population of the Salt River Pima-Maricopa Indian Community consists of two tribes: the Pimas and the Maricopas. Pima occupancy of central Arizona dates back hundreds of years whereas the Maricopas migrated from the Colorado River at a much later date. By the early 1800s, the two tribes had established friendly relations and close social and political ties through intermarriage and cooperation. These Indians were farmers who relied on an extensive canal system to irrigate their fields of maize, beans, squash and cotton in the fertile lands along the Gila River. To supplement their diet, they gathered wild plant foods in the desert, fished in the river and hunted small game animals.[6]

Direct contacts with Europeans were minimal throughout the Hispanic era, and the Pima and Maricopa social structure remained relatively unaltered. Villages consisted of family units that farmed adjoining acreages and used the same water source. These villages were economically and politically self-sufficient, governed by the unanimous decision of the council of male elders. In addition, each village had a headman, one or more shamans, and other male officials in charge of ceremonies and festivals. Warfare against the Apaches and Yumans united villages politically but did not figure prominently in the culture.[7]

Labor in Pima and Maricopa society was sexually divided with men and women taking responsibilities that complemented each other. Women's duties included the household: they prepared food, gathered wood and water, and weaved cotton into fabric. Pima women made intricate baskets for household and ceremonial purposes while Maricopa women were known for their pottery. These articles eventually became important trade items with settlers, increasing women's economic contributions. Through their ownership of the household utensils and their control of food preparation women could exert considerable influence in the community. They derived further authority from their responsibility for the upbringing and education of the children. In contrast, men's power came from their role as providers; they hunted, fished, and worked the fields, although planting and harvesting were communal efforts in which all able-bodied women and men participated. Trade with the incoming settlers underscored the sexual division of labor, and men took over all the farm work while women concentrated on manufacturing. Prestige in all roles, male and female, was associated with maturity and experience.[8]

In 1853, Pima and Maricopa lands fell under United States jurisdiction with the Gadsden Purchase, and after the Civil War increasing numbers of American settlers were moving to the Gila and Salt River Valleys. The tribes now came into close contact with Western culture and Christianity, and the American efforts to convert the local Indians began to succeed in the 1880s. Women played a significant role in this conversion to Christianity, often persuading their more resistant husbands to join them. Women also emphasized the importance of education and sent their sons and daughters to government day schools. After the Phoenix Indian School opened its doors in 1891, many Pima and Maricopa children went to the city for education. The proximity of Phoenix—a rapidly growing urban center—also had an impact in the Indian villages. New food products, tools, and European-style clothing altered material conditions; Western medicine replaced traditional healing practices; children learned English; old ceremonies and legends as well as the traditional crafts of pottery and basketry became less relevant to everyday life. Women were especially eager to accept new techniques and tools, such as sewing machines, to facilitate their work while they continued their efforts to maintain a link with the past. Grandmothers still told stories; mothers still emphasized the Indian values of family and hard work; and to their daughters, they stressed the importance of women's work.[9]

To satisfy the settlers' growing demand for land and the removal of Indians from the Salt River Valley, President Rutherford B. Hayes signed an executive order to create the Salt River reservation in 1879. Federal supervision and control of life on the reservation often contradicted tradition, and in this conflict between two divergent ways of conceptualizing the world the educated Indians became the mediators. Their efforts to manage the reservation formed a transitional phase in the process toward American-style representative government, completed with the enactment of the Indian Reorganization Act in 1934. After considerable debate, the Salt River Indians adopted a constitution and by-laws on June

15, 1940. They also took the official title "Salt River Pima-Maricopa Indian Community."[10]

The new constitution brought little immediate change. The BIA maintained its influence in reservation affairs, and the role of the tribal council was marginal. World War II prompted closer contacts with American society, accelerating the process of cultural change and accommodation. The war also marked the beginning of rapid development for central Arizona and opened up opportunities for some Pimas and Maricopas to work in the neighboring cities. Women found employment in the service sector and as domestics and entered the labor force in growing numbers. There were fewer jobs available for men, and women often became the primary providers for the family. Though increasing their work load, steady income gave women a new sense of independence and power which translated into an assertive attitude. Women realized this assertiveness in the community by involving themselves in tribal affairs more directly than before. In 1957, Martina Schurz became the first woman elected to the Salt River tribal council and Myra Rice served as vice president in 1960–1961. By 1964, two out of the seven council members were women and a woman headed the Health, Education, and Welfare Board.[11]

Looking back at these post-war developments, many women and men in the community felt that women's sense of empowerment may have adversely affected men's self-esteem. Agatha Thomas, Director of Head Start, expressed this view, explaining that husbands "probably felt somewhat useless because they often didn't have skills for employment. Women made men what they are, or were, in those days." Fred Wilson, former president of the tribal council, also commented on this social change in the community. According to Wilson, the father, traditionally the provider, became displaced when he could no longer provide for the family. This displacement often led to feelings of frustration and discouragement which, in turn, were expressed in excessive use of alcohol and general apathy.[12]

When the Economic Opportunity Act passed in 1964, Salt River was a distinctly rural community with a population of 1,650. However, Indians farmed only four percent of the irrigable acreage while the rest were leased to non-Indian farmers. There were six cattle herds and one flock of sheep on the reservation, all Indian-owned. Other business enterprises included a barbershop, a store, and a service station/restaurant/curio shop. In addition, Pima-Maricopas operated several seasonal roadside produce stands. The only industrial enterprise, processing rock products for the construction industry, was owned by a non-Indian.[13]

The proximity of metropolitan Phoenix alleviated the employment situation on Salt River, but lack of transportation and marketable skills limited opportunities for work in the city. The Arizona State Employment Service, which had helped place Native Americans in industry, commerce, and agriculture since before World War II, also failed to reach the Pima-Maricopas. In a 1964 survey of the reservation, the Arizona Commission of Indian Affairs reported the total number of the work force as 481. Thirteen percent of this labor force desired, but was unable, to find work; twenty percent worked on the reservation, and most of the remaining work force held a wage or salaried job off the reservation. Only four community members, one of whom was female, were self-employed. Women made up approximately twenty-seven percent of the labor force; fourteen percent of them were unemployed. In the Phoenix area, the growing tourist industry employed women in service occupations; others worked as domestics. Only one woman was in a managerial position, six held clerical jobs, and eight women worked in skilled crafts. A small number of women were employed as farm and other laborers, whereas approximately one-half of the male labor force were farm or other unskilled laborers, thus facing seasonal unemployment.[14]

Because of the lack of resources, the Salt River community could not provide adequate social services to its members. According to surveys of the reservation between 1961 and 1964, fifty-eight percent of the families lived below the poverty level; seventy percent of the housing was substandard; health problems included diabetes, diarrhea, and excessive drinking. The tribal council reported in 1964 that there was a desperate need for a sanitation program and "nurse-sponsored education programs in health." In addition, council president Vernon Smith pointed to problems of communication between the Public Health Service staff and the council. Salt River had only one day school, and most Pima-Maricopa children attended off-reservation public or BIA schools; a small number were in mission schools. However, this education did not meet the needs of the children, and the tribal council reported problems with adjustment, parental encouragement and high drop-out rates. Lack of job opportunities in the community further discouraged attendance. According to the Arizona Commission of Indian Affairs, only five Salt River residents attended college and twenty-five participated in vocational training in 1961.[15]

Salt River clearly qualified for EOA grants, and the tribal council saw in them an opportunity to enhance its authority in the community. BIA influence in tribal affairs was still strong, and the council acted more as a figurehead than a decision-making body. Fred Wilson was in the council at the time, and he agreed that "[the council] had no real mission that it wanted to establish in the community." Dennis Johnson, Director of the Salt River Health and Human Services, pointed to the inexperience of council members to exercise power as one reason for this lack of direction. He also emphasized the prominent role of the BIA superintendent and that "the tribe probably felt dependent on the BIA, too, since it was the only source of services and funding."[16]

Community action programs gave the council the opportunity to assert itself in tribal affairs, independent of the BIA, and in 1965 the seven council members organized as a community action agency. The grant proposals reflected the major concerns of Salt River residents: children and their education and the needs of the elderly. With the first grant in June 1965, the tribal council established the Neighborhood Youth Corps, a program for high school drop-outs; in September, the council received a grant for CAP program development and another to establish a Head Start program to prepare Pima-Maricopa children for school. Council members felt optimistic about these developments, reporting to the Arizona Commission of Indian Affairs in 1966 their belief that CAP programs "are truly tribal enterprises with full council authority."[17]

In 1965, the Office of Economic Opportunity established a three-university consortium to assist Native American communities in developing and managing CAP programs. Arizona State University (ASU), located in the city of Tempe in the Phoenix metropolitan area, was part of the consortium, and Salt River now had easy access to consultants. In its first year, the consortium spent twelve consultant days on Salt River. Council members and other Pimas and Maricopas involved in CAP participated in training sessions and workshops on leadership and administration; three community women spent the summer of 1966 in training for teacher-aides in Head Start. Consultants also helped conduct a labor force survey on the reservation.[18]

During the remainder of the 1960s, funding and the scope of CAP programs expanded, reaching the peak in 1969 when Salt River received a total of $259,227. The programs that year included Head Start; Neighborhood Centers, which provided a variety of services including job and training referrals, day care, and health services; and Aid to the Elderly. Monies were also awarded to economic development and recreational programs. Head Start received approximately one-third of the total funding, and it had become a popular component of community action on Salt River. In 1966, for example, sixty preschool children participated in

Head Start, reflecting the need for such a program in the community. Fred Wilson indicated the sense of urgency "that something had to be done about the children and their problems. This community participated in the effort to salvage the young generation and accepted Head Start as a way to help children."[19]

The tribal council also took advantage of VISTA (Volunteers in Service to America), a program that employed young, educated Americans to assist communities in CAP programs. In 1965, Salt River received the first grant to hire a VISTA worker. A committee that consisted of community members interviewed the applicants and made the recommendation to the tribal council. Frank Smith, Director of Community Development, came to Salt River through VISTA in 1970. He had worked in the California barrios before coming to Salt River and thus had experience in community work. Yet, he recalled his experience with the interviewing committee on Salt River as very unnerving; he especially remembered an elderly woman who reminded him of his status as an outsider to the community and promised to watch his actions closely. Smith concluded: "I guess we [VISTA workers] were looked at as radical by the community; [after all] we were trying to change the world."[20]

Indeed, community members at first felt ambivalent about the desirability of CAP programs. They were federal programs, and as such, the approach was questionable as just another effort to direct reservation affairs. This sentiment was enforced by the participation of non-Indians. Elizabeth Clarence came to Salt River in 1968 with her husband, a Salt River Pima, and worked for the daycare center. She indicated that, although she did not have any problems in the work place, it took her a long time to get close to her colleagues and be accepted as a member of the community. Frank Smith confirmed the observation that because of the history of federal-Indian relations, the community tended to be suspicious of non-Indians.[21]

The tribal council encouraged community participation and arranged meetings to discuss program plans with Salt River residents. These meetings generally accepted the proposals suggested by the council, but offered little input on how to run the programs. Fred Wilson suggested that one reason might have been that community members did not have enough knowledge to realize the full potential of community action, and it was thus left to the reservation leaders to make the decisions. And residents of Salt River were generally satisfied with the programs as they provided services desperately needed in the community. According to Agatha Thomas, Salt River soon "adopted the approach as a brand new thing . . . and people were happy to learn about the programs [because] nothing was around."[22]

The Salt River tribal council recruited community members as employees for CAP programs. Of those who applied and were eventually hired, a large number were women. There were several reasons why women formed the bulk of this new labor force on the reservation. First, Pima-Maricopa women pursued CAP jobs more actively than men. Many women were already working as primary breadwinners, giving them self-confidence in seeking new employment. The proximity of work close to home was also crucial for these women as they continued to be the caretakers in their families while working outside the home. Economic necessity motivated women with no previous work experience to apply for CAP jobs. These women were either single or had husbands who worked jobs in which they faced seasonal unemployment.

The second reason for women's prominence in CAP jobs was that they were more employable for the types of positions available. The bureaucracy involved in program management and implementation created many clerical jobs, and although most women had little—if any—education past high school, they often had acquired typing and other skills necessary for office work. Finally, social programs became an important component of community action on Salt River, including Head Start, youth counseling, health care, and services to the elderly. Women had traditionally taken care of these spheres of life and had maintained their responsibilities in the family despite their growing participation in the labor force. It was in these tasks that they felt comfortable and competent, while men tended to shy away from jobs they identified as women's work. Community action programs thus afforded women the occasion to practice the role of the caretaker in the larger context of the reservation. The male interviewees referred to women's "nurturing instinct" as a reason they became involved in the social programs. Or as Dennis Johnson explained, women had "the ability to step forward and fight for services that are important to their families." Agatha Thomas's opinions were representative of the women's point of view. According to her, women had always been community-minded and their involvement in community action was an extension of their strong presence in Pima-Maricopa homes. "Women did not really do anything new or extraordinary when they ventured out but they expanded [this] presence when men failed to do so. Women took responsibility of the community," Thomas concluded.[23]

Thus, during the 1960s women became more active in tribal government, especially in implementing education, health and child care programs. The Salt River Education Board, which in 1964 changed its name to Health, Education, and Welfare Board, was under female leadership between 1962 and 1969. The receptionist's position, created in 1965, belonged to a woman as did the position of the secretary of the tribal council between 1967 and 1969. After the inception of community action, women also increased their share in the employed work force on the reservation. By 1968, approximately forty percent of the Salt River labor force consisted of women as opposed to the twenty-seven percent only four years earlier.[24]

Women who were employed in community action programs can be divided into three distinct groups. First, there were the young, single women for whom community action provided their first job opportunity and a stepping stone to an economically independent life. The second group consisted of married, divorced or single women with children who had to work to support the family. Finally, a small number of elderly women worked in Head Start and in child care.

Young Pima-Maricopa men and women generally expressed interest in the community action concept. The older generation was often suspicious of these new federal efforts and concerned about the disappearing community cohesiveness. The young people had more contact and experience with life outside the reservation than their parents, and they saw potential for themselves in the CAP programs. Community action afforded meaningful employment on the reservation and a chance to continue their education. For Angela Brown, the Neighborhood Youth Program opened the door to employment and education. Brown came from a family of eight children; after her father died, her mother had to work to support the family. Brown had attended a BIA day school after which she transferred to the public school system. At the age of sixteen, she dropped out because of peer pressure and because "school just got harder for me." Brown then enrolled in the Neighborhood Youth Program that operated with community action funds to provide jobs and encourage high school drop-outs to return to school. In 1970, she started working part-time in Head Start. The program paid for her to go back to school and take the GED exam and later sent her to receive additional training at Arizona State University. After her marriage, Brown continued to work for Head Start as her husband, a construction worker, was seasonally unemployed, and she became the primary provider of family income.[25]

Economic reasons also motivated married women with children to take CAP jobs. Their husbands were either in seasonal occupations or unemployed altogether, and the wife's salary provided vital income for family survival. Often with little education and work experience, these women found employment as receptionists, teacher-aides in Head Start and day-care, and in services to the elderly. Women with previous work experience applied for CAP jobs for various reasons: proximity to home, work for the community, or more meaningful employment. For single mothers, community action projects afforded the perfect opportunity to earn money to support themselves while staying close to their families.

Rhoda Barnes began working as teacher-aide in Head Start in 1966 to help supplement the family income. At the time, her husband worked in construction and was periodically unemployed, and he fully supported her decision to work outside the home. Barnes had graduated from Mesa High School, and after getting married and having two children, she went back to school while her mother attended to the children. However, she never received her degree as she found it increasingly hard to juggle between family and school. In Head Start, she saw an opportunity to earn money while staying close to her children. Barnes was one of the first three Pima-Maricopa women to participate in teacher-aide training at ASU in the summer of 1966, and she received additional training at Mesa Community College. In 1968, she applied for a secretarial position in the Education Department, because "I didn't really like the [teaching] job but I took it because it was there and I needed a job. I am not the teacher type, but I loved the children."[26]

The third distinct group of women in community action programs were elderly women who worked in Head Start. After retiring from her housekeeping job of fourteen years in the city of Scottsdale, Florence Seely was asked to work as teacher-aide in Head Start. She helped with daycare and programs that taught children about their Pima-Maricopa heritage. Similarly, Alma Lewis worked as teacher-aide, instructing the children in Pima language. Concern for the disappearance of Pima and Maricopa traditions fueled these women's involvement in Head Start. They had grown up speaking the language, but their education in government boarding schools had denied its legitimacy as a medium of communication. Seely and Lewis saw in Head Start an opportunity to remind young Pima-Maricopas of the importance of their heritage. In a sense, they considered themselves community grandmothers in the face of the disintegration of the traditional extended family. Because the median life expectancy was low, many children did not have grandparents; in other cases, the grandparents did not live with the family. Mothers worked outside the home more often than before and fathers failed to take responsibility for children and their education. Having older women as authority figures provided some stability and a link to the past generations for children in daycare and Head Start programs.[27]

Salt River residents readily accepted women's involvement in community action programs as an extension of their roles of mother and wife. With the transformations in the economic structure, the requirements of these roles had changed and women's employment became a necessity. Traditionally, Pima and Maricopa women had also been teachers and leaders of opinion in their villages, and their participation in community action was an expansion of these duties in the reservation context. All the interviewees agreed that in the 1960s the community as a whole needed care and attention which women were better prepared to provide than men. Rhoda Barnes expressed this perspective on women's roles in the community, explaining that "a woman does more healing for the community [and sees] the needs of the community better than men."[28]

While endorsing women's increased employment and involvement in community action, the interviewees also expressed ambivalence about these developments. The overriding concern in the community was the breakdown of the traditional family structure, and women's absence from the home was interpreted as part of the problem. Elizabeth Clarence, who came to the community after her marriage to a Pima-Maricopa member, attributed such concerns as single-parent and female-headed households and teenage pregnancies directly to women's employment: "Women work out of necessity, but this has led to a breakdown in the family structure." Pima-Maricopa women took a more moderate position. Vivian Jones, for example, recognized that "families are less strong than before, perhaps partly because women work more." Pima-Maricopas also perceived the absence of male role models in the community as contributing to the problems of the family. Fred Wilson expressed this opinion: "Kids had problems because mothers were not home. The father did not have the experience nor interest nor understanding necessary to deal with the kids and their problems." The mother's role was thus accentuated and her responsibilities grew as she had to be both the mother and the father.[29]

Some Pima-Maricopa men were concerned about, and even resented, women's increased employment in community action programs. This resentment grew out of their frustration to find employment for themselves and was emphasized under female leadership. Rhoda Barnes confirmed that "some Indian men are uncomfortable about being supervised by a woman [and] men sometimes try to keep them from certain positions." This was especially true of political leadership roles, and according to Barnes, men explained that "women don't have the business mind needed for running tribal government." Dennis Johnson agreed that some Pima-Maricopa men were concerned about women's increasing power, especially in tribal politics, but he also emphasized that for other men it served as an incentive and stimulus for becoming involved themselves.[30]

The response of individual families to the mother's outside employment depended on the particular life situation of each woman. Husbands generally accepted the wife's outside employment as an economic necessity. Donald Jones, a construction worker at the time, fully supported his wife's decision to apply for a CAP job: "That was a good move for her." He also shared household chores with his wife while most men questioned the necessity of sharing in what they considered women's duties. Rhoda Barnes similarly acknowledged her husband's encouragement in her decision to work in community action but also confirmed that "[my] decision to work didn't really change family relationships," and she continued to take care of the household and the finances of the family. Angela Brown's husband "grumbled about women's work," but he eventually began to share in the household chores.[31]

The older children of working mothers proved helpful as they could take care of their siblings and attend to other household tasks; women could also rely on the extended family if no other help was available. However, inadequate child care facilities on the reservation remained an obstacle to women's employment. The Head Start program was too limited to handle all the eligible children, and it only kept children for part of the day after which they were bussed home. In 1968, a total of 140 women in the community had no child care substitutes available to them and could not consider work outside the home despite the need to do so. Because of these daycare problems, employed mothers also had to stay home in the case of their children's illness, and absenteeism became a problem in the work place.[32]

Pima-Maricopa women's responses to their work in community action programs were uniformly positive and attested to a significant change in their attitudes about themselves and the community. Women not only found jobs and a steady income in the programs, but they derived a new sense of self-worth from their responsibilities in the community. Agatha Thomas credited her community involvement with her personal growth and development. Thomas had graduated high school in Phoenix and attended college for a year. After her marriage, she dropped out of school and stayed home to take care of her two daughters. In 1966, she participated in the summer training program for teacher-aides in Head Start at ASU. Thomas worked in the program for a year but quit her job after getting pregnant with her third child. However, she remained active in the parental committee for Head Start and in her church. This involvement helped elect Thomas to the tribal council in 1971, and she served on the council for three years. In 1973, she also became Director of Head Start. Thomas confirmed that all these experiences helped her develop a sense of community service: "I was not so much wrapped up in my own woes any more. I began to see myself in relation to other people." One result of this newly gained self-esteem was Thomas's decision to divorce her alcoholic husband of fifteen years: "[I realized] I don't need this any more."[33]

Community action work also promoted women's education. To ensure maximum community participation in the programs, the tribal council stressed the hiring of Salt River residents for CAP jobs. As Vivian Jones said: "In the 1960s, it was important to get tribal members into positions. [Formal] education was not as important [a requirement] as today." And since applicants rarely had education past high school, managerial and skills training became integral components of the council's approach. The goal was not only to provide for the immediate needs of the community action programs but also to train people for self-determination. Frank Smith pointed out that this training "provided the basis for the finetuning of tribal government as many CAP trainees stayed in tribal management." In addition to the formal workshops, on-the-job training was an integral part of this educational process.[34]

This educational experience in CAP jobs increased women's confidence in their potential, and the security of permanent employment afforded them an opportunity to think ahead and consider other options. Vivian Jones concluded that "opportunities in CAP helped women see opportunities in other areas as well." Jones herself worked for community action projects until 1972. When she returned to the work force after having another child, she was employed by the Indian Development District of Arizona and the Indian Health Service in Phoenix. In 1983, she returned to work for the tribe and was eventually appointed to a managerial position. More women also applied their newly-acquired skills in tribal politics. In 1966 and in 1968–1969, three of the seven council members were women; at other times between 1965 and 1972, when the number of council members increased to nine, there was at least one woman on the tribal council.[35]

Community action not only created paid jobs on the reservation, but tribal members participated as unpaid volunteers in the programs. The advisory committees to CAP programs consisted of community volunteers, who in many cases were women. Again, women tended to take interest in health, education, and welfare, whereas men opted for issues such as economic development and land management. Volunteers also helped raise funds for community projects and contributed their labor.

The building of a youth center for children from broken homes exemplified the community's volunteer efforts. In 1965, the Office of Economic Opportunity and the U.S. Department of Health, Education, and Welfare funded a study of juvenile delinquency on the Salt River reservation. This study concluded that an unstable home was a major contributing factor to delinquency. Pima-Maricopas decided to fight the problem by building a youth center to house ten boys and ten girls who otherwise would be committed to correctional institutions. Because OEO funds for the project were limited, volunteers became crucial in raising money for the enterprise. The use of traditional materials and community labor kept the cost down, and the center opened in late 1966. Anna Moore Shaw, who became a driving force behind many volunteer efforts when she and her husband retired to Salt River, described the extent of the community's involvement:

> Finally all was finished but the plastering of the walls. The men prepared the traditional mixture of mud and straw, but the plastering had always been women's work. Where would we find women of today with the skill and patience to work with sticky plaster? Then someone thought of the old people. . . . The aged ladies turned out in force, anxious to show their old art.[36]

Local churches provided a ready volunteer force for community action. Church members had previously been involved in socially oriented programs, and CAP gave them a chance to contribute to the development of the whole community. They served on advisory committees, advocating health care and services to the elderly in particular. The Aid to the Elderly program, for instance, grew out of the efforts of women on the Medicare committee to provide health care services and help for elderly members of the community. They also expressed concern for the disappearance of Pima and Maricopa culture and languages. To revive Pima basketry, a group of community women started a basket weaving group and organized women's weaving classes. Elderly women who still knew Pima language and legends spoke to day care and Head Start classes, helping the staff in encouraging children to appreciate their tribal heritage. Shaw emphasized that "we must retrieve our Pima heritage before it is lost completely. Teaching little children the old language is one important step toward this goal."[37]

◆ ◆ ◆

The war on poverty was a passing phase in the history of Salt River, but it had a permanent influence on the development of the community. CAP programs prepared the Pima-Maricopas for self-determination, forming an important transitional period in the history of this community. Dennis Johnson confirmed that "Community action programs helped bring about a more structural power base on which Salt River developed to what it is today. . . . CAP involved people in the exercise to use the resources available and to make decisions." Frank Smith agreed that Salt River CAP programs contributed significantly to the development of the present-day tribal structure: "[The programs] provided stability and consistency in tribal management, and more importantly, training out of which present-day tribal leadership emerged. . . . CAP money was used to provide lot of the basic facilities for more effective functioning of the tribe."[38]

In 1970, the Pima-Maricopas and the Zuni of New Mexico were the first tribes to contract with the BIA for the management of services on their reservations. That same year, the Salt River constitution was revised to create a departmentalized tribal government. Frank Smith lamented that "one drawback of all this was that we developed like any other government. [There was] a loss of creativeness and spontaneity." The other interviewees agreed with Dennis Johnson's conclusion that while the present governmental structure is an imposed structure, "the community has adapted to it because it operates well." They criticized community action for its emphasis on the quantity, not quality, of programs which created a false sense of accomplishment. In addition, the whole concept of community action came too fast and without sufficient preparation in the community, resulting in inefficiency and a waste of money. Even though the war on poverty failed to reach its goal, the eradication of poverty, Salt River fared better than many other communities in successfully adapting the concept of community action to its day-to-day functioning. By the time CAP phased out, the tribal government was able to replace community action agencies as employer and continue services in the community. In 1973, tribal president Paul Smith could write that "during the past decade the Salt River Pima-Maricopa Indian Community has developed a sophisticated ability to plan and develop programs to meet the needs of the members of the community."[39]

For women, CAP programs meant greater visibility in the community. The experience and skills they acquired in community action programs increasingly translated into an interest in tribal politics, and the number of women on the council and in leadership positions grew steadily. Women's traditional roles as opinion leaders and educators had always afforded them indirect influence in the day-to-day affairs of the tribe, but community action provided an impetus and an opportunity to run for office themselves. Although the council had no female members between 1975 and 1979, women's involvement in program management and direction increased. Women continued to concentrate on the issues of health, education, and social services, but they also made strides into traditionally male spheres. Christine Owens chaired the Industrial Development Committee in 1973–1974; Alfretta Antone headed the Land Management Board in 1975; and in 1978, Marilyn Baptisto was appointed Juvenile Judge for Salt River, and the position remained in female hands until 1987. Alfretta Antone became the first woman vice president in 1980, serving in that capacity for ten years. Merna Lewis, whose career began as teacher-aide in Head Start, has held the position of vice president since 1990. "It is only a matter of time before we get our first woman president," Vivian Jones commented, also expressing a widespread agreement in the community that women on the council are strong and that their leadership attitudes seem more assertive than those of the men.[40]

As a result of their involvement in community action, women also became increasingly interested in education and career development. Not only were women gainfully employed outside the home, but their choice of occupations diversified. Donald Jones attested that today women "work as heavy equipment operators, in tribal law enforcement and other occupations that would have been unimaginable twenty years ago."[41] Pima and Maricopa women also found employment in highly skilled occupations in the Phoenix electronic industry, and the first tribal member to graduate from law school was a woman. Women seemed as eager to embrace novel ideas and innovative concepts as they did early in the American period when they accepted the idea of education and accommodated new tools and techniques to facilitate their work. Their involvement in the community was not new, but the choices available for women expanded and they adapted their roles to the changing circumstances.

Despite women's sense of themselves as a distinct group within the community, they did not profess any brand of feminism nor did they advocate specifically women's issues. As Vivian Jones said, "women seem to be pretty content with what they are and what they have." Issues such as abortion and birth control were taken up only by health educators. Jones shared the general feeling among Pima and Maricopa women that "I have no personal interest in feminism or 'women's issues.' It's more important to be part of the community."[42]

This sense of community identity informs women's continued involvement in tribal affairs. Today Pima and Maricopa women are a vital part of the Salt River community, participating in economic, social, and political decisions as council members and as directors and managers of tribal programs. In these capacities, women provide strong role models while they are looked upon as mothers who hold the power to educate children about their heritage. They are thus in a position to contribute to the survival of Pima-Maricopa identity and the ongoing efforts to bring economic growth and social stability to the community.

NOTES

I would like to thank the Salt River Pima-Maricopa Indian Community for permission to conduct research for this essay and for sharing their views of community action and its impact in their lives. My special thanks go to Vice President Merna Lewis for her time and enthusiasm for the project and to Public Relations Director Janet Johnson. I would also like to thank Michael Duchemin, Gretchen Harvey, Peter Iverson, Mary Melcher, Nancy Shoemaker, and David Ware for their helpful comments in preparing this essay.

1. Angela Brown, interview by author, 20 January 1993. For the purposes of this essay, I conducted twenty interviews in the Salt River Pima-Maricopa Indian Community in central Arizona. The first eight interviews took place in February-June 1991, and I returned to conduct another twelve in January 1993. Of the fourteen interviewees, seven women and five men participated in the community action programs between 1966 and 1972 and remained active in tribal affairs at the time of the interviews. The other two interviewees were retired women who took part in community action. To protect the privacy of the participants, I have changed their names.

2. Public Law 88–452, the Economic Opportunity Act of 1964, 20 August 1964, in *United States Statutes at Large. Volume 78* (Washington, D.C.: Government Printing Office, 1965), 508.

3. For details on the origins of the war on poverty and the content of the programs, see Sar A. Levitan, *The Great Society's Poor Law: A New Approach to Poverty* (Baltimore: Johns Hopkins Press, 1969); Peter Morris and Martin Rein, *Dilemmas of Social Reform: Poverty and Community Action in the United States* (Chicago: Aldine Publishing Company, 1973); Daniel P. Moynihan, *Maximum Feasible Misunderstanding: Community Action in the War on Poverty* (New York: Free Press, 1969); James L. Sundquist, *Politics and Policy; The Eisenhower, Kennedy, and*

Johnson Years (Washington, D.C.: Brookings Institution, 1968); Tax Foundation, *Antipoverty Programs Under the Economic Opportunity Act* (New York, 1968); Carl M. Bauer, "Kennedy, Johnson, and the War on Poverty," *Journal of American History* 69 (June 1982): 98–119; Mark I. Gelfand, "The War on Poverty," in *The Johnson Years*, ed. Robert A. Divine, vol. 1 (Lawrence: University of Kansas Press, 1987), 126–154; and *Statutes*, 508–534. Evaluations on the success of community action include Kenneth B. Clark and Jeannette Hopkins, *A Relevant War Against Poverty: A Study of Community Action Programs and Observable Social Change* (New York: Harper and Row, 1968); Robert H. Haveman, ed., *A Decade of Federal Antipoverty Programs: Achievements, Failures, and Lessons* (New York: Academic Press, 1977); and Ralph M. Kramer, *Participation of the Poor: Comparative Community Case Studies in the War on Poverty* (Englewood Cliffs, N.J.: Prentice Hall, 1969).

4. For the economic and social conditions of reservation Indians in the 1960s, see Helen W. Johnson, *Rural Indians in Poverty* (Washington, D.C.: Government Printing Office, 1969); Alan R. Sorkin, *American Indians and Federal Aid* (Washington, D.C.: Brookings Institution, 1971); and Paul Stuart, *Nations Within a Nation: Historical Statistics of American Indians* (New York: Greenwood Press, 1987). For Native Americans and the war on poverty, see Sar A. Levitan and Barbara Hetrick, *Big Brother's Indian Programs—With Reservations* (New York: McGraw-Hill Book, Co., 1971); Levitan, "Helping the Original Americans," *Great Society's Poor Law*, chapter 12; "Indians in the Great Society," *Indian Affairs* 59 (June 1965), 1–2; "War on Poverty: Two Views," *Indian Affairs* 61 (December 1965): 1–3; Office of Economic Opportunity, *Annual Reports, 1965–1971*.

5. Emma R. Gross argues that federal spending related to war-on-poverty funding helped create an effective Indian leadership that provided an impetus for Congress to pass extensive Indian legislation in the 1970s. Emma R. Gross, "Setting the Agenda for American Indian Policy Development, 1968–1980," in *American Indian Policy and Cultural Values: Conflict and Accommodation* (Los Angeles: American Indian Studies Center, University of California, 1986), 47–63. Alfonso Ortiz similarly points to the emergence of a more assertive and experienced Indian leadership as a major development between 1964 and 1980. The other major change was the emancipation of women from the home within the reservation setting. Alfonso Ortiz, "Half A Century of Indian Administration: An Overview," in *American Indian Policy*, 7–23.

6. *The Pima Indians and the San Carlos Irrigation Project* (Washington, D.C.: Government Printing Office, 1924), 2; Edward H. Spicer, *Cycles of Conquest: The Impact of Spain, Mexico, and the United States on the Indians of the Southwest, 1533–1960*, 9th printing (Tucson: University of Arizona Press, 1989), 10–13; Robert A. Hackenberg, *Aboriginal Land Use and Occupancy of the Pima-Maricopa Indians*, volume 1 (New York: Garland Publishing, Inc., 1974), 107–26; Paul H. Ezell, *The Maricopas: An Identification From Documentary Sources* (Tucson: University of Arizona Press, 1963); William H. Kelly, *Indians of the Southwest: A Survey of Indian Tribes and Indian Administration in Arizona* (Tucson: University of Arizona Press, 1953), 6–9; Paul H. Ezell, "History of the Pima," in *Handbook of North American Indians*, general ed. William C. Sturtevant, *Southwest*, Volume 10, volume ed. Alfonso Ortiz (Washington, D.C.: Smithsonian Institution, 1983),

149–51; Robert A. Hackenberg, "Pima and Papago Ecological Adaptations," in *Handbook. Southwest*, 161–63; and Claire Seota, "Life of the Early Pimas," *Special Centennial Issue*, 14 June 1979, 8–9. See also Peter Iverson, "The Pima-Maricopas of Central Arizona," unpublished essay prepared for the Arizona Historical Society in Tempe, Arizona (1991), and John Myers and Robert Gryder, *The Salt River Pima-Maricopa Indians* (Phoenix: Life's Reflections, Inc., 1988).

7. Kelly, *Indians of the Southwest*, 7–9; Spicer, *Cycles of Conquest*, 12–13; Hackenberg, *Aboriginal Land Use and Occupancy*, 59–61, 94–97, 139–140; Ezell, "History of the Pima," 152–56; Hackenberg, "Ecological Adaptations," 168–70; Donald M. Bahr, "Pima and Papago Social Organization," in *Handbook of North American Indians*, Southwest, 178–92; Henry O. Harwell and Martha S. Kelly, "Maricopa," in *Handbook of North American Indians*, Southwest, 71–85; Seota, "Life of the Early Pimas," 8–9. See also the autobiographies of George Webb and Anna Moore Shaw, Pima Indians born in the late nineteenth century, for information on Pima and Maricopa life in the mid- and late-nineteenth century. George Webb, *A Pima Remembers*, (Tucson: University of Arizona Press, 1959); and Anna Moore Shaw, *A Pima Past* (Tucson: University of Arizona Press, 1974).

8. Information on the male and female roles in Pima and Maricopa society is sparse. See Ezell, "History of the Pima," 149–54; Howell and Kelly, "Maricopa," 77–85; and Seota, "Early Pima," 9. Also helpful are the autobiographies of Shaw and Webb. Myers and Gryder, *Pima-Maricopas*, includes several oral histories of Pima and Maricopa men and women that shed light on their roles. Finally, exhibits at the Hoo-Hoogam Ki Museum on the Salt River reservation provide insights into the division of labor and social power in Pima and Maricopa society.

9. Spicer, *Cycles of Conquest*, 146–48; "The Pimas: A Century of Dishonor," *Indian Affairs* 89 (June August 1975): 2–7; Ezell, "History of the Pima," 156–59; Hackenberg, "Ecological Adaptations," 170–71. See also Robert A. Trennert, "Educating Indian Girls at Nonreservation Boarding Schools, 1878–1920," in *Unequal Sisters: A Multi-Cultural Reader in U.S. Women's History*, ed. Ellen Carol DuBois and Vicki L. Ruiz (New York: Routledge, 1990), 224–37.

10. "The Pimas: A Century of Dishonor," 3; "History of Creating the Salt River Reservation," *Special Centennial Issue*, 14 June 1979; and "Akmul Auauthm [Pima] History," ibid, 2–4.

11. Alison R. Bernstein, *American Indians and World War II: Toward a New Era in Indian Affairs* (Norman: University of Oklahoma Press, 1991) discusses Native Americans in the war. For the impact of the war in the American West and Arizona in particular, see Richard White, "World War II and Its Aftermath: Reshaping the West," *It's Your Misfortune and None of My Own: A New History of the American West*, chapter 18 (Norman: University of Oklahoma Press, 1991), 496–533; and Bradford Luckingham, "The Boom Years, 1941–1960," *Phoenix: The History of A Southwestern Metropolis*, chapter 6 (Tucson: University of Arizona Press, 1989), 136–76. For Indian women in the work force, consult Patricia K. Ourada, "Indians in the Work Force," *Journal of the West* 25 (April 1986): 52–58; and Teresa Amott and Julie Matthaei, "I Am the Fire of Time: American Indian Women," *Race, Gender, and Work: A Multicultural Economic History of Women in the United States*, chapter 3 (Boston: South End Press, 1991), 31–61. For the Pima-Maricopa tribal council, see Arizona Commission of Indian Affairs, *Tribal*

Directory (Phoenix, AZ, issued annually since 1962); and, Salt River Community Council, *Code of Ordinances of the Salt River Pima-Maricopa Indian Community* (Tallahassee, FL: Municipal Code Corporation, 1981).

12. Agatha Thomas, interview by author, 22 January, 1993; Fred Wilson, interview by author, 22 January, 1993.

13. Arizona Commission of Indian Affairs (ACIA), *Salt River Pima-Maricopa Community Report 1961* (Phoenix, AZ: 1961); ACIA, *Economic Survey Report 1963* (Phoenix, AZ: 1963); ACIA, *Survey of the Salt River Reservation 1964* (Phoenix, AZ: 1964).

14. ACIA, *Survey 1964*; Arizona State Employment Service, *Manpower Services to Arizona Indians: Thirteenth Annual Report* (Phoenix, AZ: 1965).

15. Arizona Affiliated Tribes, *Self-Determination: A Program of Accomplishments* (Phoenix, AZ: May 1971), 98; and the following ACIA publications: *Report 1961*; *Reservation Survey 1963: Health* (Phoenix, AZ: 1963); *Reservation Survey 1963: Welfare* (Phoenix, AZ: 1963); *Survey 1964*; *Reservation Survey 1964: Education* (Phoenix, AZ: 1964).

16. Fred Wilson, 20 January 1993; Dennis Johnson, interview by author, 19 January 1993.

17. Office of Economic Opportunity, *Poverty Program Information*, volume 1 (Washington, D.C.: Government Printing Office, 1966), 28–29; ACIA, *1966 Reservation Survey of OEO Programs in Arizona* (Phoenix, AZ: 1966); ACIA, *Survey of the Salt River Reservation 1965* (Phoenix, AZ: 1965).

18. ACIA, *Survey 1965*; Three University Consortium, *Indian Reservation Community Action and the Role of the Three-University Consortium in Providing Technical Assistance and Training* (Tempe, AZ: n.d.); Three University Consortium, *Indian Community Action Project: Annual Report*, July 1966 through June 1967 (Tempe, AZ: 1967); Three University Consortium, *Community Action Progress* (Tempe, AZ: 15 March 1966).

19. State Office of Economic Opportunity, *Annual Reports, 1967–1972* (Phoenix, AZ); ACIA, *Survey 1965*; Fred Wilson, 20 January, 1993.

20. Office of Economic Opportunity, *Poverty Program Information*, 28; Frank Smith, interview by author, 7 February 1991.

21. Elizabeth Clarence, interview by author, 20 January, 1993; Frank Smith, 21 January 1993.

22. Frank Smith, 21 January 1993; Fred Wilson, 20 January 1993; Agatha Thomas, 12 February 1991.

23. Dennis Johnson, 19 January 1993; Agatha Thomas, 22 January 1993.

24. ACIA, *Tribal Directories, 1962–1969* (Phoenix); ACIA, *Survey 1964*; Simon Eisner and Associates, *Background for Planning and Policy Recommendations* (1969), 8–9.

25. Angela Brown, 20 January 1993.

26. Rhoda Barnes, 13 January 1993.

27. Florence Seely, interview by author, 13 January 1993; Alma Lewis, interview by author, 13 January 1993.

28. Rhoda Barnes, 13 January 1993.

29. Elizabeth Clarence, 20 January 1993; Vivian Jones, 19 January 1993; Fred Wilson, 20 January 1993.

30. Rhoda Barnes, 13 January 1993; Dennis Johnson, 19 January 1993.

31. Donald Jones, interview by author, 15 January 1993; Rhoda Barnes, 13 January 1993; Angela Brown, 20 January 1993; Vivian Jones, 19 January 1993.
32. Eisner and Associates, *Planning and Program Recommendations*, 8.
33. Agatha Thomas, 22 January 1993; ACIA, *Tribal Directories, 1971–1974* (Phoenix, AZ).
34. Vivian Jones, 19 January 1993; Frank Smith, 21 January 1993.
35. Vivian Jones, 19 January 1993; ACIA, *Tribal Directories, 1965–1972* (Phoenix, AZ).
36. Shaw, *A Pima Past*, 222–23; *Arizona Republic*, 24 January 24 1966; *Arizona Republic*, 21 November 1966; *Phoenix Gazette*, 27 April 1967.
37. Shaw, *A Pima Past*, 212. Shaw discusses her own and other women's involvement in the community in her book, 202–12.
38. Dennis Johnson, 19 January 1993; Frank Smith, 21 January 1993.
39. Paul Smith, letter from the Tribal Council to the community, printed in *Salt River Community Action News*, October 1973.
40. Vivian Jones, 19 January 1993. ACIA, *Tribal Directories, 1962–1992*.
41. Donald Jones, 15 January 1993.
42. Vivian Jones, 19 January 1993.

CONTRIBUTORS

HELEN M. BANNAN, Director of the Center for Women's Studies at West Virginia University, has published widely in women's history, especially on issues of multiculturalism and women in the Southwest. She is now working on a multicultural history of grandmothers in America.

KATHLEEN M. BROWN is Assistant Professor of History at Rutgers University, New Brunswick. She was a 1990–91 and 1992–93 fellow at the Institute of Early American History and Culture, which will also be publishing her book, *Good Wives and Nasty Wenches: The Politics of Gender in Race in Colonial Virginia.*

PÄIVI H. HOIKKALA is a doctoral candidate in history at Arizona State University, where she is working on her dissertation, "Native American Women in the Urban Southwest: A Study of Social and Political Activism in Phoenix, Arizona, 1965–1980."

HARRY A. KERSEY, JR., Professor of History at Florida Atlantic University, has published many books on Florida Seminole history including *Pelts, Plumes, and Hides: White Traders Among the Seminole Indians, 1870–1930* and most recently *The Florida Seminoles and the New Deal, 1933–1942.*

CLARA SUE KIDWELL is on leave as Associate Professor of Native American Studies at the University of California, Berkeley. She is currently Assistant Director for Cultural Resources at The National Museum of the American Indian. Among her publications are two articles in Indian women's history: "The Power of Women in Three American Indian Societies," published in the *Journal of Ethnic Studies* in 1979, and Kidwell's 1991 presidential address to the American Society for Ethnohistory, "Indian Women as Cultural Mediators," published in *Ethnohistory* in 1992.

CONTRIBUTORS

LUCY ELDERSVELD MURPHY is a Ph. D. candidate at Northern Illinois University. Her dissertation is a frontier study of the Fox-Wisconsin Riverway. However, she has also researched and published in the history of women in business. She is currently co-editing a collection of essays on midwestern women for Indiana University Press.

KATHERINE M.B. OSBURN is currently a Visiting Assistant Professor at Fort Lewis College. She is in the process of revising her dissertation in history at the University of Denver about change and continuity in Ute women's lives during the implementation of the Dawes Act, for publication with University of New Mexico Press. Her other publications include an article about the Navajos at Bosque Redondo in the *New Mexico Historical Review*.

THEDA PERDUE, Professor of History at the University of Kentucky, is a well-known scholar of Cherokee history. Her publications include *Slavery and the Evolution of Cherokee Society, 1540–1866*, and she is now completing a book on Cherokee women in the eighteenth and early nineteenth centuries.

NANCY SHOEMAKER, Visiting Assistant Professor of history at the State University of New York at Plattsburgh, has published several articles on the history of American Indian women, families, and demography. Her current research project is a study of gender and justice in the nineteenth-century Cherokee Nation court system.

CAROL DOUGLAS SPARKS is a doctoral candidate in history at Northern Arizona University. Her master's thesis was on Anglo-American images of Navajos in the first half of the nineteenth century. Her dissertation, expanding on this earlier research, examines nineteenth-century Anglo images of Navajo, Apache, and Pueblo women.

CLIFFORD E. TRAFZER is Professor and Chair of Ethnic Studies and Director of Native American Studies at the University of California, Riverside. He is a member of the California Native American Heritage Commission, which protects sacred sites and remains. He is the author of *Renegade Tribe: The Palouse Indians and the Invasion of the Inland Pacific Northwest* (with Richard Scheuerman); *Earth Song, Sky Spirit*, and a forthcoming book, *Death Stalks the Yakima*.

DATE DUE